Dad —

Thanks for everything.

Love,

Jason

6/98

THE MUHAMMAD ALI READER

Also by Gerald Early

Tuxedo Junction: Essays on American Culture

Speech and Power: The African-American Essay and Its Cultural Content from Polemics to Pulpit, Volumes 1 & 2 (editor)

The Culture of Bruising: Essays on Prizefighting, Literature, and Modern American Culture

One Nation Under a Groove: Motown & American Culture

THE
MUHAMMAD ALI
READER

EDITED BY
GERALD EARLY

THE ECCO PRESS

This book is dedicated to Sylvia Green, my aunt, a fighter.

Copyright © 1998 by Gerald Early

THE ECCO PRESS
100 West Broad Street
Hopewell, New Jersey 08525

Published simultaneously in Canada by
Penguin Books Canada, Ltd., Ontario

Printed in the United States of America

All photographs are reprinted by permission courtesy UPI/Corbis-Bettmann except
for "Muhammad Ali lights the flame at 1996 Olympic Games" and "Muhammad Ali
with President Bill Clinton at the 1996 Olympic Games" courtesy Agence France
Presse/Corbis-Bettmann.

I would like to thank Zack Falck, my undergraduate research assistant. Without his
labors, this book would not have been possible.

Library of Congress Cataloging-in-Publication Data

The Muhammad Ali reader / edited by Gerald Early.—1st ed.
       p. cm.
    ISBN 0-88001-602-7
    1. Ali, Muhammad, 1942– . 2. Boxers (Sports)—United States—Biography.
3. Newspapers—Sections, columns, etc.—Boxing. I. Early, Gerald Lyn.
    GV1132.A44M83   1998
    796.83'092—dc21   97-36846
    [B]

Book design by The Typeworks.
The text of this book is set in Poliphilus

9 8 7 6 5 4 3 2 1

FIRST EDITION 1998

CONTENTS

INTRODUCTION:
TALES OF THE WONDERBOY

Part One

Such latter-day disfigurements leave out
All mention of those older scars that merge
On any riddled surfaces about.
　　—Weldon Kees, "A Good Chord on a Bad Piano"

There exists a great fear today, or at least there should, that Muhammad Ali, no stranger to the most intense sort of adulation reserved usually for certain psychopaths, mystics, and movie stars, may become absolutely overesteemed by the society in which he lives. This would put him in danger not only of having his considerable significance misunderstood, but also, ironically, of being diminished as both a public figure and a black man of some illustrious complexity. Ali, as a result of his touching, or poignant, or pathetic, or tragic (take your pick) appearance at the torch-lighting ceremony at 1996 Olympics Games in Atlanta has become, for new generations that did not grow up with him and for the older generations that did, the Great American Martyr, our new Lincoln, our new Martin Luther King, Oh, Father Abraham, Oh, Father Martin, Oh, Father Muhammad: the man whose hands, once unerring pistons of punishment in the prizefighting ring, tremble from boxing-induced Parkinson's disease; the man whose voice is such a slurred whisper that he, who was once called the Louisville Lip because he loved talking so much, does not like to speak in public and rarely does; the once-uncompromising black nationalist now reduced, like Orson Welles at the end, to performing magic tricks for the crowd as if he were parodying his own pop-culture greatness, exposing it as an illusion, just as his nationalism had been, just as his cultist/religious self had been. Everything in popular culture writhes with the throb of impermanence, its significance

threatened by the triteness it cannot hide, by the banality it bloats into emi￫
nence through a personality that blends the public and the private. And no
one embodied American popular culture, its excesses, its barbarities, and its
disarming densities, more than Muhammad Ali.

The public rarely responds to this sort of demise of a great popular per￫
former with anything approaching good sense or objectivity, and almost cer￫
tainly with nothing approaching a kind of gracious humor, something that,
in this case, the subject himself may very much embrace and seems to be try￫
ing to instruct us in how to achieve. This is even less likely to happen when
the figure in question is a black man, a cunning archetype who is already so
burdened by a baggage of both sentimentality and taboo as to be likely a vir￫
tual walking expression of the culture's irrationality even if his old age had
been a bit less marked by illness. And Ali had been a lightning rod for the
culture's irrationality all of his life, sometimes provoking it purposely, some￫
times a veritable representation of it himself. This was, after all, the man who
not only brilliantly playacted a combination panic attack/nervous break￫
down at the weigh￫in of his first championship fight with the dreaded Sonny
Liston in 1964; served as the redoubtable, tricksterlike black comic to
Howard Cosell's liberal Jewish straight man; had a highly publicized reli￫
gious conversion to a strange, if influential, cult that disliked whites but
wanted to be a perfect imitation of them, aggrandizing their importance
while humanizing their stark doctrine; and who said that no Vietcong ever
called him "nigger"; but who also believed for some several years that a mad
scientist named Yacub invented white people by grafting them from blacks,
that satellites from Allah circled the earth and would imminently destroy the
United States, and that blacks who dated or married whites should be killed.

Now the public, because of Ali's illness, wants to drown him in a bathos
of sainthood and atone for its guilt. This is principally true of whites who
spend a good deal of their time when they think about race (and to think
about Ali is to think about race because Ali made it such a prominent subject
in his public rantings and sermons, so successfully that he, in fact, succeeded
in making over his most inner￫city￫like black opponents, the blackest of the
black, into white men), either denying that it is a problem they caused or con￫
fessing that they have committed such atrocities against blacks that only the
most abject deference to them can make up for it all. (For a black person to ex￫
perience this is a great deal like being caught between benign neglect and

affirmative action, tough love and a comforting paternalism, the amputation of virulent racism and the gangrene of liberal racism.) This guilt arises largely from Ali's stance against the Vietnam War, a war we have come to see as at best misguided and as at worst evil, and his subsequent three-and-one-half year exile from boxing; and from a feeling that somehow, we, the American public, or the white American public (since blacks were in no position to abuse him through a rather capricious application of the Selective Service Act), are the cause of his current affliction. And we did this to him because he became a Black Muslim and spoke out frankly against racism and white double-dealing, something no black athletic hero had ever done before (or since, really). He was severely maimed by and for our racial sins, our racist use of the system against him.

Thus, it seems no accident at all that Muhammad Ali should be re-awakened in the public's mind, largely as the subject of the Academy Award-winning documentary, *When We Were Kings*, along with Jackie Robinson, as we celebrated in 1997 the fiftieth anniversary of his breaking the color line in major league baseball with the Brooklyn Dodgers. Yoked together in the public's consciousness this year were, arguably, the two most influential American athletes of the twentieth century, the American century, the first and maybe not the last, hallowed nearly as handsome, transcendent, boyish American angels hovering over our leveled playing fields of dreams (where merit and romance walk hand-in-hand), sacrifices on the altar of our hypocritical democracy, emblems of the double V, the victory on two fronts, the real world of social relations and the fantasy world of athletics: the noble black American male as inventor of a heretical Americanism, demonstrating what it cost a black to have democratic ideals and to force whites to live up to them. Ironically, Robinson did this by insisting he was an American and Ali by insisting he was victimized because he was never considered an American, but both paid the price. What do we remember most about Robinson but that he suffered, that he endured insults and provocation, that he died at the relatively young age of 52, prematurely aged, we feel, from the abuse he took as a player in order to integrate the Great American Game. In the dim lighting of the distressing paradox of American race relations, we forget, though, that Robinson received more universal acclaim during his life than virtually any black person had before him.

It is no slight schizophrenia that besets us when in today's society young black men are so often represented in our popular culture as buffoonish thugs or coonlike clowns, in our collective imagination as real, certifiable thugs and rapists. When the police mistreat a black man like Rodney King or when a sports hero like O. J. Simpson falls from grace, we hardly know whether to be outraged or relieved. Yet when it comes to Jackie Robinson and Muham-mad Ali these days, the public, especially whites, nearly weep. James Bald-win was right: that a certain insistence that the black male figure represent his humanity through the narrow prism of social protest elicits this contradic-tion, a blunting of the very effects that his social protest was meant to induce. This white response to Ali and Robinson may be a reflection of racism, but it seems more profoundly to be a sign of some organic confusion, a mythic yet turbulently defective pietism, at that very heart of our perception of our-selves. We cannot see in the way Captain Delano of Melville's "Benito Cereno" could not see, in all our tragic innocence.

Muhammad Ali, in truth, does not make a very good martyr, as Wilfrid Sheed once observed, or cannot quite be taken seriously as one. Doubtless, as Sheed points out, Ali had a martyr's complex, which is why he became a member of the Nation of Islam, not because he felt the slings and arrows of outrageous racism (Ali had a very indulged life, from boyhood on) but be-cause he wanted "to [take] on the scars of his brothers." For a man with a great sense of public mission and public consciousness, as Ali had, an act of such solidarity with the most bitter blacks on the bottom was a theatrical and vividly condensed bit of risk-taking. What Ali had, in this regard, is exactly what Malcolm X claimed to have near the end of his life: not truth, not vision, not wisdom, but sincerity. This counts for a great deal in an age of rel-ativism and cynicism, in an age when we have given ourselves over to the adolescent's version of reality, instead of the Heminway-esque version: One's measure of authenticity was not how one lived one's life in the face of what made it impossible, but how deeply one felt about something. Intensity of feeling equaled real experience. As David Riesman asserted in *The Lonely Crowd*, sincerity had become the emotion of our post-World War II, other-directed age. And no one made his inner-directed compulsions and puritani-cal hedonism more of an outer-directed exhibition than Muhammad Ali. Ali always had a portion of something Hemingway-esque but he had more than a bit of sheer adolescent emotionalism. Ali's reasons for not wanting to join the Army were never terribly convincing, but they had a potency because he was so sincere, movingly and petulantly so. He had the strength of a simplistic, unreal orthodoxy for which he seemed prepared to die in an age when the simplistic, unreal orthodoxy that held this country together was beginning to unravel, violently and quickly. Ali, despite all the talk of his brilliance, was not a thoughtful man. He was not conversant with ideas. Indeed, he hadn't a single idea in his head, really. What he had was the faith of the true believer, like a Jehovah's Witness or a Mormon or a Hasadic Jew or a communist, a grand public stage, an extraordinary historical moment, amazing athletic gifts, and good looks. But Ali cannot be taken seriously as a martyr because: first, other athletes, such as Jackie Robinson, Joe Louis, Ted Williams, Bob Feller, Hank Greenberg, Christy Mathewson, and many others lost several years of their athletic prime, *serving* in the Armed Forces during World War I, World War II, or the Korean War. No one seems to think this was tragic. Granted, we have a different view of those wars, but Ali did not pay anything more for his dissent, in relation to his career as an athlete, than other star athletes in the past have paid for not dissenting. Plus, he had the luxury of not being in danger in combat, although he was always open to the crazed assassin's bullet. And Ali never went to prison for his pacifist beliefs, like his leader, Elijah Muhammad, or like Bayard Rustin. He wasn't killed for his beliefs like his onetime mentor, Malcolm X, or his admirer, Martin Luther King.

For instance, when Ali appeared at Randolph-Macon College for Men in Virginia on April 17, 1969 to give a speech, one of 168 campuses he was planning to visit that year in order to raise legal funds for his defense against the draft, although there was some considerable outcry from the alumni and the locals about his visit, there was virtually no protest when he arrived on campus. He gave his speech, largely a kind of rote Nation-of-Islam homage to Elijah Muhammad, answered questions at some length, rather tactlessly asked the dean of men for his check when he was through, and, despite being worn out, was talked into appearing at a inner city school in the vicinity. According to the account given in *The Catholic World*, "The content of the speech itself was standard Black Muslim rhetoric, but the presentation was pure Cassius Clay entertainment. . . . Perhaps one might, in fact, criticize Ali for making his address so entertaining and amusing that the seriousness of his subject was somewhat obscured." It was this quality of Ali's, his ability to put a certain humor and, thus, a profoundly human face as well as a kind of pop culture sheen on black anger and indignation that, I think, saved his life. Like the Marxist or the deconstructionist, he made ideology self-evident where it had once been invisible, but he seemed more amused by his discovery than belligerent, more deeply struck by its wondrous expression of a benighted humanity than outraged by its expressions of unjustified power and dominance. This is the full dimension of the shallow, simplistic sincerity that protected him rather like amulet or a juju. So, in fact, after his exile, he went to make an incredible amount of money, to star in a movie of his life, and to become one of the most famous people, and surely the most famous Muslim, in the world. By the mid-1970s, after redeeming himself and regaining the title by defeating the fearsome, sullen George Foreman, Ali had become such an accepted figure in the American mainstream that DC Comics put out a special edition Superman where "that draft dodger," as he had been called in the 1960s, beat the Man of the Steel, the Great White American Hero, in a prizefight to save humanity from an alien invasion. Martyrdom, where is thy sting?

Second, there is no indication that had Ali left boxing sooner, he would have avoided suffering the brain damage he did suffer, if he had not been exiled, very unfairly, from boxing between the ages of 27 and 30. It is a rare boxer, especially one as good as Ali was and who so wanted and needed public attention, who quits before he is literally beaten into retirement. What Ali had was an irresistible combination of talent, showmanship, and a genius conceit of himself that bordered on both the heroically self-possessed and the insufferably megalomanic. He not only believed in God, to paraphrase the lyric from the musical, *Hair*, but he believed that God believed in him. Though Ali makes a poor saint, he makes a very good fallen prince, the daring, flamboyantly ignorant cavalier, which is exactly what he is: the weary, enigmatic sovereign of our time, of our realm, of our racialized imagination. What unnerves us now about Ali and brings out the insipidness of victimology is that he wound up like an old, broken-down prizefighter. The guilt we feel is that we used him as a commodity and that he used us to create great dramas of his fights, dragon-slaying heroics, extraordinary crises of our social order. It mattered greatly whether he won or lost and we are guilty about having been conned into believing a prizefight means much of anything in this world, about what our being conned did to the confidence man. But Ali, far from being a victim, is perhaps the one of the most remarkable examples of triumph over racism in our century. It is not surprising that so many white people hated him but that before his career ended a good many had come to love him. Ali was a public figure mostly shaped by two decisions: in 1964, he chose to stay with Elijah Muhammad's Nation of Islam and not defect with Malcolm X and become, in effect, a leftist Pan-Africanist, a decision that made it possible for him to weather his exile years of 1967-1970 by being surrounded by a tight community of disciplined believers; in 1977, he chose to stay with Wallace D. Muhammad who de-racialized the Black Muslims instead of defecting with Louis Farrakhan's revitalized Nation of Islam with Elijah Muhammad's old racist tenets. Had he joined Farrakhan, Ali would not be nearly as revered today as he is.

Ali has been compared to a number of famous people, from Oscar Wilde to Jack Johnson, from Elvis Presley to Jay Gatsby. I think he bears no small resemblance to our two finest jazz musicians, Louis Armstrong and Duke Ellington, and perhaps his genius might be best understood in relation to theirs. Like both of them, Ali was a southerner. Like Ellington, he came from the border South and so did not experience the most brutal sort of racism, but like Armstrong, who came from New Orleans, he came from a mythic southern place, Kentucky, with its Thoroughbreds, its bluegrass, its mint juleps, its colonels, so he experienced a deeply self-conscious white South, which may explain why he felt the oppression of racism so deeply without having to endure a great deal of it. Being a southerner, I think, explains his showmanship. Who could have been given the name of Cassius Marcellus Clay, the original an eccentric of the sort that only an antislavery, nigger-hating Southern politican could be, and not be a showman? Like Armstrong, Ali was essentially a comic. This explains why, although he was deeply hated by many whites at one point in his career, he was able to come back. He rarely said anything without a certain kind of mocking quality, and his rage, like his incessant bragging and egoism, was often that of the adolescent. Ali offered the public the contradictory pleasure of having to take him seriously while not having to take him seriously. He was deeply aware of this himself and played a game of public relations deceit as cleverly as anyone. In retrospect, Ali struck intense chords of ambiguity as a black public figure, though somewhat different ones, like Armstrong. Was Armstrong just an old-time minstrel or, through his genius, the utter undermining of minstrelsy? Was Ali a star boxer, or, through his genius, the utter undermining of boxing? Was he a militant or the complete unmasking of militancy? Joe Louis might have seemed an Uncle Tom to many compared to Ali, but Ali laughed and smiled more in public in a week than Louis did in his entire life. Ali actually seemed to like white people (which he did; he liked everyone), whereas Louis never seemed comfortable around them and never much appeared to like them. He simply contained himself in their presence. How was it that a black man could openly show how much he enjoyed white people and yet not be branded an Uncle Tom by his own people and be seen as a threat by whites? What Ali did with sheer brilliance was become the center of laughter but never the object of it. He controlled what his audiences laughed at when he made himself a source of humor. Ali's laughter was meant to signify something different from Armstrong's, not exactly an expression of deference to audience (although Ali certainly wanted to please his audiences, even as he may have exasperated them), but rather an expression of boyish joy in his own freedom and strength, a casual astonishment at the refulgence of his own extraordinary gifts that seemed to strike him simultaneously as both miraculous and absurd. Like Ellington, Ali had a certain charm and elegance, both in and out of the ring, a need to baby himself and to womanize because both were equalled captivated by their own beauty and the way people were captivated by them. Both men were highly photogenic. Ali loved to hear himself talk, as did Ellington and he loved having people around him, not because they were the best possible people at what they did, but because they did one or two things that amused or intrigued him or that he admired and felt he could use, much as Ellington saw his musicians, some of whom were not the best possible players Ellington could have had on those instruments. They did well something Ellington had a great need of for his orchestra, and Ali lived his life largely as if he were conducting a very large orchestra. Ali did this for his opponents, too. He brought out the best of what they had. He was enormously generous and this touches us deeply. Ali, like Armstrong and Ellington, had magnetism, inventiveness, a heroism that did not evade the trickster black of black folklore or the minstrel black of the nineteenth century American stage but embodied them as both the antithesis and fulfillment of himself, not as a person but as his own individualized archetype. That is why Ali is loved so much today. Like all great heroes he showed us the enormous possibility of the true meaning, the incendiary poetics, of actual self-determination.

Part Two

And is this then (said I) what the author calls a man's life? . . .
Only a few hints, a few diffused faint clews and indirections . . .
    —Walt Whitman, "When I Read the Book"

I cant say who I am
unless you agree I'm real.
    —Amiri Baraka, "Numbers, Letters"

Muhammad Ali could barely read. He certainly never read books. Yet his was the religion of the book—not only the Koran but Elijah Muhammad's *Message to the Blackman in America*. (He fervently advocated for the book, *One Hundred Years of Lynching*, a popular book among certain knowing coves in the black community, as I remember from my boyhood, used to convince those who were casual or apathetic about the Unspeakable Negro Massacres that they had better get with the truth and quit having the white man brainwash them with the white Jesus and movies like *King Solomon's Mines*.) What fascinated Ali, like many of the poorly educated, was the authority of books or their failure as authority. When I met Ali a few years ago, he went on at some length about the contradictions in the Bible. As a devout Muslim, this seemed to please him greatly, as he must have felt he was deflating the power of that text. I told him that as a Christian I hardly expected the Bible to be anything more than a messy and messed-up book. "Now you see how tough it is to be a Christian," I said. He smiled at that. There was probably something both miraculous and absurd about having a theological discussion with an ex-prizefighter who couldn't talk and had actually read very little of the Bible, a rich illustration of the uses and disadvantages of having athletes serve as all-purpose black icons.

Ali scored a 16 on the Army intelligence tests, indicating that he had a low IQ. A man of his wit and quickness could not be that dumb, we protest. Yet I think the score was an honest reflection of Ali's mental abilities. Ali was not literate, nor was he analytical. When he was younger he could successfully debate those who were much smarter, or at least had read more books, because he had the zealot's set of answers to life's questions. His mind worked through formulas and clichés. His personality gave them a life and vibrancy that they would otherwise have lacked. He was intuitive, glib, richly gregarious, and intensely creative, like an artist. He would have scored better on the test had he been better educated, but still he would never have had a score that reflected the range of his curiosity or his humanity. But it is perhaps no surprise for a man so taken by the authority of the book that he would be so attractive to people who wrote books for a living or that a book itself may possess some small authority in telling us about him.

This reader is composed of some of the best writing about and the best interviews with Muhammad Ali. Some of our finest writers—Norman Mailer, Tom Wolfe, Ishmael Reed, Irwin Shaw, Joyce Carol Oates, A. J. Liebling—have written about Ali. Ali has also given lengthy and very insightful interviews with magazines such as *Playboy*, *Black Scholar*, and *Sport*. I thought it would be useful, as we begin to revisit Ali, to think on the best that has been written about him. I have tried to include a variety, from the little-known pieces by Jackie Robinson and George Schuyler to work from the well-known George Plimpton. The pieces are arranged in strictly chronological order and are divided by decades. What is amazing is that Ali has managed to fascinate so many first-rate writers for so long, nearly forty years. There are no academic articles included here, largely for the sake of symmetry and coherence. Several of the essays and interviews were edited for space considerations. I wanted to get in as many pieces as possible, but a six-hundred-page book was clearly unfeasible and such a book would have proven something of an embarrassment, as if there had been no real editing at all. In some cases, matters extraneous to Ali were cut; in others, redundant material. What is here is a strong representative core of what these writers and interviewers were trying to capture: the elusive, often theatrical, ever-eroding, ever-reconstructing surfaces of the mind and body of Muhammad Ali. No collection of this sort can ever include everything that the editor would like to have: Space limitations, permission costs, and outright refusals always make these kinds of anthologies less than perfect. And I am more aware than any reader of what isn't here. Yet of the several books I have edited, this has given me the greatest satisfaction as a reader, as an editor, as a writer because its riches are abundant, because it is informed with a mission and a passion, because to write about someone whose like is not to be seen again in our lifetime perhaps brings out an urgent brilliance in the writers who tackled Ali as a subject; all of this makes this work greater than the sum of its parts. I have never believed in the purpose of a book more than this one. And I have never believed more in a book's meaning—a truth so basic that I, of course, did not discover it; I have simply transmitted it. To do this book was not a labor but a rare privilege.

Part Three

But you, a new brood, native, athletic, continental, greater
        than before known,
Arouse! for you must justify me.
        —Walt Whitman, "Poets to Come"

"I'm just a typical American boy from a typical American town," folksinger Phil Ochs sang in his "Draft Dodger Rag," and perhaps I was or thought I was, once. The summer of my fourteenth year was the last that I played baseball regularly. It was that spring that a Jewish friend gave me Bernard Malamud's novel *The Natural* to read. I am not sure why he gave it to me, because he did not care much for baseball. I didn't think that he cared much for novel-reading, either. But he liked *The Natural* a lot. I guess he just liked the story. He thought it was funny and said a lot about losing and life. He was my boxing friend, though, not my baseball friend. I spent many an hour with him talking about fighters and more than a few talking about Muhammad Ali. I so loved the novel that I wanted to make a bat like the Roy Hobbs's Wonderboy, for I loved the name of it, the splendor of omniscient innocence it carried. I told all the boys, all the fellas, as we all read comic books together, (and little else), that Batman's ward, Robin, was misnamed. "He's not the boy wonder. He's the Wonder boy!" And they all agreed for they had never heard of a boy wonder, but everyone, everyone knew about the Wonderboy. And they all believed because I had read *Tom Sawyer* and *Huckleberry Finn* and *Tarzan of the Apes* and Howard Pyle's *Men of Iron* and *Treasure Island* and Sherlock Holmes, and had seen all those Steve Reeves movies like *Goliath and the Barbarians* and *The White Warrior* and *Morgan the Pirate*, and knew about these things.

I was no good at wood-working and the like, so I saved my paper route money and simply bought a bat, the best bat I could find, a genuine Louisville Slugger, the first one I ever owned. I sanded that bat, restained it dark, retaped the handle, and decided to give it a name. I carefully carved, scratched, really, into the bat the word, *Ali*. I tried to carve a lightning bolt but my limited artistic skill would not permit it. I wanted to carry it in a case, but I didn't have one. I just slung it on a shoulder like the great weapon it was, my knight's sword. And I felt like some magnificent knight, some great protector of honor and virtue, whenever I walked on the field with it. I called the bat the Great Ali.

I used that bat for the entire summer, and a magical season it was. I was the best hitter in the neighborhood. I had a career year. There was no pitch I couldn't hit. My preparation was such, so arduous, and now so perfect in its justification, so inspired in its execution, that, like Conrad's Jim, "the unexpected couldn't touch me." At the plate, I could do no wrong. Doubles, triples, home runs. I could hit at will. This probably would have happened with any bat I might have used. I had grown bigger and stronger over the last year and had practiced a great deal over the winter. My hand-eye coordination was just superb at that moment in my life. Once, I won a game in the last at-bat with a home run and the boys just crowded around me as if I were a spectacle to behold, as if I were, for some small moment, in this insignificant part of the world, playing this meaningless game, their majestic, golden prince. O wondrous boy was I!

In any case, the bat broke. Some kid used it without my permission. (I jealously guarded that bat, but a kid from an opposing team grabbed it while I was in the field.) He hit a foul ball and the bat split, the barrel flying one way, the splintered handle still in the kid's hands. It was the end of the Great Ali. I screamed when it broke, for I realized only too late that the boy was using it. "You broke my bat! You broke my bat!"

It was 1966 and Ali seemed not simply the best boxer of the day but the best boxer who could ever possibly be imagined. He had, the previous fall, beaten Floyd Patterson; that spring he beat George Chuvalo and Henry Cooper. During that summer, he beat Brian London. He was so good that it was an inspiration to see him fight, to see even a picture of him. My body shivered when I saw him as if an electric shock had pulverized my ability to feel. It was the good feeling of boyish hero worship I had. He was the Wonderboy. No fighter could touch him. His self-knowledge was glorious, so transcendentally fixed was he on the only two subjects he knew: himself and boxing. He so filled me with his holy spirit that whenever, late in a game, our side needed a rally, I would chant out loud to my teammates, "Float like a butterfly, sting like a bee. Rumble, young man, rumble!" (Ah, good, teary-eyed, ever loyal Bundini Brown, Ali's assistant trainer, recommended by Sugar Ray Robinson, who gave the world that slogan and who died broke and broken, only able to move his eyelids.) That made little sense metaphori-cally in relation to baseball, but it seemed to work more often than not. It was for me, this 1966, Ali's absolute moment of black possibilities fulfilled. And I wanted that and had it for a moment, too, had it, perhaps, among the neigh-borhood fellows, the touch and glory of the Wonderboy.

When the bat broke, it seemed as if a certain spell was broken, too. I still continued to hit in the little time that was left that season before school started, but I was not as interested in baseball anymore. I drifted away from it after that summer by steps and bounds. The next summer, 1967, Ali was con-victed of draft-dodging. Martin Luther King came out against the Vietnam War. Baseball did not seem very important. Something else was. For you see, I could never be sure, before that spring when Ali refused to be drafted, if he really would, really would actually refuse to go, refuse to take that step. Maybe Ali would turn out to be another Roy Hobbs. Maybe he was just some mis-erable, talented hick who would sell out and strike out. So when he refused, I felt something greater than pride: I felt as though my honor as a black boy had been defended, my honor as a human being. He was the grand knight, after all, the dragon-slayer. And I felt myself, little inner-city boy that I was, his ap-prentice to the grand imagination, the grand daring. The day that Ali refused the draft, I cried in my room. I cried for him and for myself, for my future and his, for all our black possibilities. My poor broken bat, the evaporating mem-ories of my great season, all ghostly in the well-lighted reflections of the fires of some politics and principles that I did not understand, made me feel as if I had a new nervous system, as if my cerebral cortex had become a new an-tenna for a newer reality. If I could sacrifice like that, I thought. If I could sacrifice my life like Ali! "To fling away your daily bread," Joseph Conrad wrote, "so as to get your hands free for a grapple with a ghost may be an act of prosaic heroism." And to me, fighting whites in a way was like fighting ghosts, an arch absurdity. (What would my life be if it were not wasted in defense of its right to be a life, after all!) One could never be sure if one were broken as a result of the fight or if one were broken even before entering the lists. You see, it was, I was sure, then, the end of the Wonderboy, the utter and complete end, the final breaking of the bat. But it was, as things turned out, only the end of the beginning. It wasn't even that the best was yet to come, or even the grand second act, but rather everything that was to give 1967 meaning was to come. The year 1967 was only the first death, the germinal crisis. The grand knights always live twice. Like a hitter with a magical bat, the unexpected couldn't touch him. Nothing breaks the Wonderboy.

Gerald Early
St. Louis, Missouri
December 15, 1997

THE 1960S

"And boxing made me feel like sombody different."

*—Cassius Clay on his attraction to boxing
as a boy in "Growing Up Scared in Louisville"
by Jack Olsen,* Sports Illustrated, *February 24, 1964*

"I don't think it's bragging to say I'm something a little special. Where do you think I would be next week if I didn't know how to shout and holler and make the public sit up and take notice? I would be poor, for one thing, and I would be down in Louisville, my home town, washing windows or running an elevator and saying "yes suh" and "no suh" and knowing my place."

—Cassius Clay, "I'm a Little Special,"
Sports Illustrated, *February 24, 1964*

"You got to love your own kind. I just love my people and their children. I hug the little Negro children when they come around the yard. They're so humble and sweet and they don't bother nobody. They don't have a future, and nobody really teaches 'em the truth. I couldn't feel the same way about a white child, 'cause he's not my kind, and then later when he gets bigger he'll have to turn away from me or else give up everything he's got, just to be with some poor Negro. He's got brothers and sisters and friends that'd condemn him for being with me. Kennedy got killed. Lincoln got killed. They meant right, but they were surrounded by the other whites."

*—Cassius Clay, quoted in Jack Olsen, "Learning Elijah's
Advanced Lesson in Hate,"* Sports Illustrated, *May 2, 1965*

"Throughout history the white man has acted like the devil."

*—Muhammad Ali, from "'Yes Sir, Mr. Ali'—The Tale of a Talk"
from* Christian Century, *October 23, 1968*

POET AND PEDAGOGUE

A. J. LIEBLING

When Floyd Patterson regained the world heavyweight championship by knocking out Ingemar Johansson in June 1960, he so excited a teenager named Cassius Marcellus Clay, in Louisville, Kentucky, that Clay, who was a good amateur light heavyweight, made up a ballad in honor of the victory. (The tradition of pugilistic poetry is old; according to Pierce Egan, the Polybius of the London Prize Ring, Bob Gregson, the Lancashire Giant, used "to recount the deeds of his Brethren of the Fist in heroic verse, like the Bards of Old." A sample Gregson couplet was "The British lads that's here / Quite strangers are to fear." He was not a very good fighter, either.) At the time, Clay was too busy training for the Olympic boxing tournament in Rome that summer to set his ode down on paper, but he memorized it, as Homer and Gregson must have done with their things, and then polished it up in his head. "It took me about three days to think it up," Clay told me a week or so ago, while he was training in the Department of Parks gymnasium, on West Twenty-eighth Street, for his New York debut as a professional, against a heavyweight from Detroit named Sonny Banks. In between his composition of the poem and his appearance on Twenty-eighth Street, Clay had been to Rome and cleaned up his Olympic opposition with aplomb, which is his strongest characteristic. The other finalist had been a Pole with a name that it takes two rounds to pronounce, but Cassius had not tried. A book that I own called *Olympic Games: 1960,* translated from the German, says, "Clay fixes the Pole's punch-hand with an almost hypnotic stare and by nimble dodging renders his attacks quite harmless." He thus risked being disqualified for holding and hitting, but he got away with it. He had then turned professional under social and financial auspices sufficient to launch a bank, and had won ten tryout bouts on the road. Now he told me that Banks, whom he had never seen, would be no problem.

I had watched Clay's performance in Rome and had considered it attractive but not probative. Amateur boxing compares with professional boxing as college theatricals compare with stealing scenes from Margaret Rutherford.

Clay had a skittering style, like a pebble scaled over water. He was good to watch, but he seemed to make only glancing contact. It is true that the Pole finished the three-round bout helpless and out on his feet, but I thought he had just run out of puff chasing Clay, who had then cut him to pieces. ("Pietrzykowski is done for," the Olympic book says. "He gazes helplessly into his corner of the ring; his legs grow heavier and he cannot escape his rival.") A boxer who uses his legs as much as Clay used his in Rome risks deceleration in a longer bout. I had been more impressed by Patterson when *he* was an Olympian, in 1952; he had knocked out his man in a round.

At the gym that day, Cassius was on a mat doing sit-ups when Mr. Angelo Dundee, his trainer, brought up the subject of the ballad. "He is smart," Dundee said. "He made up a poem." Clay had his hands locked behind his neck, elbows straight out, as he bobbed up and down. He is a golden-brown young man, big-chested and long-legged, whose limbs have the smooth, rounded look that Joe Louis's used to have, and that frequently denotes fast muscles. He is twenty years old and six feet two inches tall, and he weighs a hundred and ninety-five pounds.

"I'll say it for you," the poet announced, without waiting to be wheedled or breaking cadence. He began on a rise:

> "You may talk about Sweden
>   [down and up again],
> You may talk about Rome
>   [down and up again],
> But Rockville Centre is Floyd Patterson's home
>   [down]."

He is probably the only poet in America who can recite this way. I would like to see T. S. Eliot try.

Clay went on, continuing his ventriflexions:

> "A lot of people say that Floyd couldn't fight,
> But you should have seen him on that comeback night."

There were some lines that I fumbled; the tempo of sit-ups and poetry grew concurrently faster as the bardic fury took hold. But I caught the climax as the poet's voice rose:

> "He cut up his eyes and mussed up his face,
> And that last left hook *knocked his head out of place!*"

Cassius smiled and said no more for several sit-ups, as if waiting for Johansson to be carried to his corner. He resumed when the Swede's seconds had had time to slosh water in his pants and bring him around. The fight was done; the press took over:

> "A reporter asked: 'Ingo, will a rematch be put on?'
> Johansson said: 'Don't know. It might be postponed.'"

The poet did a few more silent strophes, and then said:

> "If he would have stayed in Sweden
> He wouldn't have took that beatin'."

Here, overcome by admiration, he lay back and laughed. After a minute or two, he said, "That rhymes. I like it."

There are trainers I know who, if they had a fighter who was a poet, would give up on him, no matter how good he looked, but Mr. Dundee is of the permissive school. Dundee has been a leading Italian name in the prizefighting business in this country ever since about 1910, when a manager named Scotty Monteith had a boy named Giuseppe Carrora whom he rechristened Johnny Dundee. Johnny became the hottest lightweight around; in 1923, in the twilight of his career, he boiled down and won the featherweight championship of the world. Clay's trainer is a brother of Chris Dundee, a promoter in Miami Beach, but they are not related to Johnny, who is still around, or to Joe and Vince Dundee, brothers out of Baltimore, who were welterweight and middleweight champions, respectively, in the late twenties and early thirties, and who are not related to Johnny, either.

"He is very talented," Dundee said while Clay was dressing. It was bitter cold outside, but he did not make Clay take a cold shower before putting his clothes on. "He likes his shower better at the hotel," he told me. It smacked of progressive education. Elaborating on Clay's talent, Dundee said, "He will jab you five or six times going away. Busy hands. And he has a left uppercut." He added that Clay, as a business enterprise, was owned and operated by a syndicate of ten leading citizens of Louisville, mostly distillers. They had given the boy a bonus of ten thousand dollars for signing up, and paid him a monthly allowance and his training expenses whether he fought or not—a research fellowship. In return, they took half his earnings when he had any. These had been inconsiderable until his most recent fight, when he made eight thousand dollars. His manager of record (since somebody has to sign contracts) was a member of this junta—Mr. William Faversham, a son of the old matinee idol. Dundee, the tutor in attendance, was a salaried employee. "The idea was he shouldn't be rushed," Dundee said. "Before they hired me, we had a conference about his future like he was a serious subject."

It sounded like flying in the face of the old rule that hungry fighters make the best fighters. I know an old-style manager named Al Weill, who at the beginning of the week used to give each of his fighters a five-dollar meal ticket that was good for five dollars and fifty cents in trade at a coffeepot on Columbus Avenue. A guy had to win a fight to get a second ticket before the following Monday. "It's good for them," Weill used to say. "Keeps their mind on their work."

That day in the gym, Clay's boxing had consisted of three rounds with an amateur light heavyweight, who had been unable to keep away from the busy hands. When the sparring partner covered his head with his arms, the poet didn't bother to punch to the body. "I'm a head-hunter," he said to a watcher who called his attention to this omission. "Keep punching at a man's head, and it mixes his mind." After that, he had skipped rope without a rope. His flippancy would have horrified Colonel John R. Stingo, an ancient connoisseur, who says, "Body-punching is capital investment," or the late Sam Langford, who, when asked why he punched so much for the body, said, "The head got eyes."

Now Cassius reappeared, a glass of fashion in a snuff-colored suit and one of those lace-front shirts, which I had never before known anybody with nerve enough to wear, although I had seen them in shirt-shop windows on Broadway. His tie was like two shoestring ends laid across each other, and his smile was white and optimistic. He did not appear to know how badly he was being brought up.

Just when the sweet science appears to lie like a painted ship upon a painted ocean, a new Hero, as Pierce Egan would term him, comes along like a Moran tug to pull it out of the doldrums. It was because Clay had some of the Heroic aura about him that I went uptown the next day to see Banks, the *morceau* chosen for the prodigy to perform in his big-time debut. The exhibition piece is usually a fighter who was once almost illustrious and is now beyond ambition, but Banks was only twenty-one. He had knocked out nine men in twelve professional fights, had won another fight on a decision, and had lost two, being knocked out once. But he had come back against the man who stopped him and had knocked *him* out in two rounds. That showed determination as well as punching power. I had already met Banks, briefly, at a press conference that the Madison Square Garden corporation gave for the two incipient Heroes, and he seemed the antithesis of the Kentucky bard—a grave, quiet young Deep Southerner. He was as introverted as Clay was extro. Banks, a lighter shade than Clay, had migrated to the automobile factories from Tupelo, Mississippi, and boxed as a professional from the start, to earn money. He said at the press conference that he felt he had "done excellently" in the ring, and that the man who had knocked him out, and whom he had subsequently knocked out, was "an excellent boxer." He had a long, rather pointed head, a long chin, and the kind of inverted-triangle torso that pro-proletarian artists like to put on their steelworkers. His shoulders were so wide that his neat ready-made suit floated around his waist, and he had long, thick arms.

Banks was scheduled to train at two o'clock in the afternoon at Harry Wiley's Gymnasium, at 137th Street and Broadway. I felt back at home in the fight world as soon as I climbed up from the subway and saw the place—a line of plate-glass windows above a Latin American bar, grill, and barbecue. The windows were flecked with legends giving the hours when the gym was open (it wasn't), the names of fighters training there (they weren't, and half of them had been retired for years), and plugs for physical fitness and boxing instruction. The door of the gym—"Harry Wiley's *Clean* Gym," the sign on it said—was locked, so I went into the Latin-American place and had a beer while I waited. I had had only half the bottle when a taxi drew up at the curb outside the window and five colored men, one little and four big, got out, carrying bags of gear. They had the key for the gym. I finished my beer and followed them.

By the time I got up the stairs, the three fellows who were going to spar were already in the locker room changing their clothes, and the only ones in sight were a big, solid man in a red jersey, who was laying out the gloves and bandages on a rubbing table, and a wispy little chap in an olive-green sweater, who was smoking a long rattail cigar. His thin black hair was carefully marcelled along the top of his narrow skull, a long gold watch chain dangled from his fob pocket, and he exuded an air of elegance, precision, and authority, like a withered but still peppery mahout in charge of a string of not quite bright elephants. Both men appeared occupied with their thoughts, so I made a tour of the room before intruding, reading a series of didactic signs that the proprietor had put up among the photographs of prizefighters and pinup girls. "Road Work Builds Your Legs," one sign said, and another, "Train Every Day—Great Fighters Are Made That Way." A third admonished, "The Gentleman Boxer Has the Most Friends." "Ladies Are Fine—At the Right Time," another said. When I had absorbed them all, I got around to the big man.

"Clay looks mighty fast," I said to him by way of an opening.

He said, "He may not be if a big fellow go after him. That amateur stuff don't mean too much." He himself was Johnny Summerlin, he told me, and he had fought a lot of good heavyweights in his day. "Our boy don't move so fast, but he got fast hands," he said. "He don't discourage easy, either. If we win this one, we'll be all set." I could see that they would be, because Clay has been getting a lot of publicity, and a boxer's fame, like a knight's armor, becomes the property of the fellow who licks him.

Banks now came out in ring togs and, after greeting me, held out his hands to Summerlin to be bandaged. He looked even more formidable without his street clothes. The two other fighters, who wore their names on their dressing robes, were Cody Jones, a heavyweight as big as Banks, and Sammy Poe, nearly as big. Poe, although a Negro, had a shamrock on the back of his robe—a sign that he was a wag. They were both Banks stablemates from Detroit, Summerlin said, and they had come along to spar with him. Jones had had ten fights and had won eight, six of them by knockouts. This was rougher opposition than any amateur light heavyweight. Banks, when he sparred with Jones, did not scuffle around but practiced purposefully a pattern of coming in low, feinting with head and body to draw a lead, and then hammering in hooks to body and head, following the combination with a right cross. His footwork was neat and geometrical but not flashy—he slid his soles along the mat, always set to hit hard. Jones, using his right hand often, provided rough competition but not substitute for Clay's blinding speed. Poe, the clown, followed Jones. He grunted and howled "Whoo-huh-huh!" every time he threw a punch, and Banks howled back; it sounded like feeding time at a zoo. This was a lively workout.

After the sparring, the little man, discarding his cigar, got into the ring alone with Banks. He wore huge sixteen- or eighteen-ounce sparring gloves, which he held, palm open, toward the giant, leading him in what looked like a fan dance. The little man, covering his meager chest with one glove, would hold up the other, and Banks would hit it. The punch coming into the glove sounded like a fastball striking a catcher's mitt. By his motions the trainer indicated a scenario, and Banks, from his crouch, dropped Clay ten or fifteen times this way, theoretically. Then the slender man called a halt and sent Banks to punch the bag. "Remember," he said, "you got to keep on top of him—keep the pressure on."

As the little man climbed out of the ring, I walked around to him and introduced myself. He said that his name was Theodore McWhorter, and that Banks was his baby, his creation—he had taught him everything. For twenty years, McWhorter said, he had run a gymnasium for boxers in Detroit—the Big D. (I supposed it must be pretty much like Wiley's, where we were talking.) He had trained hundreds of neighborhood boys to fight, and had had some good fighters in his time, like Johnny Summerlin, but never a champion. Something always went wrong.

There are fellows like this in almost every big town. Cus D'Amato, who brought Patterson through the amateurs and still has him, used to be one of them, with a one-room gym on Fourteenth Street, but he is among the few whoever hit the mother lode. I could see that McWhorter was a good teacher—such men often are. They are never former champions or notable boxers. The old star is impatient with beginners. He secretly hopes that they won't be as good as he was, and this is a self-defeating quirk in an instructor. The man with the little gym wants to prove himself vicariously. Every promising pupil, consequently, is himself, and he gets knocked out with every one of them, even if he lives to be eighty. McWhorter, typically, said he had been an amateur bantamweight in the thirties but had never turned pro, because times were so hard then that you could pick up more money boxing amateur. Instead of medals, you would get certificates redeemable for cash—two, three, five dollars, sometimes even ten. Once you were a pro, you might not get two fights a year. Whatever his real reason, he had not gone on.

"My boy never got nothing easy," he said. "He don't expect it. Nobody give him nothing. And a boy like that, when he got a chance to be something, he's dangerous."

"You think he's really got a chance?" I asked.

"If we didn't think so, we wouldn't have took the match," Mr. McWhorter said. "You can trap a man," he added mysteriously. "Flashy boxing is like running. You got a long lead, you can run freely. The other kid's way behind, you can sit down and play, get up fresh, and run away from him again. But you got a man running after you with a knife or a gun, pressing it in your back, you feel the pressure. You can't run so free. I'm fighting Clay my way." The substitution of the first for the third person in conversation is managerial usage. I knew that McWhorter would resubstitute Banks for himself in the actual fight.

We walked over to the heavy bag, where Banks was working. There was one other downtown spectator in the gym, and he came over and joined us. He was one of those anonymous experts, looking like all his kind, whom I have been seeing around gyms and fight camps for thirty years. "You can tell a Detroit fighter every time," he said. "They're well trained. They got the fundamentals. They can hit. Like from Philadelphia the fighters got feneese."

Mr. McWhorter acknowledged the compliment. "We have some fine *trainers* in Detroit," he said.

Banks, no longer gentle, crouched and swayed before the bag, crashing his left hand into it until the thing jigged and clanked its chains.

"Hit him in the belly like that and you got him," the expert said. "He can't take it there."

Banks stopped punching the bag and said, "Thank you, thank you," just as if the expert had said something novel.

"He's a good boy," McWhorter said as the man walked away. "A *polite* boy."

When I left to go downtown, I felt like the possessor of a possibly valuable secret. I toyed with the notion of warning the butterfly Cassius, my fellow-littérateur, of his peril, but decided that I must remain neutral and silent. In a dream the night before the fight, I heard Mr. McWhorter saying ominously, "You can trap a man." He had grown as big as Summerlin, and his cigar had turned into an elephant goad.

The temperature outside the Garden was around fifteen degrees on the night of the fight, and the crowd that had assembled to see Clay's debut was so thin that it could more properly be denominated a quorum. Only fans who like sociability ordinarily turn up for a fight that they can watch for nothing on television, and that night the cold had kept even the most gregarious at home. (The boxers, however, were sure of four thousand dollars apiece from television.) Only the sportswriters, the gamblers, and the fight mob were there—nonpayers all—and the Garden management, solicitous about how the ringside would look to the television audience, had to coax relative strangers into the working-press section. This shortage of spectators was too bad, because there was at least one red-hot preliminary, which merited a better audience. It was a six-rounder between a lad infelicitously named Ducky Dietz—a hooker and body puncher—and a light heavy from western Pennsylvania named Tommy Gerarde, who preferred a longer range but punched more sharply. Dietz, who shouldn't have, got the decision, and the row that followed warmed our little social group and set the right mood for the main event.

The poet came into the ring first, escorted by Dundee; Nick Florio, the brother of Patterson's trainer, Dan Florio; and a fellow named Gil Clancy, a physical education supervisor for the Department of Parks, who himself manages a good welterweight named Emile Griffith. (Griffith, unlike Clay, is a worrier. "He is always afraid of being devalued," Clancy says.) As a corner, it was the equivalent of being represented by Sullivan & Cromwell. Clay, who I imagine regretted parting with his lace shirt, had replaced it with a white robe that had a close-fitting red collar and red cuffs. He wore white buckskin bootees that came high on his calves, and, taking hold of the ropes in his corner, he stretched and bounced like a ballet dancer at the bar. In doing so, he turned his back to the other, or hungry, corner before Banks and his faction arrived.

Banks looked determined but slightly uncertain. Maybe he was trying to remember all the things McWhorter had told him to do. He was accompanied by McWhorter, Summerlin, and Harry Wiley, a plump, courtly colored man, who runs the clean gym. McWhorter's parchment brow was wrinkled with concentration, and his mouth was set. He looked like a producer who thinks he may have a hit and doesn't want to jinx it. Summerlin was stolid; he may have been remembering the nights when he had not quite made it. Wiley was comforting and solicitous. The weights were announced: Clay, 194½; Banks, 191¼. It was a difference too slight to count between heavyweights. Banks, wide-shouldered, narrow-waisted, looked as if he would be the better man at slinging a sledge or lifting weights; Clay, more cylindrically formed—arms, legs, and torso—moved more smoothly.

When the bell rang, Banks dropped into the crouch I had seen him rehearse, and began the stalk after Clay that was to put the pressure on him. I felt a species of complicity. The poet, still wrapped in certitude, jabbed, moved, teased, looking the *Konzertstück* over before he banged the ivories. By nimble dodging, as in Rome, he rendered the hungry fighter's attack quite harmless, but this time without keeping his hypnotic stare fixed steadily enough on the punch-hand. They circled around for a minute or so, and then Clay was hit, but not hard, by a left hand. He moved to his own left, across Banks's field of vision, and Banks, turning with him, hit him again, but this time full, with the rising left hook he had worked on so faithfully. The poet went down, and the three men crouching below Banks's corner must have felt, as they listened to the count, like a Reno tourist who hears the silver dollar jackpot come rolling down. It had been a solid shot—no fluke—and where one shot succeeds, there is no reason to think that another won't. The poet rose at the count of two, but the referee, Ruby Goldstein, as the rules in New York require, stepped between the boxers until the count reached eight, when he let them resume. Now that Banks knew he could hit Clay, he was full of confidence, and the gamblers, who had made Clay a 5–1 favorite, must have had a bad moment. None of them had seen Clay fight, and no doubt they wished they hadn't been so credulous. Clay, I knew, had not been knocked down since his amateur days, but he was cool. He neither rushed after Banks, like an angry kid, nor backed away from him. Standing straight up, he boxed and moved—cuff, slap, jab, and stick, the busy hands stinging like bees. As for Banks, success made him forget his whole plan. Instead of keeping the pressure on—moving in and throwing punches to force an opening—he forgot his right hand and began winging left hooks without trying to set Clay up for them. At the end of the round, the poet was in good shape again, and Banks, the more winded of the two, was spitting a handsome quantity of blood from the jabs that Clay had landed going away. Nothing tires a man more than swinging uselessly. Nevertheless, the knockdown had given Banks the round. The hungry fighter who had listened to his pedagogue was in front, and if he listened again, he might very well stay there.

It didn't happen. In the second round, talent asserted itself. Honest effort and sterling character backed by solid instruction will carry a man a good way, but unearned natural ability has a lot to be said for it. Young Cassius, who will never have to be lean, jabbed the good boy until he had spread his already wide nose over his face. Banks, I could see, was already having difficulty breathing, and the intellectual pace was just too fast. He kept throwing that left hook whenever he could get set, but he was like a man trying to fight off wasps with a shovel. One disadvantage of having had a respected teacher is that whenever the pupil gets in a jam he tries to remember what the professor told him, and there just isn't time. Like the Pole's in the Olympics, Banks's legs grew heavier, and he could not escape his rival. He did not, however, gaze helplessly into his corner of the ring; he kept on trying. Now Cassius, having mixed the mind, began to dig in. He would come in with a flurry of busy hands, jabbing and slapping his man off balance, and then, in close, drive a short, hard right to the head or a looping left to the slim waist. Two-thirds of the way through the round, he staggered Banks, who dropped forward to his glove tips, though his knees did not touch canvas. A moment later, Clay knocked him down fairly with a right hand, but McWhorter's pupil was not done.

The third round was even less competitive; it was now evident that Banks could not win, but he was still trying. He landed the last, and just about the hardest, punch of the round—a good left hook to the side of the poet's face. Clay looked surprised. Between the third and fourth rounds, the Boxing Commission physician, Dr. Schiff, trotted up the steps and looked into Banks's eyes. The Detroit lad came out gamely for the round, but the one-minute rest had not refreshed him. After the first flurry of punches, he staggered, helpless, and Goldstein stopped the match. An old fighter, brilliant but cursed with a weak jaw, Goldstein could sympathize.

When it was over, I felt that my first social duty was to the stricken. Clay, I estimated, was the kind of Hero likely to be around for a long while, and if he felt depressed by the knockdown, he had the contents of ten distilleries to draw upon for stimulation. I therefore headed for the loser's dressing room to condole with McWhorter, who had experienced another almost. When I arrived, Banks, sitting up on the edge of a rubbing table, was shaking his head, angry at himself, like a kid outfielder who has let the deciding run drop through his fingers. Summerlin was telling him what he had done wrong: "You can't hit anybody throwing just one punch all the time. You had him, but you lost him. You forgot to keep crowding." Then the unquenchable pedagogue said, "You're a better fighter than he is, but you lost your head. If you can only get him again . . ." But poor Banks looked only half convinced. What he felt, I imagine, was that he *had* had Clay, and that it might be a long time before he caught him again. If he had followed through, he would have been in line for dazzling matches—the kind that bring you five figures even if you lose. I asked him what punch had started him on the downgrade, but he just shook his head. Wiley, the gym proprietor, said there hadn't been any one turning point. "Things just went sour gradually all at once," he declared. "You got to respect a boxer. He'll pick you and peck you, peck you and pick you, until you don't know where you are."

[March, 1962]

THE MARVELOUS MOUTH

TOM WOLFE

One thing that stuck in my mind, for some reason, was the way that Cassius Clay and his brother, Rudy, and their high school pal, Tuddie King, and Frankie Tucker, the singer who was opening in Brooklyn, and Cassius's pride of "foxes," Sophia Burton, Dottie, Frenchie, Barbara, and the others, and Richie Pittman and "Lou" Little, the football player, and everybody else up there in Cassius's suite on the forty-second floor of the Americana Hotel kept telling time by looking out the panorama window and down at the clock on top of the Paramount Building on Times Square. Everybody had a watch. Cassius, for example, is practically a watch fancier. But, every time, somebody would look out the panorama window, across the City Lights scene you get from up high in the Americana and down to the lit-up clock on that whacky twenties-modern polyhedron on top of the Paramount Building.

One minute Cassius would be out in the middle of the floor reenacting his "High Noon" encounter with Sonny Liston in a Las Vegas casino. He has a whole act about it, beginning with a pantomime of him shoving open the swinging doors and standing there bowlegged, like a beer delivery man. Then he plays the part of the crowd falling back and whispering, "It's Cassius Clay, Cassius Clay, Cassius Clay, Cassius Clay." Then he plays the part of an effete Las Vegas hipster at the bar with his back turned, suddenly freezing in mid-drink, as the hush falls over the joint, and sliding his eyes around to see the duel. Then he plays the part of Cassius Clay stalking across the floor with his finger pointed at Sonny Liston and saying, "You big ugly bear," "You big ugly bear," about eighteen times, "I ain't gonna fight you on no September thirtieth, I'm gonna fight you right now. Right here. You too ugly to run loose, you big ugly bear. You so ugly, when you cry, the tears run down the back of your head. You so ugly, you have to sneak up on the mirror so it won't run off the wall," and so on, up to the point where Liston says,

"Come over here and sit on my knee, little boy, and I'll give you your orange juice," and where Cassius pulls back his right and three guys hold him back and keep him from throwing it at Liston, "And I'm hollering, 'Lemme go,' and I'm telling them out the side of my mouth, 'You better *not* lemme go.' " All this time Frankie Tucker, the singer, is contorted across one of the Americana's neo-Louis XIV chairs, breaking up and exclaiming, "That's my man!"

The next minute Cassius is fooling around with Rudy's phonograph-and-speaker set and having some fun with the foxes. The foxes are seated around the room at ornamental intervals, all ya-ya length silk sheaths, long legs and slithery knees. Cassius takes one of Rudy's cool jazz records or an Aretha Franklin or something like that off the phonograph and puts on one of the 45-r.p.m. rock-and-roll records that the singers keep sending to him at the hotel.

"Those are Rudy's records, I don't *dig* that mess. I'm just a boy from Louisville"—he turns his eyes up at the foxes—"I dig rock and roll. Isn't that right?"

All the girls are hip, and therefore cool jazz fans currently, so most of them think the whole thing over for a few seconds before saying, "That's right."

Cassius puts a 45-r.p.m. on and says, "This old boy's an alley singer, nobody ever heard of him, he sings about beans and bread and all that old mess."

Cassius starts laughing at that and looking out over the city lights, out the panorama window. The girls aren't sure whether he is laughing with or at the alley singer.

Cassius scans the foxes and says, "This is *my* crowd. They don't dig that other mess, either."

The girls don't say anything.

"Is that your kinda music? I know it's *hers*," he says, looking at Francine, who is sitting pretty still. "She's about to fall over."

And maybe at this point somebody says, "What time is it?" And Rudy or somebody looks out the panorama window to the clock on the Paramount Building and says, "Ten minutes to ten."

Cassius had just come from the Columbia Records studio, across from the hotel at Seventh Avenue and Fifty-second, where he was making an album, *I Am the Greatest,* a long pastiche of poems and skits composed wholly in terms of his impending fight with Sonny Liston. The incessant rehearsing of his lines for two weeks, most of them lines he had sprung at random at press conferences and so forth over a period of a year and a half, had made Cassius aware, as probably nothing else, of the showman's role he was filling. And made him tempted by it.

After cutting up a little for Frankie Tucker and the foxes and everybody—showing them how he could *act,* really—he went over to one side of the living room and sat in a gangster-modern swivel chair and propped his feet up on the panorama-window ledge and talked a while. Everybody else was talking away in the background. Somebody had put the cool jazz back on and some husky girl with one of those augmented-sevenths voices was singing "Moon Over Miami."

"What's that club Leslie Uggams was at?" Cassius asked.

"The Metropole."

"The Metropole, that's right. That's one of the big ones out there, ain't it?"

His designation of the Metropole Café as "a big one" is an interesting thing in itself, but the key phrase is "out there." To Cassius, New York and the hot spots and the cool life are out there beyond his and Rudy's and Tuddie's suite at the Americana and beyond his frame of reference. Cassius does not come to New York as the hip celebrity, although it would be easy enough, but as a phenomenon. He treats Broadway as though these were still the days when the choirboys at Lindy's would spot a man in a white Palm Beach–brand suit heading up from Forty-ninth Street and say, "Here comes Winchell," or "Here comes Hellinger," or even the way Carl Van Vechten's Scarlet Creeper treated 125th Street in the days of the evening promenade. Cassius likes to get out among them.

About ten-fifteen P.M. he motioned to Sophia and started leaving the suite. All five girls got up and followed. The procession was spectacular even for Seventh Avenue on a crowded night with the chocolate-drink stands open. Cassius, six feet three, two hundred pounds, was wearing a black-and-white-checked jacket, white tab-collared shirt and black tie, light gray Continental trousers, black pointed-toe Italian shoes, and walking with a very cocky walk. The girls were walking one or two steps behind, all five of them, dressed in slayingly high couture. There were high heels and garden-party hats. Down at the corner, at Fifty-second Street, right at the foot of the hotel,

Cassius stopped, looked all around, and began loosening up his shoulders, the way prizefighters do. This, I found out, is Cassius's signal, an unconscious signal, that he is now available for crowd collecting. He got none on that corner, but halfway down to Fifty-first Street people started saying, "That's Cassius Clay, Cassius Clay, Cassius Clay, Cassius Clay," the way he had mimicked it back in the hotel. Cassius might have gotten his crowd at Fifty-first Street—he was looking cocky and the girls were right behind him in a phalanx, looking gorgeous—but he headed on across the street, when the light changed, over to where two fellows he knew were standing a quarter of the way down the block.

"Here he comes. Whatta you say, champ?"

"Right, man. Hey," said Cassius, referring the girls to the taller and older of the two men, "I want you all to meet one of the greatest singers in New York." A pause there. "What is your name, man, I meet so many people here."

"Hi, Pinocchio," said one of the foxes, and the man smiled.

"Pinocchio," said Cassius. Then he said, "You see all these queens are with me?" He made a sweeping motion with his hand. The girls were around him on the sidewalk. "All these foxes."

"That's sump'n else, man."

Cassius could have gotten his crowd easily on the sidewalk outside the Metropole. When it's warm, there is always a mob out there looking in through the front doorway at the band strung out along the bandstand, which is really more of a shelf. If there is a rock-and-roll band, there will always be some Jersey teenagers outside twisting their ilia to it. That night there was more of a Dixieland or jump band on, although Lionel Hampton was to come on later, and Cassius entered, by coincidence, while an old tune called "High Society" was playing. All the foxes filed in, a step or so behind. The Metropole Café has not seen many better entrances. Cassius looked gloriously bored.

The Metropole is probably the perfect place for a folk hero to show up at in New York. It is kind of a crossroads, or ideal type, of all the hot spots and live joints in the country. I can tell you two things about it that will help you understand what the Metropole is like, if you have never been there. First, the color motif is submarine green and Prussian blue, all reflected in huge wall-to-wall mirrors. If the stand-up beer crowd gets so thick you can't see over them to the bandstand, you can always watch through the mirrors. Second, the place attracts high-livers of a sort that was there that night. I particularly remember one young guy, standing there at the bar in the submarine-green and Prussian-blue light with sunglasses on. He had on a roll-collar shirt, a silvery tie, a pale-gray suit of the Continental cut, and pointed black shoes. He had a king-size cigarette pasted on his lower lip, and when the band played "The Saints," he broke into a terribly "in" and hip grin, which brought the cigarette up horizontal. He clapped his hands and hammered his right heel in time to the drums and kept his eyes on the trumpet player the whole time. The thing is, kids don't even do that at Williams Collage any-more, but they do it at the Metropole.

This same kid came over to ask Cassius for his autograph at one point. He thought "The Saints" was hip, but he must not have thought autograph-hunting was very hip. He wanted an autograph, however. He handed Cas-sius a piece of paper for his autograph and said, "It's not for me, it's for a buddy of mine, he wants it." This did not score heavily with Cassius.

"Where's your pen?" he said.

"I don't have a pen," the kid said. "It's for a friend of mine."

"You ain't got no pen, man," said Cassius.

About a minute later the kid came back with a pen, and Cassius signed the piece of paper, and the kid said, "Thank you, Cassius, you're a gentleman." He said it very seriously. "It's for a buddy of mine. You're a real gentleman."

That was the tone of things that night in the Metropole. Everything was just a little off, the way Cassius saw it.

From the moment he walked into the doorway of the Metropole, people were trying to prod him into the act.

"You *really* think you can beat Sonny Liston, man?"

"Liston must fall in eight."

"You *really* mean that?"

"If he gives me any jive, he goes in five," Cassius said, but in a terribly matter-of-fact, recitative voice, all the while walking on ahead, with the foxes moseying in behind him, also gloriously bored.

His presence spread over the Metropole immediately. As I said, it is the perfect place for folk heroes, for there is no one in there who is not willing to be impressed. The management, a lot of guys in tuxedos with the kind of Hollywood black ties that tuck under the collars and are adorned with little pearl stickpins and such devices—the management was rushing up. A guy at the bar, well-dressed, came up behind Cassius and touched him lightly at about the level of the sixth rib and went back to the bar and told his girl, "That's Cassius Clay. I just touched him, no kidding."

They sat all the foxes down in a booth at about the middle of the Metropole Café and gave Cassius a chair by himself right next to them. Lionel Hampton came up with the huge smile he has and shook Cassius's hand and made a fuss over him without any jive about when Liston must fall. Cassius liked that. But then the crowd came around for autographs, and they wanted him to go into his act. It was a hell of a noisy place.

But the crowd at the Metropole hit several wrong notes. One was hit by a white man about fifty-five, obviously a Southerner from the way he talked, who came up to Clay from behind—people were gaggled around from all sides—and stuck the blank side of a Pennsylvania Railroad receipt, the kind you get when you buy your ticket on the train, in his face and said in a voice you could mulch the hollyhocks with:

"Here you are, boy, put your name right there."

It was more or less the same voice Mississippians use on a hot day when the colored messenger boy has come into the living room and is standing around nervously. "Go ahead, boy, sit down. Sit in that seat right there."

Cassius took the Pennsylvania Railroad receipt without looking up at the man, and held it for about ten seconds, just staring at it.

Then he said in a slightly accusing voice, "Where's your pen?"

"I don't have a pen, boy. Some of these people around here got a pen. Just put your name right there."

Cassius still didn't look up. He just said, "Man, there's one thing you gotta learn. You don't *ever* come around and ask a man for an autograph if you ain't got no pen."

The man retreated and more people pressed in.

Cassius treats the fact of color—but not race—casually. Sometimes, when he is into his act, he will look at somebody and say, "You know, man, you lucky, you seen me here in living color." One time, I remember, a CBS news crew was filming an interview with him in the Columbia Records Studio A, at 799 Seventh Avenue, when the cameraman said to the interviewer, who was moving in on Cassius with the microphone: "Hey, Jack, you're throwing too much shadow on Cassius. He's dark enough already."

All the white intellectuals in the room cringed. Cassius just laughed. In point of fact, he is not very dark at all.

But he does not go for any of the old presumptions, such as, "Put your name right there, boy."

Another wrong note was hit when a middle-aged couple came up. They were white. The woman struck you as a kind of Arkansas Blanche DuBois. They looked like they wanted autographs at first. They did in a way. They were both loaded. She had an incredible drunk smile that spread out soft and gooey like a can of Sherwin-Williams paint covering the world. She handed Cassius a piece of paper and a pencil and wanted him to write down both his name *and* her name. He had just about done that when she put her hand out very slowly to caress his cheek.

"Can I touch you?" she said. "I just want to touch you."

Cassius pulled his head back.

"Naw," he said. "My girlfriends might get jealous."

He didn't call them foxes to her. He said it in a nice way. After she left, though, he let her have it. It was the only time I ever heard him say anything contemptuously of anyone.

"Can I *touch* you, can I *touch* you," he said. He could mimic her white Southern accent in a fairly, devastating way.

"Naw, you can't touch me," he said, just as if he were answering her face-to-face. "Nobody can touch me."

As a matter of fact, Cassius is good at mimicking a variety of white Southern accents. He doesn't do it often, but when he does it, it has an extra wallop because he has a pronounced Negro accent of his own, which he makes no attempt to polish. He only turns it on heavier from time to time for comic effect. Once I heard him mimic both himself, a Louisville Negro, and newspapermen, Louisville whites, in one act.

I had asked him if the cocky act he was putting on all over the country, and in England for that matter, surprised the people who knew him back home. What I was getting at was whether he had been a cocky kid in Louisville back in the days before anybody ever heard of him. He changed the direction slightly.

"They believe anything you tell 'em about me back in Louisville. News-papermen used to come around and I'd give 'em predictions and they'd say, 'What is this boy doing?'

"I had a fight with Lamar Clark, I believe it was, and I said [*Clay mimicking Clay, heavy, high-flown, bombastic Negro accent*]: 'Lamar will fall in two.' I knocked him out in two, and they said [*Clay mimicking drawling Kentucky Southern accent*]: 'Suht'n'ly dee-ud.' " (Certainly did.)

"I said, 'Miteff will fall in six.'

"They said, 'Suht'n'ly dee-ud.'

"I said, 'Warren will fall in four.'

"They said, 'Suht'n'ly dee-ud.' "

Clay had a lot better look on his face when people came by to admire what he had become rather than the funny act he puts on.

One young Negro, sharp-looking, as they say, in Continental clothes with a wonderful pair of Latin-American sunglasses, the kind that are narrow like the mask the Phantom wears in the comic strip, came by and didn't ask Cassius when Liston would fall. He shot an admiring, knowing look at the foxes, and said, "Who are all these girls, man?"

"Oh, they just the foxes," said Cassius.

"Man, I like your choice of foxes, I'm telling you," the kid said.

This tickled Cassius and he leaned over and told it to Sophia.

The kid, meantime, went around to the other side of the booth. He had a glorified version of how Cassius was living. He believed Cassius as he leaned over to the girls when the waiter came around and said, "You get anything you want. I own this place. I own all of New York." (Sophia gave him a derisive laugh for that.)

The kid leaned over to one of the girls and said: "Are you all his personal property?"

"What are you talking about, boy. What do you mean, his *personal property?*"

"You know, *his,*" said the kid. He was getting embarrassed, but he still had traces of a knowing look salivating around the edges.

"Why do we have to be his personal property?"

"Well, like, I mean, you know," said the kid. His mouth had disintegrated completely into an embarrassed grin by now, but his eyes were still darting around, as if to say, "Why don't they level with me. I'm a hip guy."

Cassius also liked it when a Negro he had met a couple of nights before, an older guy, came around and didn't ask when Liston would fall.

"I saw a crowd on the sidewalk out there, and I might have *known* you'd be Linside," he told Cassius. "What's going on?"

"Oh, I'm just sitting here with the foxes," said Cassius.

"You sure are," the fellow said.

A young white kid with a crew cut said, "Are you afraid of Liston?"

Cassius said mechanically, "That big ugly bear? If I was worried, I'd be out training and I'm out partying."

Cassius had a tall, pink drink. It was nothing but Hawaiian Punch, right out of the can.

"How you gonna beat him?"

"I'll beat that bear in eight rounds. I'm strong and I'm beautiful and I'll beat that bear in eight rounds."

"You promise?" said the kid. He said it very seriously and shook Cassius's hand, as though he were getting ready to go outside and drop off a couple of grand with his Weehawken bookmaker. He apparently squeezed pretty hard. This fellow being a fighter and all, a guy ought to shake hands like a man with him.

Cassius pulled his hand away suddenly and wrung it. "Don't ever squeeze a fighter's hand, man. That hand's worth about three hundred thousand dollars," he said, making a fist. "You don't have to shake hands, you doing good just to lay eyes on me."

The kid edged off with his buddy and he was saying, "He said, 'Don't ever squeeze a fighter's hand.' "

By now Cassius was looking slightly worse than gloriously bored.

"If they don't stop worrying me," he said, "I'm gonna get up and walk out of here."

Sophia leaned over and told me, "He doesn't mean that. He loves it."

Of all the girls, Sophia seemed to be closest to him. She found him amusing. She liked him.

"You know, he's really a normal boy," she told me. She threw her head to one side as if to dismiss Cassius's big front. "Oh, he's got a big mouth. But aside from that, he's a real normal boy."

The foxes were beginning to stare a little morosely into their Gin Fizzes and Brandy Alexanders and Sidecars, and even the stream of autograph seekers was slowing down. It was damned crowded and you could hardly hear yourself talk. Every now and then the drummer would go into one of those crazy skyrocketing solos suitable for the Metropole, and the trumpet player would take the microphone and say, "That's what Cassius Clay is going to do to Sonny Liston's head!" and Cassius would holler, "Right!" but it was heavy weather. By this time Richie Pittman had dropped in, and Cassius motioned to him. They got up and went out "for some air." At the doorway there was a crowd on the sidewalk looking in at the band-stand, as always. They made a fuss over Cassius, but he just loosened his shoulders a little and made a few wisecracks. He and Richie started walking up toward the Americana.

It was after midnight, and at the foot of the hotel, where this paseo-style sidewalk pans out almost like a patio, there was a crowd gathered around. Cassius didn't miss that. They were watching three street musicians, colored boys, one with a makeshift bass—a washtub turned upside down with a cord coming up out of the bottom, forming a single string; a drum—a large tin-can bottom with spoons as sticks; and one guy dancing. They were playing "Pen-nies from Heaven," a pretty good number for three guys getting ready to pass the hat. Cassius just walked up to the edge of the crowd and stood there. One person noticed him, then another, and pretty soon the old "That's Cassius Clay, Cassius Clay, Cassius Clay" business started. Cassius's spirits were ris-ing. "Pennies from Heaven" stopped, and the three colored boys looked a little nonplussed for a moment. The show was being stolen. Somebody had said something about "Sonny Liston," only this time Cassius had the 150-watt eyes turned on, and he was saying, "The only thing I'm worried about is, I don't want Sonny Liston trying to crash *my* victory party the way I crashed his. I'm gonna tell him right before the fight starts so he won't forget it. 'Sonny,' I'm gonna tell him, 'Sonny Liston, I don't want you trying to crash my victory party tonight, you hear that? I want you to hear that now, 'cause you ain't gonna be able to hear anything eight rounds from now.' And if he gives me any jive when I tell him that, if he gives me any jive, he must fall in five."

A soldier, a crank-sided kid who looked like he must have gone through the battered syndrome at about age four, came up to take the role of Cassius's chief debater. Cassius likes that when he faces a street crowd. He'll hold a press conference for anybody, even a soldier on leave on Seventh Avenue.

"Where you gonna go after Sonny Liston whips you?" the kid said. "I got some travel folders right here."

"Boy," said Cassius, "you talk about traveling. I want you to go to that fight, 'cause you gonna see the launching of a human satellite. Sonny Liston."

The crowd was laughing and carrying on.

"I got some travel folders," the kid said. "You better look 'em over. I can get you a mask, too."

"You gonna bet against me?" said Cassius.

"Every cent I can get my hands on," said the kid.

"Man," said Cassius, "you better save your money, 'cause there's gonna be a total eclipse of the Sonny."

Cassius was standing there looking like a million dollars, and Richie was standing by, sort of riding shotgun. By this time, the crowd was so big, it was spilling off the sidewalk into Fifty-second Street. All sorts of incredible people were moving up close, including sclerotic old men with big-lunch ties who edged in with jag-legged walks. A cop was out in the street going crazy, trying to prod everybody back on the sidewalk. A squad car drove up, and the cop on the street put on a real tough tone. "All right, goddamn it," he said to an old sclerotic creeper with a big-lunch tie, "get up on the sidewalk."

Cassius looked around at me as if to say, "See, man? That's only what I predicted"—which is to say, "When I walk down the street, the crowds, they have to call the police."

The autograph business had started now, and people were pushing in with paper and pens, but Cassius wheeled around toward the three colored boys, the musicians, and said, "Autographs are one dollar tonight. Everyone puts one dollar in there" (the musicians had a corduroy-ribbed box out in front of the tub) "gets the autograph of Cassius Clay, the world's strongest fighter, the world's most beautiful fighter, the onliest fighter who predicts when they will fall."

The colored boys took the cue and started up with "Pennies from Heaven" again. The kid who danced was doing the merengue by himself. The kid on the bass was flailing away like a madman. All the while Cassius was orating on the corner.

"Come on, man, don't put no fifty cents in there, get that old dollar bill outa there. Think at all you're getting free here, the music's so fine and here you got Cassius Clay right here in front of you in living color, the next heavy-weight champion of the world, the man who's gon' put old man Liston in orbit."

The dollar bills started piling up in the box, and the solo merengue kid was dervishing around wilder still, and Cassius wouldn't let up.

"Yeah, they down there right now getting that Medicare ready for that old man, and if I hit him in the mouth he's gonna need Denticare. That poor ol' man, he's so ugly, his wife drives him to the gym every morning 'fore the sun comes up, so nobody'll have to look at him 'round home. Come on, man, put yo' money in that box, people pay good money to hear this—"

The bass man was pounding away, and Cassius turned to me and said, behind his hand, "Man, you know one thing? If I get whipped, they gonna run me outa the country. You know that?"

Then he threw his head back and his arms out, as if he were falling backward. "Can you see me flat out on my back like this?"

The colored kids were playing "Pennies from Heaven," and Cassius Clay had his head thrown back and his arms out, laughing, and looking straight up at the top of the Americana Hotel.

[1963]

MIAMI NOTEBOOK: CASSIUS CLAY AND MALCOLM X

GEORGE PLIMPTON

1.

The press was incensed at Cassius Clay's behavior before the Liston fight. You could feel it. They wanted straight answers, and they weren't getting them. Usually, particularly with fighters, the direct question of extreme sim-plicity—which is of great moment to the sportswriters—will get a reply in kind. "Champ," asks the sportswriter, "how did you sleep last night and what did you have for breakfast?" When the champ considers the matter and says he slept real fine and had six eggs and four glasses of milk, the sports-writer puts down, *"gd sleep 6 eggs 4 gl milk,"* on his pad, and a little while later the statistic goes out over Western Union.

But with Clay, such a question simply served to unleash an act, an enter-tainment which included poetry, the brandishing of arms and canes, a cho-rus thrown in—not a dull show by any standard, even if you've seen it a few times before. The press felt that the act—it was constantly referred to as an "act"—was born of terror or lunacy. What *should* have appealed, Cassius surely being the most colorful, if bizarre, heavyweight since, well, John L. Sullivan or Jack Johnson, none of this seemed to work at all. The press's atti-tude was largely that of the lip-curling disdain the Cambridge police have to-ward the antics of students heeling for the *Harvard Lampoon.*

One of the troubles, I think—it occurred to me as I watched Clay at his last press conference on February 24 before the fight—is that his appearance does not suit his manner. His great good looks are wrong for the excessive things he shouts. Archie Moore used the same sort of routine as Clay to get himself a shot at both the light-heavyweight and heavyweight champi-onships—self-promotion, gags, bizarre suits, a penchant for public speak-

27

ing—but his character was suited to it, his face with a touch of slyness in it, and always humor. So the press was always very much in his support, and they had much to do with Moore's climb from obscurity. At his training camp outside San Diego—the Salt Mines it is called, where Cassius himself did a tour at the start of his career—Moore has built a staircase in the rocks, sixty or seventy steps, each with a reporter's name painted in red to symbolize the assistance the press gave him. Clay's face, on the other hand, does not show humor. He has a fine grin, but his features are curiously deadpan when the self-esteem begins, which, of course, desperately needs humor as a soften-ing effect. Clay himself bridled at the resentment he caused. It must have puz-zled him to be cast as the villain in a fight with Liston, who on the surface at least, had absolutely no flair or panache except as a symbol of destructiveness.

Clay made a short, final address to the newspapermen. "This is your last chance," he said. "It's your last chance to get on the bandwagon. I'm keeping a list of all you people. After the fight is done, we're going to have a roll call up there in the ring. And when I see so-and-so said this fight was a mismatch, why I'm going to have a little ceremony and some *eating* is going on—eating of words." His manner was that of the admonishing schoolteacher. The press sat in their rows at the Miami Auditorium staring balefully at him. It seemed incredible that a smile or two wouldn't show up on a writer's face. It was so wonderfully preposterous. But I didn't see any.

2.

In the corridors around the press headquarters in the Miami Auditorium, one was almost sure to run into King Levinsky, a second-rate heavyweight in his prime (he was one of Joe Louis's bums of the month) who fought too long, so that it had affected him, and he is now an ambulatory tie-salesman. He would appear carrying his ties, which are labeled with a pair of boxing gloves and his name, in a cardboard box, and he'd get rid of them in jig time. His sales technique was formidable: he would single out a prospect, move down the corridor for him fast, and sweeping an arm around the fellow's neck pull him in close . . . to within range of a hoarse and somewhat wetly deliv-ered whisper to the ear: "From the King? You buy a tie from the King?" The victim, his head in the crook of the fighter's massive arm, would mumble and nod weakly, and fish for his bankroll. Almost everyone had a Levinsky tie, though you didn't see too many people wearing them. When the King appeared around a corner, the press would scatter, some into a row of phone booths set along the corridor. "Levinsky!" they'd say and move off quickly and officiously. Levinsky would peer around and often he'd pick someone *in* a phone booth, set his cardboard box down, and shake the booth gently. You'd see him watching the fellow inside, and then the door would open and the fellow would come out and buy his tie. They only cost a dollar.

Sometimes Levinsky, if he knew he'd already sold you a couple of ties, would get you in the crook of his arm and he'd recount things he thought you ought to know about his career. "Joe Louis finished me," he'd say. "In one round that man turned me from a fighter to a guy selling ties." He said this without rancor, as if Louis had introduced him to a chosen calling. "I got rapport now," he'd say—this odd phrase—and then he'd let you go. Clay came down the corridors after the weigh-in and Levinsky bounded after him. "He's gonna take you, kid," he hollered. "Liston's gonna take you, make you a guy selling ties . . . partners with me, kid, you kin be *partners* with me." Clay and his entourage were moving at a lively clip, canes on high, shouting that they were ready to "rumble," and it was doubtful the chilling offer got through.

At the late afternoon press parties in the bar of the Roney Plaza, the promoters had another fighter at hand—the antithesis of Levinsky—a personable Negro heavyweight, Marty Marshall, the only man to beat Liston. The promoters brought him down from Detroit, his hometown, to impress the writers that Liston wasn't invincible, hoping that this notion would appear in their columns and help promote a gate lagging badly since the fight was universally considered a mismatch. Marshall met Liston three times, winning the first, then losing twice, though decking Liston in the second, always baffling him with an unpredictable attack. Liston blamed his one loss on making the mistake of dropping his jaw to laugh at Marshall's maneuvers, and *bam,* getting it broken with a sudden punch.

Marshall didn't strike one as a comic figure. He is a tall, graceful man, conservatively dressed, a pleasant face with small, round, delicate ears, and a quick smile. Greeting him was a complex matter, because he was attended for a while by someone who introduced him by saying, "Shake the hand that broke Sonny Liston's jaw!" Since Marshall is an honest man and it was a left hook that did the business, his *left* would come out, and one had to consider whether to take it with one's own left or with the right, before getting down to the questions. There was almost always a circle around him in the bar. The press couldn't get enough of what it was to be in the ring with Liston. Marshall didn't belittle the experience (after all, he'd been beaten twice), and indeed some of the things he said made one come away with even more respect for the champion.

"When I knocked him down with that hook in the second fight, he got up angry," said Marshall. "He hit me three shots you shouldn't've thrown at a bull. The first didn't knock me down, but it hurt so much I went down anyway."

"Geezus," said one of the reporters.

"Does he say anything—I mean when he's angry—can you see it?"

"No," said Marshall. "He's silent. He just comes for you."

"Gee*zus,*" said the reporter again.

We all stood around, looking admiringly at Marshall, jiggling the ice in our glasses.

One of the writers cleared his throat. "I heard a story about the champion this morning," he said. "He does his roadwork, you know, out at the Normandy Golf Course, and there was this greenskeeper working out there, very early, pruning the grass at the edge of a water hazard, the mist coming off the grass, very quiet, spooky, you know, and he hears this noise behind him and there's Liston there, about ten feet away, looking out of his hood at him, and this guy gives a big scream and pitches forward into the water."

"Yeah." said Marshall. He was smiling. "I can see that."

3.

Each fighter had his spiritual adviser, his *guru* at hand. In Liston's camp was Father Murphy, less a religious adviser than a confidant and friend of the champion. In Clay's camp was Malcolm X, who was then one of the high officials of the Black Muslim sect, indeed its most prominent spokesman, though he has since defected to form his own black nationalist political movement. For months he had been silent. Elijah Muhammad, the supreme leader, the Messenger of Allah, had muzzled him since November for making intemperate remarks after the assassination of President Kennedy. But he had been rumored to be in Miami, and speculation was strong that he was there to bring Cassius Clay into the Muslim fold.

I was riding in a car just after the weigh-in with Archie Robinson, who is Clay's business manager and closest friend—a slightly built young man, not much older than Clay, one would guess, very polite and soft-spoken—and he asked me if I'd like to meet Malcolm X. I said yes, and we drove across Biscayne Bay to the Negro-clientele Hampton House Motel in Miami proper—a small-town hotel compared to the Babylon towers across the bay, with a small swimming pool, a luncheonette, a pitch-dark bar where you had to grope to find a chair, with a dance floor and a band which came on later, and most of the rooms in balconied barrackslike structures out back. It was crowded and very lively with people in town not only for the fight but also for an invitation golf tournament.

I waited at a side table in the luncheonette. Malcolm X came in after a while, moving by the tables very slowly. Elijah Muhammad's ministers—Malcolm X was one of them—are said to emulate him even to the speed of his walk, which is considerable. But the luncheonette was not set up for a swift entrance. The tables were close together, and Malcolm X came by them carefully—a tall, erect man in his thirties, a lean, intelligent face with a long pronounced jaw, a wide mouth set in it which seems caught in a perpetual smile. He was carrying one of the Cassius Clay camp's souvenir canes, and with his horn-rimmed glasses, his slow stately walk, and with Robinson half a step behind him, guiding him, I thought for a second that he'd gone blind. He sat down, unwrapped a package of white peppermints which he picked at steadily, and began talking. Robinson sat with us for a while, but he had things to attend to.

I took notes from time to time, scratching them down on the paper tablecloth, then in a notebook. Malcolm X did not seem to mind. He said he was going to be unmuzzled in March, which was only five days away. He himself wrote on the tablecloth once in a while—putting down a word he wanted to emphasize. He had an automatic pen-and-pencil set in his shirt pocket—the clasps initialed FOI on one (Fruit of Islam, which is the military organization within the Muslim temple) and ISLAM on the other. He wore a red ring with a small crescent.

Malcolm X's voice is gentle, and he often smiles broadly, but not with

humor, so that the caustic nature of what he is saying is not belied. His manner is distant and grave, and he asks, mocking slightly, "Sir?" when a question is not heard or understood, leaning forward and cocking his head. His
answers are always skilled, with a lively and effective use of image, and yet as
the phrases came I kept thinking of Cassius Clay and *his* litany—the fighter's
is more limited, and a different sort of thing, but neither of them ever *stumbles*
over words, or ideas, or appears balked by a question, so that one rarely has
the sense of the brain actually working but rather that it is engaged in rote,
simply a recording apparatus playing back to an impulse. Thus he is truly in-
tractable—Malcolm X—absolutely dedicated, self-assured, self-principled,
with that great energy . . . the true revolutionary. He does not doubt.

When give-and-take of argument is possible, when what Malcolm X says
can be doubted, his assurance and position as an extremist give him an advantage in debate. He appreciates that this is so, and it amuses him. "The extremist," he said, "will always ruin the liberals in debate—because the
liberals have something too nebulous to sell, or too impossible to sell—like the
Brooklyn Bridge. That's why a white segregationalist—what's his name,
Kilpatrick—will destroy Farmer, and why William Buckley makes a fool of
Normal Mailer, and why Martin Luther King would lose a debate with me.
Why King? Because integration is ridiculous, a dream. I am not interested in
dreams, but in the nightmare. Martin Luther King, the rest of them, they are
thinking about dreams. But then really King and I have nothing to debate
about. We are both indicting. I would say to him: 'You indict and give them
hope. I'll indict and give them no hope.'"

I asked him about the remarks that had caused him his muzzling by Elijah Muhammad. His remarks about the assassination had been taken out of
context, he said, though it would be the sheerest hypocrisy to suggest that
Kennedy was a friend to the Negro. Kennedy was a politician (he wrote
down the word on the paper tablecloth with his FOI pencil and circled it)—
a "cold-blooded politician" who transformed last year's civil rights march on
Washington into a "crawl" by endorsing the march, joining it, though it was
supposed to be a protest against the country's leaders . . . a politician's trick
which tamped out the fuse though the powder keg was there. Friend of the
Negro? There never had been a politician who was the Negro's friend. Power
corrupts. Lincoln? A crooked, deceitful hypocrite, claiming championship
to the cause of the Negro who, one hundred years later, finds himself singing

"We Shall Overcome." The Supreme Court? Its decision is nothing but an act of hypocrisy . . . nine Supreme Court justices expert in legal phraseology tangling the words of their decision in such a way that lawyers can dilly-dally over it for years—which of course they will continue to do. . . .

I scribbled these phrases, and others, on the paper tablecloth, mildly surprised to see the Muslim maxims in my own handwriting. We talked about practicality, which is the weakest area of the Muslim plans, granted the fires of resentment are justifiably banked. Malcolm X was not particularly concerned. What may be illogical or impractical in the long run is dismissed as not being pertinent to the *moment*—which is what the Negro must concern himself with. He could sense my frustration at this. It is not easy to dismiss what is practical. He had a peppermint and smiled.

I changed the subject and asked him what he did for exercise.

"I take walks," he said. "Long walks. We believe in exercise, physical fitness, but as for commercial sport, that's a racket. Commercial sport is the pleasure of the idle rich. The vice of gambling stems from it." He wrote down the word "Promoter" on the tablecloth with his FOI pencil and circled it. "The Negro never comes out ahead—never *one* in the history of sport."

"Clay perhaps."

"Perhaps." He liked talking about Clay. "I'm interested in him as a human being," he said. He tapped his head. "Not many people know the quality of the mind he's got in there. He fools them. One forgets that though a clown never imitates a wise man, the wise man can imitate the clown. He is sensitive, very humble, yet shrewd—with as much untapped mental energy as he has physical power. He should be a diplomat. He has that instinct of seeing a tricky situation shaping up—my own presence in Miami, for example—and resolving how to sidestep it. He knows how to handle people, to get them functioning. He gains strength from being around people. He can't stand being alone. The more people around, the better—just as it takes water to prime a country well. If the crowds are big in there tonight in the Miami Auditorium, he's likely to beat Liston. But they won't be. The Jews have heard he's a Muslim and they won't show up."

"Perhaps they'll show up to see him taken," I said.

"Sir?" he said, with that slight cock of the head.

"Perhaps . . ."

"When Cassius said, 'I am a man of race,'" Malcolm X went on, "it pleased the Negroes. He couldn't eliminate the color factor. But the press and the white people saw it another way. They saw him, suddenly, as a threat. Which is why he has become the villain—why he is booed, the outcast." He seemed pleased with this.

Wasn't it possible, I asked, that the braggart, the loudmouth was being booed, not necessarily the Black Muslim? After all, Clay had been heartily booed during the Doug Jones fight in Madison Square Garden, and that was before his affiliation with the Muslims was known.

"You, *you* can't tell," replied Malcolm X. "But a Negro can feel things in sounds. The booing at the Doug Jones fight was good-natured—I was there—but the booing is now different . . . defiant . . . inflamed by the columnists, all of them, critical of Cassius for being a Muslim."

"And as a fighter?"

"He has tremendous self-confidence," said Malcolm X. "I've never heard him mention fear. Anything you're afraid of can whip you. Fear magnifies what you're afraid of. One thing about our religion is that it removes fear. Christianity is based on fear."

I remarked that the Muslim religion, since it has its taboos and promises and threats, is also based on fear—one remembers that British soldiers extracted secrets from terrified Muslim captives by threatening to sew them up for a while in a pig's skin.

Malcolm X acknowledged that the Muslims had to adapt Islam to their purposes. "We are in a cage," he said. "What must be taught to the lion in a cage is quite different from what one teaches the lion in the jungle. The Muhammadan abroad believes in a heaven and a hell, a hereafter. Here we believe that heaven and hell are on this earth, and that we are in the hell and must strive to escape it. If we can adapt Islam to this purpose, we should. For people fighting for their freedom there is no such thing as a bad device."

He snorted about peaceful methods. "The methods of Gandhi?" Another snort. "The Indians are hypocrites. Look at Goa. Besides, they are the most helpless people on earth. They succeeded in removing the British only because they outnumbered them, out*weighed* them—a big dark elephant sitting on a white elephant. In this country the situation is different. The white elephant is huge. But we will catch him. We will catch him when he is asleep. The mice will run up his trunk when he is asleep.

"Where? They will come out of the alley. The revolution always comes from the alley—from the man with nothing to lose. Never the bourgeois. The poor Negro bourgeois, with his golf clubs, his golfing hat"—he waved at the people in the lunchroom—"he's so much more frustrated than the Negro in the alley; he gets the doors slapped shut in his face every day. But the explosion won't come from him. Not from the pickets, either, or the nonviolent groups—these masochists . . . they *want* to be beaten—but it will come from the people *watching*—spectators for the moment. They're different. You don't know. It is dangerous to suggest that the Negro is nonviolent.

"There *must* be retribution. It is proclaimed. If retribution came to the Pharaoh for his enslavement of six hundred thousand, it will come to the white American who enslaved twenty million and robbed their minds."

"And retribution, that is in the Koran?"

"Sir?"

"The Koran . . . ?"

He said, "Chapter 22, verse 102."

I put the numbers down, thinking to catch him out; I looked later. The verse reads: *"The day when the trumpet is blown. On that day we assemble the guilty white-eyed (with terror)."*

"These are the things you are teaching Cassius?"

"He will make up his own mind."

He popped a peppermint in his mouth. We talked a little longer, somewhat aimlessly. He had an appointment with someone, he finally said, and he stood up. The noise of conversation dropped noticeably in the luncheonette as he stood up and walked out, erect and moving slowly, holding his gaudy souvenir cane out in front of him as he threaded his way between the tables; the people in the golfing hats watched him go.

4.

I went out into the lobby of the hotel, just standing around there feeling low. A phrase from Kafka, or rather the *idea* of some phrases from *The Trial*, came to me. I looked them up the other day: "But I'm not guilty, said K. It's a mistake. Besides, how can a man be guilty? We're all men. True, said the priest: but that's how the guilty talk."

The lobby was crowded. I didn't feel comfortable. I went out to the street and stood *there,* watching the traffic. The cars came by going at sixty, none of them taxis. I went back to the lobby. The armchairs, not more than four or five, were occupied. I wouldn't have sat down anyway.

Then a fine thing happened. I was talking into the desk telephone, trying to find Archie Robinson, and a Negro, a big fellow, came up and said softly, "Hello, man, how's it?"—smiling somewhat tentatively, as if he wasn't quite sure of himself. I thought he was talking to someone else, but when I glanced up again, his eyes were still fixed on me. "We looked for you in New York when we came through," he said.

I recognized him, the great defensive back on the Detroit Lions, Night Train Lane, a good friend. "Train!" I shouted. I could sense people turn. It crossed my mind that Malcolm X might be one of them. "Hey!" I said. *"Hey!"* Lane looked a little startled. He hadn't remembered me as someone who indulged in such effusive greetings. But he asked me to come back to his room where he had friends, most of them from the golf tournament, dropping in for drinks and beans. I said that would be fine.

We went on back. Everyone we passed seemed to know him. "Hey man," they'd call, and he'd grin at them—a strong presence, an uncomplicated confidence, absolutely trusting himself. He had the room next to mine at the Detroit Lions' training camp (I was out there, an amateur among the pros, trying to play quarterback and write a book about it) and it was always full of teammates, laughing and carrying on. A record player, set on the floor, was always going in his room—Dinah Washington records. He had married her earlier in the year, her ninth or tenth husband, I think. The volume was always up, and if you came up from the practice field late, her voice would come at you across the school grounds. She had died later that year.

His room was small and full of people. I sat quietly. Train offered me some beans, but I wasn't hungry. He said, "What's wrong with you, man?"

"I'm fine," I said.

"Hey!" someone called across the room. "Was that you in the lunchroom? What you doin' talking to that guy X?"

"Well, I was listening to him," I said.

"They were telling around," this man said, "that X had a vision—he seen Cassius win in a *vision.*"

Someone else said that in a fight they'd rather be supported by a Liston left jab than a Malcolm X vision. A big fine hoot of laughter went up, and Night

Train said it was the damnedest co-in-ci-dence but a *horse* named Cassius had won one of the early races at Hialeah that afternoon—perhaps *that* was Malcolm X's vision.

They talked about him this way, easily, matter-of-factly. They could take him or leave him, which for a while I'd forgotten. Malcolm X had said about them: "They all know I'm here in the motel. They come and look at me through the door to see if I got horns . . . and you can see them turning things over in their minds.

5.

The day after he beat Liston, Cassius turned up at a news conference at the Miami Beach Auditorium. The rumor was that he had gone to Chicago for the Muslim celebrations there, and the press was surprised when he appeared—and even more so at his behavior, which was subdued. Since a microphone system had gone out, his voice was almost inaudible. Cries went up which one never expected to hear in Clay's presence: "What's that, Clay? Speak up, Cassius!"

Archie Robinson took me aside and told me that he and Clay had dropped in on the celebrations at the Hampton House Motel after the fight, but it had been too noisy, so they'd gone home. It was quieter there, and they had been up until four A.M. discussing Cassius's "new image."

I remarked that this was a rare kind of evening to spend after winning the heavyweight championship. I'd met a younger singer named Dee Some-thing-or-other who had been waiting for Clay outside his dressing room after the fight. She had some idea she was going to help Cassius celebrate. She was very pretty. She had a singing engagement at a nightclub called the Sir John. Her mother was with her. She was very anxious, and once in a while when someone would squeeze in or out of the dressing room she'd call out: "Tell Cassius that Dee . . ." The girl was calm. "I call him Marcellus," she said. "A beautiful name. I can say it over and over."

The newspapermen waiting to get into the dressing room looked admiringly at her. "Clay's little fox," they called her, using Clay's generic name for girls—"foxes"—which is half affectionate and half suspicious; he feels that girls can be "sly" and "sneaky" and are to be watched warily. When the new champion finally emerged from his dressing room in a heavy press of entourage, photographers, and newspapermen, he seemed subdued and preoccupied. He didn't glance at Dee, who was on her toes, waving shyly in his direction. "Marcellus," she called. The crowd, packed in tight around him, moved down the corridor, and photobulbs flashing. The mother looked quite put out.

6.

The living accommodations for Liston and Clay were as different as their fighting styles. Liston had a big place on the beach, a sixteenroom house next to the Yankees' owner, Dan Topping, reportedly very plush, walltowall carpeting, and each room set up like a golfclub lounge—a television set going interminably, perhaps someone in front of it, perhaps not, and then invariably a card game.

Clay's place was on the mainland, in North Miami, in a lowrent district—a small plain taterwhite house with louvered windows, a front door with steps leading up to a little porch with room for one chair, a front yard with more chairs set around and shaded by a big ficus tree with leaves dusty from the traffic on Fifth Street. His entire entourage stayed there, living dormitorystyle, two or three to a room. Outside the yard was almost worn bare. There wasn't a neighborhood child on his way home from school who didn't pass by to see if anything was up. Films were shown there in the evening, outside, the children sitting quietly until the film started. Then the questions and the exclamations would come, Clay explaining things, and you could hardly hear the soundtrack. Only one film kept them quiet. That was the favorite film shown two or three times, *The Invasion of the Body Snatchers* ... watched wideeyed in the comforting sounds of the projector and the traffic going by occasionally on Fifth Street. When the big moths would show up in the light beam, almost as big as white towels they seemed, a yelp or two would go up, particularly if a body was being snatched at the time, and the children would sway for one another.

The children were waiting for Clay when he drove up from his press conference the day after the fight. So was Malcolm X, a camera slung from his neck; his souvenir cane was propped against the ficus tree. The children came for the car, shouting, and packing in around so that the doors had to be opened gingerly. Clay got out, towering above them as he walked slowly for a chair in the front yard. The litany started almost as soon as he sat down, the children around him twelve deep, Malcolm X at the periphery, grinning as he snapped pictures.

"Who's the king of kings?"

"Cassius Clay!"

"Who shook up the world?"

"Cassius Clay!"

"Who's the ugly bear?"

"Sonny Liston!"

Who's the prettiest?"

"Cassius Clay!"

Sometimes a girl, a bright girl, just for a change would reply *"me,"* pointing a finger at herself when everyone else was shouting *"Cassius Clay,"* or she might shout *"Ray Charles,"* and the giggling would start around her, and others would join in until Clay, with a big grin, would have to hold up a hand to reorganize the claque and get things straightened out. Neither he nor the children tired of the litany. They kept at it for an hour at a time. Malcolm X left after a while. There were variations, but it was essentially the same, and it never seemed to lack for enthusiasm. The noise carried for blocks.

We went inside while this was going on. The main room, with an alcove for cooking, had sofas along the wall. The artifacts of the psychological campaign against Liston were set around—signs which read "settin' traps for the Big Bear," which had been brandished outside his training headquarters, and a valentine, as tall as a man, complete with cherubs, which had been offered Liston and which he had refused. It stood in a corner, next to an easel. Newspapers were flung around—there had been some celebrating the night before—and someone's shoes were in the middle of the room. Souvenir canes were propped up by the side of the stove in the cooking alcove. It was fraternity-house clutter.

I was standing next to Howard Bingham, Clay's "official" photographer. "It was fun, wasn't it?" I asked.

"Oh, my," he said. "We have the *best* time here."

He had joined up with Clay after the George Logan fight in California, about Clay's age, younger perhaps, and shy. He stutters a bit, and he told me that he didn't take their kidding lying down. He said: "I walk around the house and sc . . . sc . . . scare people, jump out at them. Or they d . . . doze off on the c . . . couch, and I sneak around and tickle them on the nose, y'know, with a piece of string. Why I was agitating C . . . C . . . Cassius for half an hour once when he was dozing off. And I give the hot f . . . f . . . feet around here, a lot of that. We had a high time."

I asked what Cassius's winning the championship meant for him.

"Well, of course, that must make me the greatest ph . . . ph . . . photogra' pher in the world." He couldn't keep a straight face. "Oh please," he said. His shoulders shook. "Well, I'll tell you. I'm going to get me a mo . . . mo . . . mohair wardrobe, that's one thing."

At the kitchen table Archie Robinson was sorting telegrams, stacked up in the hundreds. He showed me some of them—as impersonal as an injunc' tion, from the long sycophantic messages from people they had to scratch around to remember, to the tart challenges from fighters looking to take Clay's title away from him. Clay wasn't bothering with them. He was going strong outside—his voice rising above the babble of children's voices: "Who shook up the world?"

"Cassius Clay!"

I wandered back to his room. It was just large enough for a bed, the mat' tress bare when I looked there, an armchair, with clothes including his Bear Huntin' jacket thrown across it, and a plain teak'colored bureau which had a large'size bottle of Dickinson's witch hazel standing on it. A tiny oil paint' ing of a New England harbor scene was on one wall, with a few newspaper articles taped next to it, illustrated, describing Clay at his most flamboyant. A training schedule was taped to the mirror over the bureau. It called for "all" to rise at five A.M. The bedclothes were in a corner. One corner of the mattress was covered with Cassius Clay's signature in a light'blue ink, flow' ery with the Cs tall and graceful, along with such graffiti as: "Cassius Clay Is Next Champ"; "Champion of the World"; "Liston Is Finished"; "The Next Champ: Cassius Clay" . . .

Outside, it had all come true. His voice and the answers were unceasing. "You," he was calling to the children, "you all are looking . . . at . . . the . . . champion . . . of . . . the . . . whole . . . wide . . . world."

[June, 1964]

VIEWS AND REVIEWS

GEORGE S. SCHUYLER

Cassius Clay, the new heavyweight champion who loud-mouthed and clowned his way to a shot at the top pugilistic goal, and won, has disclosed a perspicacity and discernment in excess of his youth. He proved this conclusively (if any further proof were needed) at his Miami press conference following his victory.

Dropping the pose that had caused many reporters to question his sanity and courage, and made him a seven-to-one underdog as he went into the ring, young Clay spoke intelligently, grammatically, modestly, and sincerely. It was a welcome relief after the illiterates and delinquents we have heard barking at the microphone at ringside after a victory during the past couple of decades.

What was most impressive about young Clay was the manner in which he answered loaded questions about Islam and the so-called Black Muslims. Yes, he said, he was a member and had been for the past five years. Yes, he believed in the teachings of Mr. Muhammad's sect and what he saw of good decorum, proper dress, respect for women and sobriety in the Muslim gatherings which he had attended.

Yes, he could continue to attend them. There were, he said, 750 million people in Islam, and there was no reason why he should not also be a member. He believed also in the voluntary racial segregation or communalism which the Muslims endorse.

While this writer disagrees with the Muslims on some counts, on others they are more realistic than some of the people who oppose and denounce them, without giving any sound reason for doing so.

Islam is as sound as Christianity, Judaism, or Hinduism, and I respect those who are true believers in whatever faith who live up to its tenets. Society everywhere has found religion to be desirable and necessary for the orderly progress of the race. The differences between faiths are superficial and illusory.

In a way they are fundamentally the same. If the adherents of Islam practice what they preach, I endorse them as fully as the dedicated Christians and Jews. It is idle to expect perfection in any of them, and Muslims err quite as much as the others. All of these faiths do well in their way.

I was amused that reporters sought to make much of the fact that young Clay was in the company of Malcolm X who had attended the fight; as if the Muslim teacher were some horrendous oger. All religious faiths have their preachers, exponents, and scholars, and Muhammadanism is no exception. Malcolm X is one of the most intelligent and gifted of the Muslim preachers, and has done more than any other to lift it out of more ignorant sectarianism.

This is more than I can say for some of the pixilated persons who have recently got the Negro mob to chasing rainbows and bubbles. Considering the associations and activities of other prizefighters I have known, Cassius Marcellus Clay is picking good company.

[March, 1964]

CLAY EXPLODES LISTON MYTH

JACKIE ROBINSON

It will go down in boxing history how the myth of Sonny Liston, The Great Unconquerable, was exploded in the flurry of the hammering fists of a brash, brave, and talkative young man.

Say all you will about Cassius and his great flow of language, his towering ego, his unorthodox manner of projecting himself. You must still admit that he put the deeds behind the words and came through victoriously.

Clay did more than win. He achieved the feat of outsmarting a man who had not only captured the title, but who had built a tremendous reputation for being able to scare his opponents, almost literally, to death.

Despite all those headlines about how worried Cassius was before fight time, the young Louisville Lip roared into the fray in the first round, attacking and proving that there was no fear in his heart.

Actually, Clay delivered a greater psychological beating to the now deposed champ than a physical one. His fight did not begin in the ring in Miami. It began months ago when Cassius initiated his psychological warfare, taunting Liston, making him angry and low-rating him.

I don't think there can really be any doubt or shadow cast upon Clay's clear-cut victory. Liston's failure to come out into the ring to take the rest of his beating is upheld by medical testimony.

However, most of us, who are accustomed to seeing the gladiators win their honors in the center of the ring and lose them there, could not help feeling a keen disappointment that Liston should go out like this. Frankly, I feel it was the beating he had taken and the cuts on his face which caused him to decide not to show for the next round.

Many people have asked me whether I am disturbed because, ideologically, Cassius has taken on a new trainer—Malcolm X. Why should I be disturbed? Clay has just as much right to ally himself with the Muslim religion as anyone else has to be a Protestant or a Catholic.

There are those who scoff at the claim by Muhammad's Muslims that they represent a religion. These people have the right to their opinion. On the other hand, one of the basic American principles involves the right of each individual to embrace a philosophy and call it his religion.

People who are concerned over Clay's alliance with the Muslims seem mainly worried lest great flocks of young and adult Negroes will suddenly turn to the Islam ranks. I don't believe this will happen.

I don't think Negroes en masses will embrace Black Muslimism any more than they have embraced Communism. Young and old, Negroes by the tens of thousands went into the streets in America and proved their willingness to suffer, fight, and even die for freedom.

These people want more democracy—not less. They want to be integrated into the mainstream of American life, not invited to live in some small cubicle of this land in splendid isolation.

If Negroes ever turn to the Black Muslim movement, in any numbers, it will not be because of Cassius or even Malcolm X. It will be because white America has refused to recognize the responsible leadership of the Negro people and to grant to us the same rights that any other citizen enjoys in this land.

Despite his loudness—and sometimes crudeness—Clay has brought excitement into boxing. He has also spread the message that more of us need to know: "I am the greatest," he says. I am not advocating that Negroes think they are greater than anyone else. But I want them to know that they are just as great as other human beings.

[March, 1964]

THE CHAMP
AND THE CHUMP

MURRAY KEMPTON

Just before the bell for the seventh round, Cassius Clay got up to go about his job. Suddenly, he thrust his arms straight up in the air in the signal with which boxers are accustomed to treat victory and you laughed at his arrogance. No man could have seen Clay that morning at the weigh-in and believed that he could stay on his feet three minutes that night. He had come in pounding the cane Malcolm X had given him for spiritual support, chanting "I am the greatest, I am the champ, he is a chump." Ray Robinson, that picture of grace who is Clay's ideal as a fighter, pushed him against the wall and tried to calm him, and this hysterical child turned and shouted at him, "I am a great *performer,* I am a great *performer.*"

Suddenly almost everyone in the room hated Cassius Clay. Sonny Liston just looked at him. Liston used to be a hoodlum; now he was our cop; he was the big Negro we pay to keep sassy Negroes in line and he was just waiting until his boss told him it was time to throw this kid out.

British journalists who were present remembered with comfort how helpful beaters like Liston had been to Sanders of the River; Northern Italian journalists were comforted to see on Liston's face the look that *mafiosi* use to control peasants in Sicily; promoters and fight managers saw in Clay one of their animals utterly out of control and were glad to know that soon he would be not just back in line but out of the business. There were two Catholic priests in attendance whose vocation it is to teach Sonny Liston the values of organized Christianity, and one said to the other: "Do you see Sonny's face? You *know* what he's going to do to this fellow."

The great legends of boxing are of managers like Jack Hurley, who had taken incompetent fighters and just by shouting their merits, against all reason built them up for one big payday at which they disgraced themselves and were never heard from again. Clay had created himself the way Hurley created his paper tigers. His most conspicuous public appearance in the week

45

before he was to fight had been a press conference with the Beatles. They were all very much alike—sweet and gay. He was an amateur Olympic champion who had fought twenty professional fights, some of them unimpressive; and he had clowned and blustered about how great he was until he earned his chance from a Liston who, if he could not respect him as an opponent, could recognize him as a propagandist skilled enough to fool the public. A reporter had asked Liston if he thought the seven to one odds against Clay were too long, and he answered: "I don't know. I'm not a bookmaker. I'm a fighter." But there was no hope Clay could win; there was barely the hope that he could go like a gentleman. Even Norman Mailer settled in this case for organized society. Suppose Clay won the heavyweight championship, he asked; it would mean that every loudmouth on a street corner could swagger and be believed. But if he lay down the first time Liston hit him, he would be a joke and a shame all his life. He carried, by every evidence unfit, the dignity of every adolescent with him. To an adult a million dollars may be worth the endurance of being clubbed by Sonny Liston; but nothing could pay an adolescent for just being picked up by the bouncer and thrown out.

On the night, Clay was late getting to the dressing room and he came to stand in back of the arena to watch his younger brother fight one of the preliminaries. He spoke no word and seemed to look, if those blank eyes could be said to look, not at the fighters but at the lights above them. There was a sudden horrid notion that just before the main event, when the distinguished visitors were announced, Cassius Clay in his dinner jacket might bounce into the ring, shout one more time that he was the greatest, and go down the steps and out of the arena and out of the sight of man forever. Bystanders yelled insults at him; his handlers pushed him toward his dressing room, stiff, his steps hesitant. One had thought him hysterical in the morning; now one thought him catatonic.

He came into the ring long before Liston and danced with the mechanical melancholy of a marathon dancer; it was hard to believe that he had slept in forty-eight hours. Liston came in; they met in the ring center with Clay looking over the head of that brooding presence; then Clay went back and put in his mouthpiece clumsily like an amateur and shadowboxed like a man before a mirror and turned around, still catatonic and the bell rang and Cassius Clay went forward to meet the toughest man alive.

He fought the first round as though without plan, running and slipping and sneaking punches, like someone killing time in a poolroom. But it was his rhythm and not Liston's; second by slow second, he was taking away the big bouncer's dignity. Once Liston had him close to the ropes—where fighters kill boxers—and Clay, very slowly, slipped sideways from a left hook and under the right and away, just grazing the ropes all in one motion, and cut Liston in the eye. For the first time there was the suspicion that he might know something about the trade.

Clay was a little ahead when they stopped it. Liston had seemed about to fall on him once; Clay was caught in a corner early in the fifth and worked over with the kind of sullen viciousness one cannot imagine a fighter sustaining more than four or five times in one night. He seemed to be hurt and walked back, being stalked, and offering only a left hand listlessly and unimpressively extended in Liston's face. We thought that he was done and asking for mercy, and then that he was tapping Liston to ask him to quiet down a moment and give the greatest a chance to speak, and then we saw that Clay's legs were as close together as they had been before the round started and that he was unhurt and Liston just wasn't coming to him. It ended there, of course, although we did not know it.

"I told ye'," Cassius Clay cried to all of us who had laughed at him. "I told ye'. I just played with him. I whipped him so bad and wasn't that good. And look at me: I'm still pretty."

An hour later he came out dressed; a friend stopped him and the heavyweight champion of the world smiled and said he would be available in the morning. His eyes were wise and canny, like Ray Robinson's.

[March, 1964]

IN THE RING (2)

LEROI JONES

Sonny Liston was the big black Negro in every white man's hallway, waiting to do him in, deal him under, for all the hurts white men have been able to inflict on his world. Sonny Liston was "the huge Negro," the "bad nigger," a heavy-faced replica of every whipped-up woogie in the world. He was the underdeveloped have-not (politically naive) backward country, the subject people, finally here to collect his pound of flesh.

The mock contest between Liston and Patterson was a "brushfire" limited war, Neo-Colonial policy to confuse the issue. Patterson was to represent the fruit of the missionary ethic; he had found God, reversed his underprivileged (uncontrolled) violence, and turned it to work for the democratic liberal imperialist state. The tardy black Horatio Alger offering the glad hand of integration to welcome twenty million into the lunatic asylum of white America.

In this context, Liston the unreformed, Liston the vulgar, Liston the violent, comes on as the straightup Heavy (who still had to make some gesture at the Christian ethic, like the quick trip to the Denver priest before the match, to see if somehow the chief whitie could turn him into a regular fella). "They" painted Liston Black. They painted Patterson White. And that was the simple conflict. Which way would the black man go? This question traveled on all levels through the society, if anyone remembers. Pollsters wanted the colored man in the street's opinion. "Sir, who do you *hope* comes out on top in this fight?" A lot of Negroes said Liston. A lot of Negroes said Patterson. That old hope come back on you, that somehow this *is* my country, and ought'n I be allowed to live in it, I mean, to make it. From the bottom to the top? Only the poorest black men have never fallen at least temporarily for the success story. And the poor whites still fall hard.

A white cab driver was turning to see me in his rearview mirror; he said, "You know that Liston has got the biggest hands of any boxer to come in the ring. You know his arms are six feet long. I mean six feet long each. He's like an animal. Jesus! He shouldn't even be allowed to fight normal guys." That was the word from that vector of polite society.

The match meant most to the Liberal Missionaries. It was a chance to test their handiwork against this frightening brute. So a thin-willed lower-middle-class American was led to beatings just short of actual slaughter. Twice. And each time Patterson fell, a vision came to me of the whole colonial West crumbling in some sinister silence, like the across-the-tracks House of Usher.

But, dig it, there is no white man in the world who wanted to fight Sonny Liston himself. So the Orwell Synapse takes over. What we cannot gain by experience, we will gain by *inperience,* the positing of a fantasy "event" for what is actually the case. History is changed to correspond with what we all know reality *should* be, a maneuver common to every totalitarian order. The December 1963 issue of *Esquire* fantasizes with an essay entitled "The Greatest Fights of the Century." Liston beats Marciano, "the most brutal first round ever seen," and he also beat Louis . . . "Louis flew back five feet, fell, and rolled on his face." Having set this up, Dempsey comes marching in like drunk Ward Bond whistling a cavalry tune, to straighten everything out. It is a little hectic (like in *The Spoilers* or when John Wayne is facing a really brave Indian) but the end is never in doubt. As the barbarian climbs through that chink in the wall, IBM! ". . . Liston turned and fell heavily to the floor, his right glove under his face." In the posture of sleep, like a gypsy in the desert, a *fellaheen.* "At six, he rolled over and, back now in his corner, Dempsey smiled." The muscular Neyland-Smith.

See the white man dream? Which is where the whole race has gone: to the slowest. But the mass media make the dream a communal fulfillment, so that now each man who had and has the dream in solitary can share and grow bigger at its concrete illustration. It's like the European painters when they began to paint Arab/Moorish/Semitic experience in medieval middle-European contexts. Christ is then a blond all dressed up in desert clothes but still looking like Jeffrey Hunter. Another smart Germanic type made good. (Practically speaking, for instance, if God were not white, how could He get permission from the white man to make him? If, say, God were black, there would have to be some white man somewhere to tell him what to do, right?)

So now, forget that all this is dream and wish fulfillment, and think of it as a blatant social gesture. This is how the synapse works. We erase the mad-bad big black bad guy by going back in time to get him in a dream; the drop to the canvas takes nearly the whole of the dream, it is so slow and gravityless; you can replay it over and over again—". . . heavily to the floor, his right glove under his face." "Liston vs. Dempsey. . . . Dempsey, K.O., 1:44 of the ninth."

The champ is the big strong likable immigrant who has always done American's chores. He's glad to oblige. We always get to the bad niggers . . . either kill 'em or drive 'em out of the country. Jack Johnson, Henry Highland Garnet, Du Bois, Paul Robeson, Robert Williams, Richard Wright, Sidney Bechet, Josephine Baker, Beauford Deloney, Chester Himes, so many others. The black neurotic beauties trailing dumbly through the "equal" streets of hopeless European cities. All the unclaimed fugitive corpses.

That leaves us with Cassius X. Back in the days when he was still Clay it was easy to see him as a toy manufactured by the Special Products Division of Madison Avenue. Now I think of him as merely a terribly stretched out young man with problems one hoped would have waited at least for him to reach full manhood. Clay is not a fake, and even his blustering and playground poetry are valid; they demonstrate that a new and more complicated generation has moved onto the scene. And in this last sense Clay is definitely my man. However, his choice of Elijah Muhammad over Malcolm X (if indeed such is the case) means that he is still a "homeboy," embracing the folksy vector straight out of the hard spiritualism of poor Negro aspiration. Cassius is right now just angry rather than intellectually (socio-politically) motivated.

The Liston-Clay fight seemed to be on the up and up to me. Liston was way out of shape, expecting young X to be just another weakfaced American. But Cassius can box, and even Liston in shape might have trouble spearing the very quick X. Sonny's risking jail now, where most of the white world would have him (shades of Jack Johnson!) and the possibility of a return match between Clay and Liston grows each day more remote.

But whoever has the heavyweight championship now, or in the future, it is an even remoter possibility that it will be Jack Dempsey, or for that matter any of his Irish progeny. The Dempseys in America, having graduated from the immigrant-newcomer class, don't have to knock heads for a living except as honest patrolmen; their new roles as just Anybody make them as weak and unfit for the task of defeating any of the black heavyweights as any other white Americans, even the honorary kind like Floyd Patterson.

So what kind of men are these who practice such deception on them‑
selves? Oh, they are simply Americans, and some years from now, perhaps
there will be this short addition: "you remember them, don't you?"

[June, 1964]

THE REDEMPTION OF THE CHAMPION

GORDON PARKS

London—late spring. A knock on the door as I was packing my bags and Muhammad Ali suddenly came dancing into the hotel room—"whoomp-whoomp-whoomp," throwing lefts and rights close to my head. His young face was free of the fury it had held a few hours before when he was beating Henry Cooper. Most of London was still sleeping off the defeat of its champion. And, considering the physical demands of the fight, and the yelling, shoving mobs that had clawed at him later, I thought Muhammad would be sleeping, too. But here he was, the improbable Louisville Kid, come to say a quick good-bye.

"Go-o-ord-on Pa-a-rks." He strung out my name for two seconds, then flopped across both twin beds and took a piece of paper from his pocket: "Here's the poem I've been promising you. Want to hear it?" Before I could answer, he was reading:

> Since I won't let critics seal my fate
> They keep hollering I'm full of hate.
> But they don't really hurt me none
> 'Cause I'm doing good and having fun.
> And fun to me is something bigger
> Than what those critics fail to figure.
> Fun to me is lots of things
> And along with it some good I bring.
> Yet while I'm busy helping my people
> These critics keep writing I'm deceitful.
> But I can take it on the chin
> And that's the honest truth my friend.
> Now from Muhammad you just heard
> The latest and the truest word.

So when they ask you what's the latest
Just say, "Ask Ali. He's still the greatest."

"Well, how'd you like it?" he asked proudly.

"Just fine." I edged toward the subject that was really on my mind—and, I guessed, his. "And you were good with the press after the fight."

"Yeah? Guess I said all the right things. Well, the loud talk and everything is over now. Just being myself from now on—a good-acting champ."

Right. Just right. Exactly what I wanted to hear him say. The question was how deep it all went. The situation reminded me of the final moments I had spent with my son David, before he went off to the Army. (Muhammad and David resemble one another, not only physically but in the way they walk and gesture.) Only this time I didn't offer any advice. I wanted to. I wanted to say: "Just remember—*Don't let reporters rile you. Don't always ham it up for the cameras. Listen to your trainers. Be careful about your draft situation.*" But I had learned that this boy, unlike my son, was not receptive to outright advice; even when you gave it gently you got silence—no response at all.

Now he jumped up suddenly, handed me the poem, and gave me a bear hug. "Well, so long, champ," he said. Then, throwing punches again, he danced out the door.

I had met Muhammad Ali in Miami a month earlier, when he started training for Cooper, the first of his summer series of overseas fights. His public image was then in tatters. He stood accused in the press of sins ranging from talking too much to outright anti-white bigotry. There had been rumblings of dislike for him ever since he became a Muslim after the first Clay-Liston fight in February 1964. Then, late last winter, when he declared, "I don't have no quarrel with those Vietcongs!" he became, in the public eye, not just a loudmouthed kid but a "shameless traitor," as one paper put it.

At that point I began to feel a certain sympathy for him. There was a side to this brash, poetry-spouting kid that I admired. I was not proud of him, as I had been proud of Joe Louis. Muhammad was a gifted black champion and I *wanted* him to be a hero, but he wasn't making it. I also felt, however, that he could not possible be quite so bad as he was made out to be in the press.

He lay on his bed, in the small bungalow he always rents in Miami, half-covered by a sheet, only his chest and his powerful bare shoulders exposed. He smiled broadly as I came in.

"Sit down," he said in a surprisingly soft voice. "They tell me you're the greatest."

There were no chairs, so I sat down on the bed beside him. He had a magazine in his hand and he pointed to a word in an article about him: "What's that mean?"

I studied the word for a second. "He's saying you're 'paradoxical,' that you aren't what you appear to be—sometimes."

"Uh-huh. And just what does he mean by calling me a bigot?"

I thought of the word "racist," but I said, "He's accusing you of being just as intolerant against whites as they are to us." He went on like this for a while, asking questions but never commenting on the answers I gave.

At first I was puzzled. The conversation, if it could be called that, didn't seem to be getting anywhere. But after a time I realized that we were, in fact, *talking*—person to person, without any put-on at all—and that this was his way of saying that he trusted me. I felt free to tell him quite directly that I had come to Miami to see whether he was really as obnoxious as people were making him out to be.

"No need to beat around the bush, brother," he said quickly. "I know why you came." His head slid off the pillow close to the wall. "People," he went on more softly, "have wrote a lot of bad things about me. But nothin' they write is goin' to turn *everybody* against me. Every fight, the gates just get bigger and the White Hopes get fewer."

Then, in a great swoosh, he sprang out of bed. "Come on, man, let's go see a movie!"

In my rented Cadillac he flicked on the radio and out blasted the voice of the late Sam Cooke with "Shake."

Muhammad began singing along with him. An announcer's voice cut in: "Cassius Clay [Muhammad tensed, cocked his ear] returned to Miami today to start training for his forthcoming fight with Henry Cooper in London. Cassius . . ."

The announcer went on, but the champion had stopped listening: "Cassius Clay! I'm on everybody's lips. But still they won't call me by my right name."

Muhammad's brow knitted when we hit the cinema district: "What's all those signs say?"

"There's *Cast a Giant Shadow*. Looks good," I said. "Or Paul Newman in *Harper*."

"Naw, naw. Something rough—with ghosts, no love and sex and stuff. What's that? *Goliath and the Vampires*. That's for me brother! Find out when it starts."

"It's half over," I said, hoping I was saved from the vampires.

"Come on. Let's go anyhow. The last half's always best."

Later Muhammad chose to stroll through Miami's Negro section. The rented limousine crept along the street behind us while greetings came from all the doorways and windows.

"Hi, champ."

"Hi, baby. What's shakin'?"

"Hi, Muhammad. Who's the greatest?"

"Are you blind, man?"

"Hey, champ, how many rounds for Cooper?"

"If he tries to get rough—one's enough."

"You're the greatest, baby!"

He could no more escape that last line than he could his color.

"These people like me around when they've got trouble. Patterson, Joe Louis, Sammy Davis, and other Negro bigwigs don't do that. Too busy cocktailin' with the whites. I don't need bodyguards. You don't need protec-tion from people who *love* you."

I asked myself how he could believe that the boppish, sycophantic chatter we'd just heard was "love." Did he think that a good world was one filled with smiles and flattery—one where all things were bigger than life? I began to suspect so.

He trained hard. In the ring Muhammad let the sparring partners bull and spin him about as Cooper might do. He floated and ducked, causing them to miss badly, "Dance, baby, dance," his trainer, Angelo Dundee, purred from the corner.

"Hey, Angelo, could I have whipped Jack Johnson in his time?"

"Baby, you could have taken anybody in everybody's time."

"And that's the beautiful truth, brother," Rahaman, his sparring partner, cut in. Such questions, such answers, I realized, meant more to him that I had originally imagined. Muhammad seemed to encourage it all. Often he had asked me, "Why would a big magazine like yours want to do a story on me? Am I really that big? Do people really want to know about me?" He expected affirmative answers and he nearly always got them. He clearly needed these assurances against the bad publicity he was getting.

Some days he would drive up to a schoolyard at recess. "Come here, all you beautiful black children!" And they came running as if he were about to hand out thousand-dollar bills. "Only difference in me and the Pied Piper is he didn't have no Cadillac," he would say. The adoring kids were more important to him than he was to them.

During those lazy afternoons he talked about that "crazy house" he wanted to build on a high hill—"where travelers could come by and say, 'That's where he lives, the heavyweight champion of the world.'" But just about any topic outside of Muslimism, boxing, or himself made him tune out.

One day several boys came into the yard and two of them started sparring. "Hey, stop that!" he shouted at them "You don't fight your brother—even in play. Now come on inside and I'll let you see some movies—of me beatin' up the 'Bear' and the 'Rabbit.'"

He continued the lecture as he threaded the projector: "They've been lynching your pappys and grandpappys and rapin' your mothers and sisters down here for years. There's plenty people to fight besides your brother. Catch you at it again, I'm gonna bop your heads together. Now, I'm gonna show the second Liston fight first, 'cause it last just long enough to warm up the machine."

He started the film and began announcing over the commentator's voice: "Here we go! Look, children! Looks like a turtle chasin' a jackrabbit! Now, watch close or you won't see it! Rat-a-tat! Bop! There it is! Now watch that clown fall flat on his face. There he goes. Wham!"

Muhammad ran up to the movie screen: "Git up, you bum! Get up and fight!"

When Patterson appeared on the screen Muhammad scoffed, "There's the Rabbit. Listen at 'em cheer. They love him. He's their black White Hope, children! Poor sucker! Now, here I come! Boooo! Boooo! Boooo! Boooo! Listen at 'em give it to me!"

I watched him closely. There was no joy in his heckling. Nobody could like being booed that much, especially not someone so concerned about "love."

I myself had wanted Floyd to beat him that night, and I told him so later. He smiled: "I beat him so bad his breath smelled like saddle soap."

However, that fight bugged him. He was still trying to explain it in his bedroom late that night: "Patterson had no business in that ring with me—after saying he was going to bring the title 'back to America.' But the crowd came for a show and I gave 'em one. 'Come on, sucker, git past that left,' I kept saying to him. The ref felt sorry for him and kept telling me to shut up. I felt sorry for him, too. Maybe that's why I couldn't freeze him. But if I'd took him in the first round, they'd a hollered I'm sadistic. But they didn't call that Patterson-Johansson fight sadistic. The Rabbit went down seven times."

His eyelids dropped for a few seconds. He had talked himself out. There was a little snore and he nodded himself awake. Then, looking out the window, he said, "I like Floyd. He oughta quit. He's made lots of money. They'll never treat him as bad as they treat me." Then he dug his head into the pillow and went to sleep.

Some mornings, while he was winding up his training in Miami, I came upon him with his hands lifted, facing the East, mumbling prayers to Allah. Sometimes he seemed morose and disgruntled with everything around him. Then he would be in high spirits again—laughing, chattering, dancing, shadowboxing in his yard, in the street, wherever there was room to throw a punch. It was never easy to know which of his different selves would be visible at a given moment.

I never witnessed the hate he is assumed to have for whites. But I did see him stand in the burning sun for an hour, signing autographs for Southern white children. And I did go with him on a visit to a young white hemophiliac one afternoon. On leaving the boy and his parents he remarked, "There are some good white folks around." I said it was nice of him to have made the visit. "Well," he answered, "he must have been a nice kid to want to see me."

Now and then his thoughts seemed far away. He would drop a conversation almost in midsentence without reason, leaving me in a void. Even when there was a great deal of noise around him, he would remain mute, meditative. One evening, in such a mood, he invited me for a walk. Just minutes before, he had been rearranging his scrapbook and I asked him why he didn't have a secretary.

"Oh, people don't ask me for much outside of autographs." he said. "No speeches and such things." He thought about that for a few paces.

"Do you know that Martin Luther King was the only Negro leader who sent me a telegram when I became champion of the world—the only one. I was just a dumb kid then, thinking all of them would be so proud of me—me being the champ and everything. I expected too much."

"You're so young yet. There's plenty of time to change—if you really want to."

"I want to. I'm sure I want to," he said, as though trying to convince himself. I repeated that he had plenty of time left and that the world had a lot to offer him.

After an intent pause, he said, "Nobody in this world ever offered me anything except Elijah Muhammad. Nobody."

Later that night, I went with him to the local mosque meeting. Muhammad Ali was dressed in his new blue-serge uniform of the Fruit of Islam, the tough and elite Muslim guard. And, like everyone else who attended, he raised his arms and allowed himself to be frisked according to strict custom. Here, for the first time, I saw Muhammad listening eagerly to what someone else had to say.

Lucius Bey, the Muslim minister in Miami, started slowly, in a deliberately restrained voice. But soon the intensity increased: "The black man is indeed the greatest! His genes are stronger! No white man can produce a baby darker than himself! The most beautiful women in the world are black!"

"Teach, brother, teach!" Muhammad's voice led all the rest in the chorus.

"They say we hate the white man. We don't hate the white man! We just hate the way he treats us!"

"Tell 'em like it is, brother! Preach!" Now it was a duet between Lucius Bey and Muhammad.

"Why is the white man so anxious about Elijah Muhammad changing our slave names? Why? Africans are from Africa! Japanese are from Japan! Swedes are from Sweden! Where are Negroes from? Negroia?"

"Wake us up, brother! Wake us up."

"Right NOW, the white man's being run out of all the black countries!

And—now, listen to this—he wants us black people to go fight for him to stay there!"

Lucius Bey had hit home: *"Preach the truth! They want me to go right now!"*

"When the white man asks, 'What's your name?' and you say, 'Muhammad Ali,' they say, 'That nigger's done woke up!'"

"Preach! Preach! Preach!"

Lucius Bey preached on—for an hour and a half.

Lucius Bey's "message" was still burning inside Muhammad the next day. Angelo got told off; sparring partners got their lumps; there was no horsing around in camp that day, no movies, no children. And he kept spewing the kind of comment that had already made him a villain in the press. By evening the bungalow was dead quiet.

My original notion that there might be a different kind of story in Muhammad Ali had almost evaporated. I was going back to New York the next morning and there now hardly seemed any need for me to go on to London.

Then, just before I left to go to my hotel, I took a chance and said to him, "It's not only white people, but a lot of Negroes don't like the way you act."

That cut him, deep. He erupted: "What do they want? I ain't promoting alcohol and sex-hugging on some white woman's head! So what if I am the first black athlete to stand up and say what I feel! Maybe I'm like the Japanese flier who sacrifices himself so others can live!

"Hate! Hate! Hate! Who's got time to go around hatin' whites all day! I don't hate lions, either—but I know they'll bite! What does the white man care if I hate him, anyhow? He's got everything going for him—white Swan soap, Tarzan, Jesus, White Owl cigars, the white tornado, Snow White and her Seven Dwarfs! Angel food cake is white—devil's food cake is black, naturally!"

He ranted on and on. Lucius Bey's sermon had been tepid in comparison.

"One question before I go," I said after listening to him for most of an hour. "What about your draft situation?"

"What about it? How can I kill somebody when I pray five times a day for peace? Answer me! For two years the Army told everybody I was a nut. I was ashamed! My mother and father was ashamed! Now, suddenly, they decide

I'm very wise—without even testing me again. I ain't scared. Just show me a soldier who'd like to be in that ring in my place!

"I see signs saying 'L.B.J., how many kids did you kill today?' Well, I ain't said nothing about Vietnam. Where is it anyway? Near China? Elijah Muhammad teaches us to fight only when we are attacked. My life is in his hands. That's the way it is. That's the way it's got to be!"

He was wrapped up in himself—yes: still belligerent, still the mistreated kid against a hostile world. Yet, I reflected, he made some sense. The issue had never come up in my own home, but I knew I would have been ready to back up my own son if *he* had decided to resist going to Vietnam. Muhammad, however, was the heavyweight champion of the world. Did that give him a special responsibility to think and act differently? A lot of people clearly thought that it did. Yet I wasn't sure.

I didn't expect to see Muhammad again. But early the next morning there he was at my hotel door. "Hurry up, champ. You're about to miss your plane," he said. He spent the trip to the airport urging my driver through shortcuts and around other cars. Carrying my bags, he ran all the way to the departure gate. Then his big hand held me back for an instant.

"I don't want to do anything that's going to hurt my people," he said. "I've been doing a lot of thinking since last night. I hope you'll be there in London."

I was sure he was making me a promise of some sort. "I'll be there," I said, and ran for the plane.

The London fog made Muhammad's plane four hours late. But the big crowd was still waiting. He stepped off smiling broadly, waving to all the cameras, reporters, and the cheering crowd.

"Got any predictions, champ?"

"Nope."

"Any poetry, champ?"

"Nope. I'd have to keep my fingers together so you wouldn't say I was predicting."

"You've toned down considerably—a different fellow."

"It's just me, being myself."

Two days later the *Daily Telegraph* said: "Cassius Clay presented himself to an admiring British public yesterday as Muhammad Ali, a heavyweight champion of courtesy and charm."

He smiled when I showed him the newspaper: "Wait till the folks back home get a load of this."

"Do you really care about what they think back there?"

"I got a lot of boos," he said, "but—it's still home. I have to think about home."

The British found him to be a "decent chap." "Foxes" in miniskirts, mods, and rockers chased him. His telephones rang all day and all night. The adoration finally took its toll.

"You got a extra bed at your hotel?" he asked me in desperation. I said I had.

"Then you've just took on a nonpaying guest, brother."

A nd each day after training he would come to my room, consume quarts of orange juice, check the sports pages, and sleep. We talked of things we hadn't really talked about before—my family and his family. He woke up one afternoon and simply began talking about his childhood:

"I used to lay awake scared, thinking about somebody getting cut up or being lynched. Look like they was always black people I liked. And I always wanted to do something to help these people. But I was too little. Maybe now I can help by living up to what I'm supposed to be. I'm proud of my title and I guess I want people to be proud of me."

I was astonished, and moved. It was the first time he had ever said anything like that. He went on:

"My mother always wanted me to be something like a doctor or a lawyer. Maybe I'd a made a good lawyer. I talk so much. I guess I got that from my father. I'm really kinda shy. Didn't get as much schooling as I wanted to. But common sense is just as good. My parents did what they could for me and my brother, scuffling down in Kentucky where things was hard. I bought 'em a new house and some furniture and two cars. I think they're proud of me now, no matter what people say. I'm glad I could get 'em out of a rut."

"Everybody will be proud of you if you would just give them a chance. Americans, Africans, everybody. Look how the British are treating you."

"Yeah, they sure are nice to me all right. Wonder what makes 'em so nice? Have they ever been in any big wars?"

I thought back to the awful bombings in Britain during the Second World War. He was not born at the time. "Yes, several," I said.

Two mornings before the fight Angelo telephoned me: "The Champ wants you at a press conference at ten this morning. He says he's going to say something you'll like to hear."

"I'll be there," I said. The conference would be at Isow's, a kosher restaurant where he took his meals. I went to Muhammad's room first.

"Here's what I'm going to say," he said. "Read it and tell me what you think."

It was a note, scribbled in red ink, and it began by thanking everyone from the restaurant chef to the prime minister for his "kindness and understanding." Halfway through, Muhammad got to the point: "When I was campaigning for the championship, I said things and did things not becoming of a champion. But I'm champion now. And today I'm measuring my words. I'm measuring my deeds. I'm measuring my thoughts. By the help of the Honorable Elijah Muhammad, this is the new Muhammad Ali. And last, I want to mention something that is nearest to me—the country in which I was born. . . ."

("Wouldn't just 'my country' be better?" I asked. "No," he said, "Elijah Muhammad would like it better the way it is.")

". . . I thank the President of the United States and the officials of the government. And I thank my draft board for letting me come here to defend the title. Regardless of the right or wrong back there, that is where I was born. That is where I'm going to return."

"Beautiful, brother," I said.

Minutes later, dressed in a black-silk lounge suit, Muhammad Ali sparkled with confidence and charm as he faced the battery of microphones and reporters. By now I was sure that what he would say came from an impulsive, well-intentioned heart. But I wasn't listening as he spoke. I stood in the back of the room, wondering whether his new high resolve could last.

It was possible, I decided. There would be times when he could, under the pressure of hostile questions, forget and say or do something hopelessly wrong. I decided to wait and see.

Three months is not the longest of trials but it is a summer's worth at least and a time during which Muhammad Ali managed absolutely to keep his cool, despite some easy chances to lose it. The fight with Brian London had had problems. The press welcomed the champion back to England courteously, even warmly. But as the fight drew nearer and public interest in it kept dropping, reporters tried to stir things up by needling Muhammad. Muhammad merely guzzled down more orange juice and sparred even less. At a press conference, a reporter suggested to him directly that he looked fat and undertrained. Instead of answering, Muhammad turned casually to me.

"Where'd you get that foxy suit you got on, boss?"

"At my London tailor," I said.

"Well, call him up and tell him I want six just like it—all dark and conservative." Later, in Saville Row, he selected the materials in less than ten minutes. "And make me a vest for each one. I'm a gentleman now. I've got to look like one," he instructed the happy tailor.

As matters turned out, of course, the fight answered a number of criticisms about how well Muhammad Ali had trained and how hard he could hit. On his way into the ring, he had been serenaded with boos. The catcalls had continued as he prayed briefly to Allah before the bell. But when he jogged around the ring, as attendants helped poor London off the canvas, there was nothing but cheers.

Back at the hotel he preened before the mirror in his new tailored suit. "Well, you changed their song real quick," I said.

"Yep, boss, I picked up a lot of new fans tonight. I won't be getting no more boos till I get back where I was born."

"Your face isn't even marked."

"Nope. Can't afford marks. The public likes pretty gentlemen fighters. So it looks like Muhammad has to stay pretty and be a gentleman forever and ever."

Someone laughed but the champion seemed dead serious. And he just might do it I decided. For, at least, he seemed fully aware of the kind of behavior that brings respect. Already a brilliant fighter, there was hope now that he might become a champion everyone could look up to. If only those, back where he was born, extended their patience they would help buoy that hope. From where I had watched and listened, it all seemed so worthwhile.

[September, 1966]

Please note that this piece has been edited for this volume and does not appear in its entirety.

IN DEFENSE OF CASSIUS CLAY

FLOYD PATTERSON WITH GAY TALESE

I have been called a "coward" and a "rabbit" and an "Uncle Tom" by Cas-sius Clay, and many people think that I share their contempt for him, but I do not. Cassius Clay, I think, is at heart a modest man. He can listen a long time without saying anything, he can charm you with his politeness. So much of his bragging and stomping, his histrionics and wisecracks are all part of an act. He is a kind of actor—a bad actor, some say, but an actor—and the main purpose behind his behavior is to get people to buy tickets to his fights, hoping to see him put his foot in his mouth.

He never gave them that satisfaction in the ring, he is a fine fighter, but he may have shot off his mouth too much outside the ring this year. Now he is in real trouble. At first people laughed at Clay's outrageous speeches and poetry, but then it got around that he was a member of the Black Muslims, and then he publicly denounced the draft and criticized America's policy in Vietnam. It's not so bad for politicians and Pulitzer Prize poets and certain intellectuals in this country to sign petitions and speak out against the war in Vietnam, but with Cassius Clay did it he paid a heavy price for Freedom of Speech. The draft board moved in on him, his title fight with George Chuvalo was banned from New York and Chicago and several other cities, and many closed-circuit television theaters boycotted it, and Clay earned relatively little money from the fight, which ended up in Toronto.

The prizefighter in America is not supposed to shoot off his mouth about politics, particularly when his views oppose the government's and might in-fluence many among the working classes who follow boxing. The prize-fighter is considered by most people to be merely a tough, insensitive man, a dumb half-naked entertainer wearing a muzzled mouthpiece. He is supposed to stick to his trade—fighting and keeping his mouth shut and pretending that he hates his opponent. There is so much hate among people, so much contempt inside people who'd like you to think they're moral, that they have to hire prizefighters to do their hating for them. And we do. We get into a ring and act out other people's hates. We are happy to do it. How else can Negroes like Clay and myself, born in the South, poor, and with little education, make so much money? I think boxing is a good thing. I do not think that it should be abolished, as do some hypocritical editorial writers on the *New York Times,* because the elimination of boxing will not eliminate the hate that people have and the wars. If people did not have such things as boxing they'd invent something else, maybe something that would not give poor people a chance at the big money.

So I'm all for boxing, although I admit that the existence of boxing says something about our society and the violence that it needs. When a fighter kills in the ring he does not go to jail; instead he gains a strange new respect from some people, maybe just bloodthirsty people, but this respect is something like that given to a war hero who has killed many men in battle, and when a fighter becomes a killer the boxing promoters know that more people will come out to watch him fight the next time. So violence and hate are part of the prizefighter's world, Clay's world and mine, although we do not hate one another, nor do I hate Liston or Ingemar Johansson or any other opponent, and I am sure the feeling is the same with them. We fight but we do not really hate down deep, although we try to pretend we hate. Sometimes it is all very confusing, we become very mixed up. And we are afraid.

We are not afraid of getting hurt but we are afraid of losing. Losing in the ring is like losing nowhere else. People who lose in business—get fired from their job, or lose a client, or "get kicked upstairs"—can still go down with some dignity and they might also blame their defeat on an ungrateful employer or on the unfair competition. But a prizefighter who gets knocked out or is badly outclassed suffers in a way he will never forget. He is beaten under the bright lights in front of thousands of witnesses who curse him and spit at him, and he knows that he is being watched, too, by many thousands more on television and in the movies, and he knows that the tax agents will soon visit him—they always try to get their share before he winds up flat broke—and the fighter cannot shift the blame for his defeat on his trainers or managers or anybody else, although if he won you can be sure that the trainers and managers would be taking bows.

The losing fighter loses more than just his pride and the fight; he loses part of his future, is one step closer to the slum he came from, and I am sure that before each fight Cassius Clay also goes through the mental torture and doubt. He knows how happy thousands of Americans would be if he got beaten bad, and maybe that is why Clay has to keep saying, "I'm the greatest, I'm the greatest"—day after day, hour after hour, loud and clear, on television and in the newspapers: "I'm the greatest." He wants people to say, "You're not!" and then he is forced to meet the challenge, put himself in a do-or-die frame of mind, go a little crazy maybe, crazy with some ferocious fear. So far it has worked for him. What he will be like if he loses I do not know, but the fear of losing causes strange things to happen to fighters, and it caused me to hate myself so much that I wore a fake mustache and beard and tried to hide. I did not want to face the public that I had let down. This pressure was due partly to my being built up as such a "good guy," and when I lost to Sonny Liston, the "bad guy," it was like a national disaster.

I have gotten over that beard business now, thank God, but the "good-guy" image still drives me to do strange things, to behave in ways that are a little unnatural, just as I imagine the "bad-guy" role that Cassius Clay has inherited from Sonny Liston has influenced many of the crazy things he does in public. Before my fight with Cassius Clay I remember one day he came stomping up to my camp. He was surrounded by Muslims and he came barging in, calling me "rabbit," and he held a bunch of carrots in his arms. All the television cameras and photographers moved in close to get action shots of Clay coming over to me with those carrots. I guess they were expecting a nice bloody scene. But they were disappointed. Clay handed me the carrots and I took them. The photographers took pictures, the pictures got into the papers and on television, and I guess it all helped sell tickets to the fight. But in that split second that Cassius Clay's eyes met with mine, I could sense that he was a little embarrassed by it all. He seemed to be apologizing, saying, "This is what I have to do." And later on, when we had a press conference before the fight, and Clay was screaming and bragging to a bunch of sportswriters, he leaned over and whispered to me once: "You want to make some money, don't you, Floyd? You want to make lots of money, don't you?"

He seemed to feel that he had to explain his public actions to me, maybe because he goes so much further than the rest ever have, or maybe because he is such a convincing bad guy. That has probably been part of his problem. He has been too convincing. Maybe he has overplayed his part, made it bigger than it was supposed to be, and the public is not sure that it likes its fighters, its hired haters, to go beyond the role it expects them to play, which does not include joining the Black Muslims or denouncing the draft or criticizing America's policy in the Vietnamese War.

When I first met Cassius Clay, his public image was so different. It was in 1960. I was the champion then and was traveling through Rome. I'd had an audience with the Pope, then visited the American Olympic team there and met Cassius Clay. He was the star boxer for the American team, and he was very polite and full of enthusiams, and I remember how, when I arrived at the Olympic camp, he jumped up and grabbed my hand and said, "Com'on, let me show you around." He led me all around the place and the only unusual thing about him was this overenthusiasm, but other than that he was a modest and very likable guy.

In 1965 in Las Vegas I fought against him and was stopped in a technical knockout. Before the fight he'd said that if he lost he would listen to my viewpoint on Catholicism, and if I lost I should hear him out on the Black Muslims, but this was, again, all part of the prefight buildup. In the fight itself, I did not have a chance. I boxed him well in the first round, but in the second round my back went out. I took a swing at him and missed, and got a muscle spasm, and after that I could not swing without great pain. In fact I could not even stand up straight, and the pain was unlike anything I've ever felt, and in the later rounds I was hoping that Clay would knock me out. It is not pleasant admitting this, but it is the truth: I had had such high hopes for this fight, so much riding on it, so many people cheering for me. I remember how, on the morning of the fight, Frank Sinatra had asked to see me, and I was escorted over to his suite in the Sands Hotel by Al Silvani, a friend of Sinatra's who was one of my trainers. I really did not know Silvani very well before the fight, but Sinatra had called me up earlier in the year after the death of my trainer, Dan Florio, and said that if I wanted Al Silvani to help me I could have him. I did not say yes at first. I thought it over, and decided to wait. Then Sinatra again called and said I could have Silvani, who was then working in Sinatra's film company, and finally I said okay, and Silvani, two days before the fight arrived in Las Vegas to help train me for Cassius Clay, and on the morning of the fight Silvani escorted me to Sinatra's suite, and Sinatra was very nice that morning, very encouraging, he told me I could win, how so many people in America were counting on me to win back the championship from Clay.

After I lost the fight, I paid Sinatra another visit in his suite. I told him I was sorry I had let him down, and all the others, but Sinatra was a very different guy after I lost to Clay. I was talking to him in his suite and then he did a strange thing: He got up and walked all the way over to the other side of the room, and he sat down there, so far away that I could hardly talk to him. I got the message. I left.

During the fight itself, Clay, in the clinches, said many things about white people, trying to hit me again with that Uncle Tom thing. But it was all I could do to stand up that night; as I said, I really wanted to be knocked out. I wanted to be knocked out with a good punch, though, or a good combination of punches. I wanted to go down with something that would be worthy of a knockout. But in the tenth and eleventh rounds, Cassius Clay wasn't landing anything good. He was just jabbing. Jab, jab, jab, jab, you know, and he was standing at a distance. It was strange, but Clay was taking no chances, and yet he must have known that I was in pain with my back.

Then in the twelfth round, Clay became a punching maniac. He still took no chances but he came in and began landing punches here, here, here, and here—punches began to land all over my head, and a very, very strange thing began to happen then. A happiness feeling came over me. I knew the end was near. The pain of standing up in the ring, that sharp knife in my back that accompanied every move I made, would soon end. I would soon be out. And as Clay began to land these punches, I was feeling groggy and happy. But then the referee stepped in to break us up, to stop Clay's punches. And you may remember, if you saw the fight in the films, seeing me turn to the referee, shaking my head, "No, *no!*" Many people thought I was protesting his decision to stop the fight. I *really* was protesting his stopping those punches. I wanted to be hit by one really good one. I wanted to go out with a great punch, to go down that way. It never happened, and that is why I was protesting to the referee.

After the fight many sportswriters suggested that Clay was carrying me, but this was not true. And Clay himself said nothing of the kind until, on a television show after the fight, a sportscaster named Howard Cosell, who was a very good friend of mine, watched a rerun of the fight with Clay and kept making the remark over and over that Clay seemed to be carrying me. Cosell began to put the idea in Clay's head as the two of them watched the rerun, and Cosell would say, "Cassius, you're carrying Patterson, you seem to be carrying him," and Clay said no, but by the eleventh round Clay started giv/ing in, saying, yes, he seemed to be carrying me. But I repeat, Clay did not carry me in that fight. I might have been carried out of that fight, but I defi/nitely was not carried during the fight.

Since then I have seen Clay once. We were in a photographer's studio pos/ing for the picture you see on the cover of this magazine. Clay flew into New York from Chicago just to do that, and I believe he was very happy to hear that I was saying some complimentary things about him for publication and was very surprised, too, because he's become accustomed to reading only the worst things these days. He gave me a big bear hug when I walked to the door, had a big smile on his face, and there was real warmth there. Then we sat down and he asked if my back is responding to treatment (it is), and then said that he would like to go on a boxing tour with Liston and myself to make some extra money. He didn't make much in Toronto for the Chuvalo fight, he said, not with all that bad publicity, and he added that he needed money these days to pay his alimony and settle other debts. He was very polite and gentle throughout the evening, and when he said good/bye I called him Cassius—I never call him by his Muslim name, Muhammad Ali—and then I added, "It's all right if I call you Cassius, isn't it?" He smiled and said, "Anytime, Floyd."

He seemed no different to me then than he did when I first met him in Rome in 1960, and I think that *that* Cassius Clay is the real one, but I believe that he has made some very serious mistakes since then and does not know how to get out of them now. I believe that he joined the Black Muslims with/out even knowing what it stands for, without checking into it. It just sounded good. He was very young then, twenty/one or twenty/two, and much im/pressed with Malcolm X, who *was* an impressive man, a spellbinding man who could talk faster than anybody, including Cassius.

Then Malcolm X said some very bad things and fell out with the Muslim leaders in Chicago, and then he was shot. I think this really frightened Cas/sius Clay. He'll not admit it, but I think it really got to him. Now he is trapped. He could not get out of the Black Muslims even if he wanted to, I think, because he'd never know what might happen as a result. I remember my own feeling as I entered the ring in Las Vegas last November for the Clay fight: I wondered if there might not be some shots fired into the ring. When/ever I tried to dismiss the idea as ridiculous, I kept remembering that Mal/

colm X was murdered before a large crowd of people and so was President Kennedy, and if people want to get you, they'll get you anywhere. I thought about this until the bell rang, and then I forgot about it and concentrated on the fight, but I have since thought about it again, and even now as I say these things I wonder if I might not be endangering my own life.

Joining the Muslims was one reason for Clay's decline in popularity, and his views on Vietnam and the draft are others, and I happen to disagree with everything he is saying on these three subjects, and I think the Cassius Clay viewpoint is working against the civil rights movement and the best interests of the nation. I certainly would fight willingly in Vietnam for my country, and have no soft feelings toward the Black Muslims. But what bothers me about Cassius Clay's situation is that he is being made to pay too stiff a penalty for saying and doing what he thinks is right. I happen not to agree with him, but he certainly has a right to express his opinion on Vietnam and the draft and the Muslims without having half the nation jumping on his back. Why? Because Clay was exercising his right of free speech. He did not, as far as I know, break any law. I read in the newspapers recently that he was charged with defying a police officer who stopped a car in which he was riding, and for passing a stop sign, but he has not been found guilty of any major crime, and so I think he should be getting a bigger break than he has gotten this year.

It isn't enough that he is a fine fighter, unfortunately. The public demands that its champions also be popular, and sometimes popularity is achieved by keeping your mouth shut, but Clay isn't this way. I'm more this way, and Clay isn't like me in the least, but in our democracy people have a right to be different. But I know this may just be wishful thinking on my part, and I do not see how Clay can get out of the mess he got himself into unless he quits the Muslims, and that might be dangerous, as I said. If he joined the United States Army he might be helping his cause, although he'd probably have to do something pretty dramatic—he'd have to go to Vietnam and be photographed running through the woods with a knife in his back and carrying a wounded white GI on his shoulders. Or he might retire from boxing for a while, and if he did not have the heavyweight title the Muslims might not find him so useful, and maybe he could then stay out of the spotlight until the public forgot about him a little and found a new "bad guy."

But if he does none of these things I still feel that he deserves better treatment than he is getting, and I think the public is partly to blame. The public fails to understand what he is—a twenty-four-year-old fighter, an entertainer, a very individualistic young man whose life is far from easy, and they should make allowances for him. I do not think these should be anything special, but maybe once in a while they should stop booing him, maybe even cheer him for a change, make him feel more liked, more reputable within himself, more responsible. Right now the only people in America who are not booing him are the Black Muslims, and maybe that is one reason he prefers being with them. Maybe if there were a few cheers from the other side of the fence, and a little more tolerance, too, people would realize that Cassius Clay is not as bad as he seems, and maybe then he would also return the favor once in a while and keep his mouth shut.

[August, 1966]

IN DEFENSE OF CASSIUS CLAY

JACKIE ROBINSON

Muhammad Ali—or Cassius Clay—just might be one of the greatest heavyweight champions this country has ever produced.

One thing is certain. He is the most hated.

He is hated because he is a Muslim.

He is also hated because he speaks his mind.

Some members of the sports press don't like either one of these things.

But what they seem to dislike most is that Clay is a Black Muslim and an outspoken black man.

While, in my opinion, some of the things that Clay says and does rate criticism, I do not feel that he deserves much of the bad press which he gets. I know what he is going through. For, during my own career in sports, I came to learn that there are many writers who like tame Negroes who "stay in their place." Of course, by backing up his words with deeds, Clay or Ali has clearly demonstrated where his "place" is—right up there at the top.

I think it is most significant that some of the writers, even the so-called liberals, do not want to grant this young champion his dues. One of the sportswriting fraternity whom I have considered a liberal for a long time is Howard Cosell. And Cosell has appeared to be in Clay's corner for several years. Yet, in a recent *Wide World of Sports* television interview with Clay, it struck me that Howard was being quite vicious in the way he tried to sway public opinion to his anti-Clay way of thinking.

Of course there are some liberals who always like to bow to the stands and earn the roar of the approval of the masses. If this is the way Cosell is going, I hate to see it. Clay, however, seems capable of taking care of himself in the exchange of words as well as that of blows.

[March, 1967]

MUHAMMAD ALI AND THE LITTLE PEOPLE

IRWIN SHAW

Between February 17, 1966, when it was announced that he was 1-A, and April 28, 1967, the day he was ordered up for induction into the Armed Forces, Muhammad Ali successfully defended his championship seven times. But on April 28, in Houston, Muhammad Ali refused to take the oath, saying, "I have searched my conscience and I find that I cannot be true to my belief in my religion by accepting such a call." From that moment to this, except for two three-round exhibitions on the same night in Detroit, he has been barred from the ring.

In the attempt legally to clear Muhammad Ali of the 1-A classification, his lawyers had previously filed suit in Kentucky, contending their client's constitutional rights were invaded because Negroes were systematically excluded from membership on draft boards. The hearing denied the request to set up a three-judge panel to rule on the charge of racial discrimination in the Selective Service System.

It is interesting to speculate what the ruling of the draft board would have been if Muhammad Ali had been astute enough to take up residence in Harlem prior to his original classification and had gone before a draft board there rather than in Kentucky. The young son of a friend of mine, a student at the University of Pennsylvania, who rooms in a predominantly black neighborhood, and whose draft board includes only one white man, has taken a lesson from Muhammad Ali's predicament and plans to move to a lily-white neighborhood before his student deferment is exhausted. The draft helps those who help themselves.

Muhammad Ali also pleaded for exemption on the grounds that he objected to military service as a matter of conscience and that he was a practicing minister of a recognized religious faith. This part of his plea was left up to the ruling of the Selective Service System, which decided that Clay could not claim exemption on the stated grounds because his religion was "racist and political." This last bit of modern-day religious wisdom must have caused considerable interest in Utah, a state which is the fief of the Mormon Church, a cult which teaches the eternal inferiority of the black race, members of which, if they are ever accepted within the fold, are kept among the lowest ranks of the faithful.

Clay was convicted in Houston, Texas, on June 20, 1967, for "willfully refusing to report and submit to induction into the Armed Forces." The sentence was five years imprisonment and $10,000 fine.

His lawyers appealed the conviction and he was allowed to remain at liberty pending the disposal of the appeal, but his punishment had begun even before the case was brought to trial. Even before his indictment, on the day he refused to take the soldier's oath, the great state of New York, acting through its Athletic Commission, demonstrated its lightninglike fealty to the Union by declaring the heavyweight championship vacated and up for grabs.

All the other athletic commissions in the country behaved with admirable unity of spirit, usually only demonstrated at times of national crisis, and forbade Muhammad Ali's appearance in a ring in any state of the Union. Even Nevada, whose chief glory is Las Vegas, that haunt of rectitude, sternly guarded the moral purity of the Silver State's citizens and visitors by making sure that Muhammad Ali would not "float like a butterfly, sting like a bee," anywhere within Nevada's borders. It is to be hoped that the professional gamblers, the Mafia members, the hustlers and whores of the city are grateful for the care shown by their local government for their spiritual welfare.

In a gesture of rare international solicitude, a judge in Texas preserved the citizens of Yokohama, Japan, from possible contamination by the boy from Louisville. Muhammad Ali had been offered a bout in Yokohama for $250,000, a sum that would probably cover any normal legal fees since he put in his claim for exemption. After the conviction, his lawyers pleaded for permission for him to make the trip to Japan, guaranteeing that he would report to whatever American authorities in Japan were designated for the purpose, and further guaranteeing his immediate return to the United States after the fight. The judge ruled negatively and thoughtfully went on to order the boxer to surrender his passport immediately.

The point of this piece is not to criticize the judicial processes involved in the Muhammad Ali case. The law under which he was tried and found guilty is not an unreasonable one and theoretically, at least presents no perils to Muhammad Ali that it does not present to any other healthy young man of his age. The law is not a popular one, but not all laws can be popular and the Supreme Court, in review, has found that his trial was fair and the sentence within the judge's discretion, although it did send the case back to a lower court to determine whether the admitted wiretapping of a conversation between Martin Luther King and the defendant had tainted the conviction.

In a rancorous exchange between J. Edgar Hoover and ex-members of the Department of Justice, it had been revealed that King's telephone had been tapped to discover possible Communists in King's entourage and the extent of their influence on the late pastor's actions. It is the belief of King's lawyer (who is also one of Muhammad Ali's lawyers) that the FBI's task was made easier by the hotel King patronized when he came to Washington. The management always gave the minister the same suite, an attention King naively accepted as a sympathetic gesture on their part.

As noted earlier, when the Supreme Court sent the case down for review, the lower court ruled that the intercepted conversations had had no effect on the conviction, and the sentence of five years in prison and a fine of $10,000 was confirmed. The setting for the ruling, of course, was the state of Texas where Ali could expect little popular support.

The prosecution in the Clay case admitted to having eavesdropped on five conversations. Four were read publicly. The fifth was read by the judge in chambers who decided that it was a case of legal wiretap. Rumor has it that the fifth was not read publicly because it dealt with "a foreign personality," that the "foreign personality" was a diplomat of the United Arab Republic. If any reader of this magazine feels the temptation to speak to a Nobel Prize winner or a duly accredited diplomat, he might be advised to think twice before dropping his dime in the box.

What has happened in the various courtrooms into which Muhammad Ali's action has led him can hardly justify a citizens' rebellion, but what has happened outside the courtroom—wiretapping by the FBI and the pious boycotting of a simple and courageous, if misguided, young black— must make us all take a long hard look at America today.

When Cassius Clay, as he was then called, first appeared before the draft board in Louisville, Kentucky, where he was born and where he was something of a town pet as an adolescent boxing prodigy, the draft board classified him on March 20, 1964, as 1-Y, a classification that deferred him from military service indefinitely on the grounds that he had scored too low on the Armed Forces Qualifying Test (a percentile score of 16) to be accept-able as a soldier. He was then required to take a battery of aptitude tests, which he failed. A communiqué issued by the Pentagon at that time stated that "interviews conducted by experts in the field of testing and analysis indi-cate that Clay put forth his best efforts on both occasions."

At the time he was tested the lowest possible score that the Armed Forces would accept was 30. But subsequently the passing figure was dropped to 15, one below Muhammad Ali's score. The fighter's friends have voiced the rather farfetched notion that this change was deliberately aimed at him. But even if one sees this change as the result of a persecution complex, one won-ders if the level of manpower available to the United States Army is so low that for the good of the service it is necessary to enlist a recalcitrant and a highly vocal complainer who is poorly equipped for the military trade.

Until he won the championship from Sonny Liston, Clay was regarded as a handsome and not particularly dangerous clown. But after he won the championship in Miami and announced that he had taken the name of Cas-sius X (the Muhammad Ali came a year later) and that he was a Muslim, a member of the Islam religion, the gay and likable young underdog became overnight a dark threat to the nation's security and his continued deferral from military service an insult to the Flag. Two years after his original classification as 1-Y, on February 17, 1966, he was moved up to 1-A.

This is not the place to argue the merits or demerits of the Muslim reli-gion, although the emergence in recent years of some of the more violent Black Power groups now makes the Muslims seem about as sinister as the Quakers. Whatever one's opinions may be of the sect, it is not against the law to belong to it and no sanctions can be legally pressed against a man for being a member. Yet one would have to be naive to think that Muhammad Ali's an-nouncement had nothing to do with his eventual reclassification as fit for duty by his draft board. As Muhammad Ali said when he was notified that the Army was now ready to accept him, "How can they do this without another test to see if I'm any wiser or worser than last time? Why are they so

anxious, why are they gunning for me?" Regardless of all legalistic pro-
nouncements put out by the authorities, it is hard to believe that he would not
still be fighting if he had remained Cassius Clay and kept his big mouth
closed except when he was smiling or when he got around to reciting:

> "This is the legend of Cassius Clay,
> The most beautiful fighter in the world today.
>
> He talks a great deal and brags indeedy
> Of a muscular punch that's incredibly speedy.
>
> The fistic world was dull and weary,
> With a champ like Liston things had to be dreary.
>
> Then someone with color, someone with dash,
> Brought fight fans a-runnin' with cash.
>
> This brash young boxer is something to see
> And the heavyweight championship is his destiny."

If he'd kept his out-of-the-ring oratory to these lyrical limits, it is almost
certain fans would welcome him in the rings of every arena of the country,
delighting them with his speed and prowess. In a country which honors non-
conformity and respects the individual conscience, Muhammad Ali's refusal
to go with the crowd might bring new admirers to any bout.

There is nothing in the law that forbids a man under indictment, or even a
man appealing a conviction, from working at his habitual trade, as long as it
is a legal one. Of course, if he is in a profession in which he relies upon his
popularity with the public, the public, if it wishes, can stop patronizing him.
If anyone believes that the American public is horrified at Muhammad Ali's
conduct, ask any boxing promoter in the world if he would like Muhammad
Ali to fight for him. The answer would of course be an enthusiastic and realistic yes. In fact, only recently, a Chicago promoter called the people at Madison Square Garden to inquire if the Garden would handle the television side
of a Muhammad Ali match, the bout to be staged in the Cook County Jail,
a place not previously known for its sporting events, but one which the pro-

moter evidently thought was outside the purview of the Illinois Athletic Commission.

For the record, the people at the Garden were interested and asked that they be contacted again when plans were definite, but the first call was the only one. In the years since Muhammad Ali's announcement of his Muslim affiliation, various companies which had previously sponsored television broadcasts of Ali's fights had backed off from later bouts, fearful of organized boycotts of their products. However, it was felt that there would be enough potential sponsors to make the enterprise profitable. The main concern was planning a production around the match to get in seven advertising spots of a minute apiece, at $40,000 a spot.

Muhammad Ali was quoted as saying, "I got no quarrel with them Vietcong," a feeling that is certainly shared by a large number of Americans who are not facing five years in jail, who are going about the business of earning their living unimpeded and who make no phone calls to people whose phones are monitored, even inadvertently, by the FBI. Among others figures in the world of sports there has been no noticeable rush to the flag, and even among those few professional athletes who have been trapped into some form of military service there has been no case, to my knowledge, of a halfback or a pitcher or even a Boxing Commissioner who has fallen in action or even heard a shot fired in anger. I am not suggesting that a regiment be formed of boxers and fullbacks, to be despatched immediately to the Mekong Delta, thereby depriving me of the pleasure of watching them throw a left hook or go off tackle, but to the ordinary American, especially the black American, it must seem that one man has been singled out and hounded down where hundreds of his more cautious colleagues have been allowed to drift off into safety.

[November, 1969]

Please note that this piece has been edited for this volume and does not appear in its entirety.

THE 1970S

"And I want to be the first black champion got out that didn't get whipped. . . . Boxing's just a sport. . . . They stand around and say 'Good fight, boy; you're a good boy; good goin'.' And that's it. They don't look at fighters to have brains. They don't look at fighters to be businessmen, or humans, or intelligent. Fighters are just brutes that come to entertain the rich white people."

—Muhammad Ali, "'I'm Sorry, But I'm Through Fighting Now,'"
Esquire, *May 1970*

"They're expecting me to come back looking fat, looking bad. They think they've done me in. But I'm going to fool them."

—Muhammad Ali, from "'No More Boasting,
Just the Fight,'" Life, *October 23, 1970*

"I'm like a little ant. Lots of other little ants know me, follow me. So God gives me some extra power."

—Muhammad Ali from "King of All Wisdom," by Robert Lipsyte,
New York Times Magazine, *June 29, 1975*

"This ain't the time no more to shout, 'I'm the Greatest.' Just like it's not the time for rock 'n' roll. There's a different beat. No more Rap Brown and get-the-honky stuff. It's a new time, a new season. . . . I started boxing in Eisenhower's time. What singers of that time are still big? Frank Sinatra? No others. What ballplayers? None.

—Muhammad Ali, from "Ali: Born Again!" by Pete Axthelm and Peter
Bonventre, Newsweek, *September 25, 1978*

CASSIUS CLAY
IS THE SIXTIES

JIMMY CANNON

The 1960s went out in Dallas for me. The horns were blowing down in the streets and the people in the next room in the hotel pounded on the wall and howled like dogs.

The sixties were a time of Bob Cousy going, and Lew Alcindor coming. The sixties belonged to the Jets and the Mets. The Yankees went down, and Casey Stengel walked away from baseball on his bent legs. The Celtics couldn't be beaten but Bill Russell left them and now they can't win.

The sport of football moved up, and Vince Lombardi preached a doctrine of pious violence. Television owned what it wanted and athletes became actors. It was the time for Joe Namath, and no one swung higher. Old men forgot Bronko Nagurski when Jimmy Brown carried the football, and Jack Nicklaus caught up with Arnold Palmer and passed him.

The small talk of the country concerned Bear Bryant and O. J. Simpson and Mickey Mantle hobbling around on his mangled legs and Namath and Bachelors III and Willie Mays hurt by the years and Lombardi demanding his players forget pain and Sandy Koufax throwing the fastball past batters and Johnny Unitas's maimed arm and Wilt Chamberlain arguing with the coach he worked for and the neglect of Hank Aaron's greatness and Roger Maris hitting sixty-one home runs. It seemed that every town affluent enough to support a movie house and a church turned up with a major sports franchise.

The athlete of the decade has to be Cassius Clay, who is now Muhammad Ali. He is all that the sixties were. It is as though he were created to represent them. In him is the trouble and the wildness and the hysterical gladness and the nonsense and the rebellion and the conflicts of race and the yearning for bizarre religions and the cult of the put-on and the changed values that altered the world and the feeling about Vietnam in the generation that ridicules what their parents cherish.

81

Even Malcolm X is part of what Clay was in the sixties and the historians already have celebrated the force of his philosophy on his times. It was Malcolm X who persuaded Clay to be a Black Muslim. But Malcolm X was shot in a New York dance hall by guys with x's in their names and Clay would discuss his old friend as a traitor.

The kids shriek when they protest, and Clay would open that immense mouth and scream. He goes along with the proposition that reality should be avoided and ducks into the cave of his imagination. He seriously discusses great religious philosophies and stands up for segregation and often sounds like he is shilling for the Ku Klux Klan when he explains his theories of race.

The character he used as a contender for the heavyweight championship would have been all wrong in any other decade. He called himself the greatest and the prettiest and demeaned the guys he had to fight and attempted to humiliate them. He was conceited and never stopped bragging, and then suddenly he claimed he was a minister of the Black Muslim sect and they convicted him for draft evasion.

The urge for celebrities to be martyrs was another symptom of the sixties and Clay went along with the play and seems eager to go to jail for being a devout Muslim. He never went to college but he made that scene and now travels around lecturing at universities to students who understand his con-man comedy and the unsophisticated evangelism and kindergarten philosophy.

It was logical he would be called the greatest champion in all the ages of boxing. This was a decade when the critics were afraid of things they couldn't understand and honored chaos in the arts. They praised Clay with a wild irresponsibility. He is the best around but his reputation was established by two fights with Sonny Liston.

The old head-breaker out of the St. Louis mobs quit, sitting in his corner the first time. In the second fight, an effete looping right hand knocked Liston out in the first round, as Clay yelled down at him that people would think it was a fake if he didn't get up.

The sixties were a bad time, but some of the years were wonderful. And, because I make my living writing sports, Cassius Clay is the sixties for me.

[1970]

THE BLACK SCHOLAR INTERVIEWS MUHAMMAD ALI

Black Scholar: The heavyweight championship has always meant a lot to the champion's people—especially in the case of oppressed black Americans. But you have added a new dimension to the role of a champion. You fight for us both outside and inside the ring. What made you take a revolutionary stand against the war at the risk of your title in the ring and even imprisonment?

Ali: What's wrong with me going to jail for something I believe in? Boys are dying in Vietnam for something they don't believe.

I met two black soldiers a while back in an airport. They said: "Champ, it takes a lot of guts to do what you're doing." I told them: "Brothers, you just don't know. If you knew where you were going now, if you knew your chances of coming out with no arm or no eye, fighting those people in their own land, fighting Asian brothers, you got to shoot them, they never lynched you, never called you nigger, never put dogs on you, never shot your leaders. You've got to shoot your "enemies" (they call them) and as soon as you get home you won't be able to find a job. Going to jail for a few years is nothing compared to that."

We've gone too far to turn around. They've got to go on and either free me or put me in jail, because I'm going to go on just like I am, taking my stand. If I have to go to jail, if I have to die, I'm ready.

People are always asking me what I think about the draft. I wrote a little poem on it. I said:

> Hell no,
> I ain't going to go.
> Clean out my cell
> And take my tail

> To jail
> Without bail
> Because it's better there eating,
> Watching television fed
> Than in Vietnam with your white folks dead.

Black Scholar: Still, you have sacrificed and given up a lot already by most standards. How does it feel with your title gone, not being able to do the thing you have practiced most of your life, the thing you do best, probably better than any other heavyweight ever did?

Ali: Everything they did to me backfired on them. I'm supposed to be a has been by now. Three years after the title's gone, and I haven't made a dollar yet in boxing. And they had me about broke when I started, because the draft was always hitting me (for $290,000 altogether) trying to get justice in the courts.

As long as I was yelling: "I am the greatest" and my name was Cassius Clay, "I'm pretty." The Army didn't want me. Two times they let me off. They whispered: "He's a little mentally off." They made a way to keep me out of the army. But then they heard I was a Muslim. They said: "That nigger ain't crazy." And they changed the whole draft law just to get me. Understand? Then they took the title unjustly. I'm supposed to be selling shoestrings and walking around somewhere broke. But I surprised them; I'm doing better.

I'm not protesting my title being taken away. I'm not even hanging around at the fights. Because I'm not depending on the white power structure and that boxing game for survival. Where they don't look at fighters to have brains or intelligence. Fighters are just brutes that come to entertain the rich. Beat up on each other and break each other's noses, show off like two little monkeys for the crowd, killing each other for the crowd. And half of the crowd is white. We're slaves in that ring. The masters get two of us big ones and let us fight it out while they bet, "My slave can beat your slave."

So they can't disappoint me, I mean:

> I made my play,
> And I'm going to go all the way.

So I'm happy. I wake up happy. I go to bed happy. And if I go to jail tomorrow, I'll go to jail happy. Because eighty percent of the prisoners in there are brothers, and they're waiting to be taught, too. I'd convert the whole jail.

Black Scholar: What's wrong with most of the other black celebrities, in your view? Are they failing their roles? And if so, what should they be doing differently?

Ali: We black people could become free sooner than you think, if all the athletes and entertainers just took a stand—the famous ball players and the rock-and-roll artists, the big ones—took a walk through the ghetto one day and told the white man, "We're with these people and we ain't going to sell out anymore."

I'm getting together a dope-addict program, rehabilitating addicts. And there are some black welfare women in Los Angeles who want my help because they don't have clothes, but they can't get the money. All they've got is the seven dollars a week the government gives them to live on. Me and Joe [Frazier] could put on one boxing exhibition and get them more sewing machines than they could use in a lifetime.

The same with black entertainers. It's sickening to me to watch Barbara McNair, Leslie Uggams. These women on TV. Walk right out and kiss some white man right in the mouth. P-f-ft. Aw, she's so happy to be on television with a white man. I get mad and cut the TV off. The Supremes. All of them get great singing black songs. And as soon as they get great they go where you can't see them anymore. They start singing all of those old offbeat white songs—"Swaneeee River."

I'm as big as you can get in fame and sports. (The next title to that you can get is President of the United States.) And I'm so black, man, I don't care. I'm not going to compromise. I'm not going to do anything to mislead my people. I get pleasure out of walking down the alleys, walking through the ghettos, walking up to little black children. "Say, man, I'm going to beat your head."

"Cassius Clay! Mommy, here's Cassius." The whole neighborhood comes out. They haven't ever seen a celebrity sitting on the garbage can with them. That makes them feel good and it makes me feel good, too.

Black Scholar: So you see black celebrities as occupying a crucial position.

Ali: Most blacks can protest and the news won't even get in the paper, let alone leave the country. But Arthur Ashe, for example, can raise a lot of hell. Lou Alcindor can raise a lot of hell. Jim Brown, the football player, Bill Russell, the basketball player. Those kinds of people. The Temptations. The Four Tops. Marvin Gaye. All of those big names. James Brown the singer.

Go on and join something. If it isn't the Muslims, at least join the Black Panthers. Join something bad. Because black people look up to athletes and entertainers. That's right. We look up to them. So the white man uses them to lead the little ones because the world is watching the big ones.

The reason I'm putting emphasis on this is because I hate to see black women and black men—once they get prestige and greatness, where they can go into ghettos and pick up little black babies and make them feel good, and once they big, to go leave and marry somebody else and put the money in that race. That makes me so mad. People like Lou Rawls and Eartha Kitt and Leslie Uggams.

I know these Negroes. Floyd Patterson—and his first wife, Sandra. A pretty black wife and four beautiful children. He quit her and went all the way to Sweden to marry a white woman. (That's why I gave him such a good whuppin'.)

Now the white man's got the heavyweight champion—Joe Frazier's got a white girlfriend. She's in his training camp all the time. When he's singing in those nightclubs. I went up and caught him one night. I'm not condemning white women, white women are beautiful—for white men.

Black Scholar: Do you feel that you could give Joe Frazier a whuppin', too?

Ali: Let's put it like this:

> Ali comes out to meet Frazier, but Frazier starts to retreat;
> If Frazier goes back an inch farther, he'll wind up in a ringside
>   seat;
> Ali swings with a left, Ali swings with a right,
> Look at the kid carry the fight.

Frazier keeps backin', but there's not enough room;
It's a matter of time before Ali lowers the boom;
Now Ali lands with a right, what a beautiful swing.
But the punch lifts Frazier clean out of the ring.
Frazier's still risin', but the referee wears a frown,
'Cause he can't start countin' 'til Frazier comes down.
Now Frazier disappears from view, the crowd is getting frantic;
Our radar stations have picked him up.
He's somewhere over the Atlantic.
Who would have thought when they came to fight
That they would witness the launching of a black satellite?
Yes, the crowd did not dream when they laid down their money
That Ali would retire Frazier and Sonny.
Frazier came out smoking, and Ali wasn't joking.
He was peckin' and a pokin', pourin' water on his smokin'.
It might shock and amaze ya.
But Ali destroyed Frazier.

Black Scholar: Your year's suspension from the Nation of Islam is about up now, isn't it?

Ali: Yes, I'm under a year's suspension because I said I was going back to boxing just for the money. As if to say that my god and what I believe can't take care of me. I cannot talk to any Muslim in the country, or go to any meetings. They will not speak to me on the street. They have nothing to say to me until I'm back in good standing. This is what makes the Honorable Elijah Muhammad so great. There's no favoritism. This is what destroys more religions and more movements: The leader has a couple of people he'll let do a few things because they are famous or have a lot of money and the rest of the followers are punished. People who Elijah Muhammad will down quicker than anybody are his famous followers. I know brothers that get put out of the movement constantly for committing adultery and fornicating with people they are not married to.

Black Scholar: We notice that, while colleges and universities have entire schools of theology, they tend to leave Mr. Muhammad out of even the black studies programs.

Ali: A lot of blacks don't follow him because he's here to straighten them out. They like leaders when they are dead. If Elijah Muhammad died tomorrow, he'd be the biggest thing in the world. Because the white press could take what he said and say, "Naw, he didn't mean that." "It's all right to go out and get a little if your wife doesn't know it." I know what they are like. They don't want to be righteous. But don't argue and condemn. Just say: "I'm not ready for the strict laws." Don't find fault in the man. Because he's for you. He loves black people. He doesn't even get to come out on the street. Every day he's working for black people, writing his newspaper columns. Sending lectures to all of his temples. Business forms. His house stays full of foreign ambassadors. People from the UN come to Elijah Muhammad's house every day. White people stop in front of his house on sightseeing buses. These are white people, hoping they can get a glimpse of him. And the Negro preachers next door to him don't like him.

A lot of white people know more about Muslims than black people do. They know more about the Islamic religion and it's our religion. They don't tell you anything about it. You'd be surprised. They hide things that they don't want you to have. Anybody for you ain't no good. I'm a bad nigger now. That's because I'm for you all the way. I'm no good anymore. I can't box in any state. The Las Vegas commissioner last week—somebody tried to get me a license. He said: "He can't come out here to fight. He might corrupt the city." Now how can I corrupt Las Vegas?

I go into college dormitories every day. (To show you how we've been brainwashed.) I see everybody's picture on the wall but Elijah Muhammad's. I see Rap Brown. I see Huey Newton, Eldridge Cleaver, Martin Luther King, Abernathy. I see Muhammad Ali, Stokely Carmichael. You don't see Elijah Muhammad's picture up there as someone who has done something for black people. He's done more in every city for feeding and clothing and changing pimp-players and wineheads. They don't put his picture on the wall. Converting sissies, dope addicts, whores, players, doctors, lawyers. Anybody around will admit that the Muslims are the most unified and the cleanest people in the country. But he's one leader that you're never told about.

Because the white man doesn't endorse him. If the white man said tomorrow that Elijah Muhammad is the Moses, he's the one you black people should follow, he's going to put him on *Life* magazine, on *Time* magazine, black folk will like Elijah Muhammad.

I'm not fussing, but I've got to recognize the real leader, the one who started all of it. If I mean right, if I'm not envious, if I don't want to be the leader, why not recognize the leader? You know all about everybody Elijah taught, but you don't know him. Why?

Black Scholar: You have certainly done your part to help make his teaching known and to fight an unjust draft.

Ali: Yeah, that's my life now, my satisfaction. Frazier and [Jimmy] Ellis fought for my old job. My new job is freedom, justice, and equality for black folks, to bring them the knowledge of their true selves.

Black Scholar: History will never forgive white America for barring you from the ring, Ali, and it will also ask if we blacks were really too impotent to do anything about it. Or maybe soon—if you don't get justice in the Supreme Court—we will be left with no other choice.

Ali: Well, I've caught so much hell from the white power structure and the boxing authorities when I said I had no quarrel with Vietnam and that I am the greatest. I was moderate then. But I'm not fighting now. It's all over now.

I was determined to be one nigger that the white man didn't get. One nigger, that you didn't get, white man. You understand? One nigger, you ain't going to get. *One nigger you ain't going to get.*

That was then when I was fighting and still moderate. But I'm not fighting anymore. And I can really raise hell now. I've got some ideas, and they haven't seen anything like they're going to see now.

[June, 1970]

Please note that this piece has been edited for this volume and does not appear in its entirety.

"I DON'T HAVE TO BE WHAT YOU WANT ME TO BE," SAYS MUHAMMAD ALI

ROBERT LIPSYTE

Muhammad Ali is no sharecropper's son who fought his way off barren land, always grateful to boxing for lifting the plow traces off his shoulders. He feels superior to boxing, a gift to boxing, a hero of history who has temporarily ennobled a sordid and ungrateful sport. In an accurate prediction just before his three-and-a-half-year exile from the ring, he said: "When I'm gone, boxing be nothing again. The fans with the cigars and the hats turned down will be there, but no more housewives and little men on the street and foreign presidents. I was the onliest boxer in history people asked questions like a senator."

He had been someone special from the start, a pampered firstborn in an active, accomplished Louisville family which counted teachers, musicians, college graduates, and craftsmen among the aunts and uncles, and claimed direct descent from Henry Clay. His father, Cassius Marcellus Clay, Sr., a handsome, mercurial, noisy, combative failed dreamer, gave him the gift of tongue, and time—Cassius never worked a day in his life outside the ring. His mother, Odessa, a warm, pretty, pillowy woman whose grandfather was an Irishman named Grady, still dotes on him and calls him "Gee-Gee," his first words. Muhammad Ali, dredging his childhood, remembers his mother touching her toes to trim her waist, like any nonworking suburban housewife. When he started boxing at twelve he was no sickly lad building his body for revenge against bullies, no street boy channeled by a sympathetic social worker. Someone had stolen his new $60 bicycle. Cassius, righteously angry, went looking for a policeman. He found one, teaching boxing to a class of neighborhood boys. Cassius ordered the policeman to catch the robber, so he could "whup" him. The policeman gently suggested that Cassius stay and join the class.

Had the policeman spent his off-duty hours coaching rock singers or teaching watercolors or giving a course in hotel administration, boxing might never have got its senator. The boy was bright, confident, ambitious, extroverted, and bursting with energy. Education would fail him. Years later his high school reported his IQ as 78, his only satisfactory subjects art and gym; yet still he was graduated.

To this day he reads slowly and painfully and comprehension requires enormous concentration, a marked contrast to his quick and clever gifts of word and ear. Except for tennis, he did not seem to like other sports. I asked him once if he had ever played football, and he said, "Just once, that's all. They gave me the ball and tackled me. My helmet hit the ground, POW. No sir. You got to get hit in that game, tooooo rough. You don't have to get hit in boxing, people don't understand that."

Our conversation wandered on: this was on the day before his recent fight with Oscar Bonavena, and somehow we began talking about ice hockey, a game he considers very violent. He seemed fascinated but physically uncomfortable when I told him about goalies skating off to get their faces stitched, then returning to play, and how players sometimes switch all the paper cups containing a team's dentures, then watch, laughing, as they try to fit the wrong ones in. He grimaced. "Why do people let theirselves get done like that?" Surprised at the question, I said that most hockey players were poor, rural Canadians with no other chance for money and fame. He said he could understand that, but he kept shaking his head and saying, "Games is just for a little while, your face and teeth is all your life."

Boxing absorbed him from the start; in it he found a perfect expression for his narcissism, his need for constant recognition, and his physical energy. He was good, soon, and he worked very hard, training with great dedication, badgering the more experienced for pointers, yet sifting all information through his own requirements. The style he worked out depends upon his rare speed and magnificent conditioning and he will sacrifice punching opportunities to avoid being hit—he was champion for years before people stopped trying to talk him into more conventional techniques.

After an unusually thorough apprenticeship—more then a hundred amateur bouts capped by the 1960 Olympic light-heavyweight champion-ship—he turned professional. Some three years and nineteen pro fights later he signed to meet Sonny Liston for the title.

The boxing commissioners and the sporting press expected him to be beaten badly, but no one raised too strong an objection to the mismatch. But when Ali won, the commissioners immediately called for an investigation, and found irregularities in the contract they had previously okayed. The press declared that Liston was a bum and had set back boxing a hundred years, an amusing thought for 1964.

The consternation was great even among people who admitted that Ali was bringing fresh interest and money into boxing. They were beginning to realize that control was slipping away. Liston had not been exactly what box-ing wanted as its champion, but the people around him were educable. By the time Clay got to Miami for that fight he was listening to Malcolm X, and the eleven distinguished Louisville sponsors—the men with "the connections and the complexions," according to Clay—were lame-duck managers. The strutting and the posturing and the poems and the predictions—especially the predictions when they came true!—had never rested easily on boxing's fearful little heart, but it was generally accepted that Clay would bring in a few paydays before being carried out.

Now he was going to loom over all their award dinners, he was going to wear their cherished championship belt, he was going to antagonize all the politicians on whose sufferance boxing exists. The World Boxing Associa-tion was the first to act, withdrawing its recognition of the Liston-Clay fight as a title fight, retroactively, on a contract technicality.

As Ali is the first to point out, there is precedent in cheating a champion of his rightful title. "My case revives his story," he once crowed as Jack Johnson's picture flashed on a movie screen. The differences between Johnson and Ali, however, seem as revealing as the similarities.

America's gladiators were white men for the most part when Jack John-son took over the title in 1908. Blacks had been the original prizefighters, jockeys, and oarsmen in America, but as soon as money, prestige, and mythic symbolism were offered to sports heroes, the blacks were squeezed out. Box-ing promoters claimed that the fans didn't want to see blacks fight: trainers claimed blacks couldn't take punishment, and white champions quite simply refused to fight them. As usual, hard commerce was draped with an ethic: A black man in the heavyweight throne would endanger the morals of the young, the safety of the women, and the image of the nation in the world. Had Jack Johnson preferred black women and been as humble as Floyd Patterson, they still would have found a way to junk him.

From Joe Louis in 1937 to Cassius Clay in 1964, there were eight champions, six of them black. The racism of economics still existed—matchmakers were eager for black-white bouts, and advertising agencies, television sponsors, and the press still prayed for white hopes—but the black man was not America's gladiator. In fact, it was now possible to differentiate between black men, so that Patterson could be a white hope in fights against Liston and Ali, and even against a white second-generation Croatian-Canadian, George Chuvalo.

However, part of the deal for a modern black champion is his obligation to be a credit to his race; that is, he must serve as an example to his brothers of what a hardworking man can achieve through the system. He is living proof that it can be done, that failure is an individual shame.

Jack Johnson's persecution was racially and economically motivated. Muhammad Ali's was basically political. He had gained the white-controlled sports world's greatest prize, then laid it at the feet of the Muslims' Elijah Muhammad, feared in those days as the commando-in-chief of black rage.

During the thirty-eight months of his active championship, Ali responded to the increasing pressures and demands by developing and nurturing a fever of the spirit, a kind of self-winding madness. No sweetly reasonable mind would have endured. How could he explain the constant diatribe against the cleanest-living, most dedicated athlete in the country? Why should white men feel threatened by the only major black celebrity who publicly announced he had no intention of moving into, a white neighborhood or getting a white woman? Why should cities close their gates to a man who fights drew big money? How could he be attacked for blurting, "I got no quarrel with them Vietcong," on the very day Senators were making more critical statements on network television? It made no sense at all unless . . . unless . . . "THEY'RE ALL AFRAID OF ME BECAUSE I SPEAK THE TRUTH THAT CAN SET MEN FREE."

Feverish, he created some of the most stunningly virtuoso heavyweight title defenses ever seen, he married and divorced, and he began to measure himself against other sorely beset heroes of history—Jesus, Columbus, Davey Crocket, Wyatt Earp.

His marriage to Sonji Roi, described as a Chicago barmaid, was surprising and seemed uncharacteristic. She was five years older than he, divorced, a mother, a non-Muslim, a glamorous and worldly woman. Ali had often fantasized about the beautiful natural girl he would find in a backwood cabin, court with songs and gentle play, and after she fell in love with his soul, reveal "WHO I REALLY AM," and whisk her off to share his throne. Now, suddenly clumsy and callow, he walked five steps ahead of a siren with flashing thigh. Once, during an impromptu press conference at poolside, Sonji appeared above us, on the balcony in front of their motel room. "Ah-leeeee," she crooned.

"What is it?" he snapped, glancing up from the corner of his eye. "What you want?"

"You, Ahhhh-leeeeeee. Now."

Sheepishly mumbling apologies, he rose and left.

A person close to Ali has explained that strange marriage and divorce with an interesting hypothesis. Sonji, according to this hypothesis, was a good friend of Herbert Muhammad, who is Elijah's son and still Ali's closest business adviser. Ali and Sonji met when Herbert installed her at the newspaper, *Muhammad Speaks.* The natural attraction of two appealing and spirited people was encouraged by the Muslim hierarchy, which envisioned Sonji as a control on their leading personality. But they had underestimated her strong character and his religious involvement. Sonji wanted Ali to be "more of a man" and stand up to Elijah, to take a greater role in decision-making that concerned him. Ali, in turn, wanted Sonji to be more of a Muslim wife in clothing and conduct, to complement his own pious posture.

He was hurt and depressed after the failure of his marriage, but he had his two great vehicles of expression, his religion and his boxing, and he rode them into new lands. He toured Europe and Africa and the Mideast, felt the sympathy of foreign crowds, had audiences with heads of state, listened to black intellectuals. He finally understood what his friend and assistant trainer, Drew (Bundini) Brown, had often told him: "The world is a black shirt with a few white buttons."

America's first truly international sports hero, he was a celebrity on the streets of the world. In Accra they named mammy wagons Cassius Clay, children in Istanbul wore sweatshirts bearing his likeness, and he once had a sweaty hour in Stockholm trying to convince the local press that his prefer- ence for black women was a positive idiosyncrasy. He had nothing against blondes.

Two events, less than three months apart, forced him out of American rings for most of 1966. On November 22, 1965, he tortured and humiliated [Floyd] Patterson, who had allowed himself to be merchandised as the repre- sentative of whites, liberals, moderate blacks, Christians, and Americans in a holy war against the antichrist. The fight was an incredible display of ab- solute mastery. Until the referee threw himself between the fighters in the twelfth round. Ali jabbed just hard enough to swell Floyd's face, slugged just hard enough to make him groggy, holding up whenever Patterson seemed about to fall, when he would yell, "No contest, get me a contender." Specta- tors were on their feet screaming at Ali to end it, to put Floyd out of his misery.

The second event, his Vietcong remark on February 17, 1966 was then used as the excuse to cancel his Chicago date with Ernie Terrell. No boxing commission or veterans group would have protested, however, if there had been any chance that Terrell, or anyone then available, could have beaten Ali.

Ali's metaphysical baggage, rather than weighing him down, has given him an added dimension of strength. Fight managers talk about "hunger" as if it is only the ambition to climb out of poverty into a secure and comfortable life. Ali's hunger is his mystical sense of responsibility to his destiny. He steps into the ring spooked, he is fighting for all the little children, all the toothless old women on tumbledown back porches, all the winos in garbage alleys "ALL OVER THE WORLD." The fantastic will this unleashes in the ring is ter- rifying to an opponent who is fighting for something so simple as food or lavender Caddies. Thus, maddened or misguided or tuned in to divine wave lengths, Ali moved untouched through nine title defenses, and then through the trough of his life, the long exile after he refused to submit to the draft on April 28, 1967.

The speed with which he was stripped of his title was amazing; within minutes of the news flash that day, the chairman of the New York State Athletic Commission had withdrawn recognition "in the best interests of boxing." (A Legal Defense Fund lawyer, Ann Wagner, recently pointed out that those same best interests had been served by the licensing of ninety convicted felons, including rapists and murderers; her brief persuaded a federal judge to order the commission to reinstate Ali as a boxer in New York, paving the way for tomorrow's fight.)

Soon after Ali's title was removed, the World Boxing Association, bankrolled by ABC-TV, organized its own heavyweight elimination tournament, eventually won by Ali's sparring partner, Jimmy Ellis. The New York commissioner, Edwin B. Dooley, declaring that New York was as deserving of a heavyweight title as any of the WBA member states, arbitrarily sanctioned a fight between Frazier and Buster Mathis as a world championship match. Several years later, Frazier beat Ellis and was hailed as the new champ; but in private moments Frazier admitted he would never feel entirely comfortable until he proved himself a better man than Ali in the ring.

On the afternoon of his fight against Jerry Quarry, Ali lounged on a sofa in a wooden cottage outside Atlanta, answering phone calls from Whitney Young and Sidney Poitier, watching a movie of Jack Johnson's life and times, and issuing short, personal weather reports. "You know something," he said when his certified public accountant dropped by to wish him luck, "the best thing that ever happened to me was lose my title a few years and live like an ordinary man. I learned the value of a dollar, what to buy, what not to buy."

He never lived like an ordinary man; he traveled extensively, first for court appearances and Muslim meetings, later on campus-speaking tours that further broadened his awareness and honed his speaking style. He appeared in a Broadway musical, *Buck White* and was not a success, although his voice was pleasant and his presence professional. He contracted to write his autobiography with Richard Durham, a television dramatist, he appeared live in some scenes of a / k / a ("also known as"), a documentary of his life, and he sparred with Rocky Marciano in a computer's version of a match between them in their primes. They stayed even until the thirteenth round, when Marciano, "bleeding" from both eyes, cornered him and knocked him out. Ali does not encourage discussion of that entertainment. Sometimes he says that he had not known he would lose, sometimes he says, "It don't matter, nobody gonna believe a movie."

Among the visitors to the cottage before the Quarry fight was the Jesse Jackson, who said that Ali's victory that night would be a blow against the forces of blind patriotism that had tried to railroad him into jail and break his spirit and body. Jackson, tall and electric, was only one of a glittering array of black celebrities at a fight which the white mayor called a "demonstration in democracy." The engineer of the evening, State Senator Leroy Johnson, had apparently brandished his black voting bloc like a war club; he also shared in the profits of the promotion.

Quarry, terribly outclassed by an Ali who seemed no slower and definitely stronger, bled badly enough to have the fight stopped after three rounds. Ali shared his postfight press conference with Mrs. Coretta King and Ralph Abernathy, who presented him with the Dr. Martin Luther King Memorial Award for his "contributions to the cause of human dignity." Mrs. King called him "a champion of justice and peace and unity" and Dr. Abernathy said Ali was "the March on Washington all in two fists."

Some Ali-ologists found great significance in the presence of such political figures. It tended to give substance to rumors that Ali's one-year suspension from the Muslims, which began early in 1969, was actually the first public step in a gradual disinvolvement between the sect and the fighter. The reason for the suspension seemed obscure. Through *Muhammad Speaks,* Elijah declared it had to do with Ali's declaration he would seek to fight again so he could clear up his debts, estimated then at $300,000. When asked why this should warrant suspension, Ali explained that he had momentarily forsaken Allah by trying to solve his own problems.

Whatever the reason for the suspension, observers point to signs they feel indicate that Ali has outgrown the Muslims and the Muslims, their growth peaked out, no longer need a personality that can only bring them unwanted attention. Among those signs: Ali has established his second wife and their three daughters in Philadelphia, after years of living within summoning distance of Elijah, in Chicago; Cassius, Sr., estranged during the period of Ali's most emotional involvement with Elijah, is now a highly visible member of his entourage, and the flying wedge of hard-eyed Muslims that once attended Ali has given way to a genial assembly of show-business friends and footmen.

The Quarry fight reestablished Ali's credibility with the closed-circuit

television network that has become the most important element in a success/
ful prizefight. He was alive, he showed up, no federal marshals blocked him
at the ring steps, he was fit to fight, and he filled the screen. Now the promot/
ers could scramble to make the Ali/Frazier match the so/called "fight of the
century."

Since neither fighter owed too much to the boxing industry—the corpo/
ration that owns Frazier's contract, Cloverlay, is a cross section of Philadel/
phians, and with the Louisville Sponsoring Group long gone, Ali owns
himself—the fight became a show/business deal; Jack Kent Cooke, the West
Coast sports impresario, and Jerry Perenchio, a Los Angeles talent booker,
joined forces to buy rights to the fight by guaranteeing each boxer $2.5 mil/
lion, sports' biggest payday. On the glamour of that alone, the fight has
become a historic event.

Fight buffs previewed this match for years. For the first time since Sonny
Liston, the public believes there is an opponent who can beat Ali. Like Ali,
Frazier has never lost a pro fight; like Ali, he has a psychological stake in win/
ning. Although he has added a little ring style in recent years, Frazier is basi/
cally a slugger who keeps coming until he gets inside an opponent's reach.
Then he hammers at the body till the head drops into range. This, of course,
is theoretically how the experts think Ali can be beaten.

Ali came out of the Quarry fight fully aware that he wasn't quite ready
yet, and he signed to meet Oscar Bonavena. Frazier was not impressed with
that matchup. "Oscar Bonavena," said Joe "couldn't hit Clay with a 30/30
rifle. If he hits Clay once all night, it's because Clay wants to be touched up
to get his body in shape for me."

Ali used the rough/hewn Bonavena, as a training aid, particularly for
defensive body work, but apparently underestimated the Argentine fighter's
strength. It wasn't until the fifteenth round that Bonavena was tired enough
for Ali to leave himself open and knock him out. Frazier, dismissing his
earlier insight, now claims the fight proved there was no way he could lose to
Ali.

But fight buffs alone can't support a $5 million guarantee; there is an an/
ticipation of live unrehearsed allegory here that transcends a simple
punch/up. There are millions of people who, for years, have wanted to see
both Cassius Clay and Muhammad Ali cut down; he is too boastful, they

cried, button that Louisville Lip. Some of them gagged at calling him Muhammad Ali, and others could not understand how a man can refuse to serve his country, yet reap its material rewards.

Some whites felt he would stir the blacks, some blacks felt he would bring whitelash upon them. And some felt, quite simply, that the heavyweight champion of the world, an idol who owes everybody something, could at least be humble and accommodating enough to walk through two easy years as an Army boxing instructor. Didn't Joe Louis the Brown Bomber, do that?

And there are millions of people who want Ali to win. Most of them have no feeling at all about the bright, decent Frazier; Ali is the only character on stage. For some of them he is the Third World or the Noble Savage or the Child who will Show us the Way. For others he is the man who stood firm, who was willing to suffer for his convictions. For black athletes, especially, he provided a painful, but liberating lesson; if the champion of the world could be shamefully persecuted before he was convicted of a crime, no one's hard-earned achievements should be traded for promises and phony glory. There are those who see him as youth and light and magic, a Technicolor genie in a bottle-green world. And there are those who simply see him as the man who told the Establishment to stuff itself and is now getting $2.5 million for hanging tough.

The future looks like his. The five-year sentence for draft evasion seems less sure than it once did: The Supreme Court is reviewing his conviction, and some lawyers do not see how it can fail to overturn a ruling made before the 1970 Welsh decision in which moral and ethical objection to war was judged as legally valid as religious objection. If he beats Frazier, as he should, the undisputed title will be worth interesting and rewarding business and entertainment contracts. Debt-free, without legal restraints, perhaps without Muslim prohibitions, Ali's near future could be a joyous crest after the trough, one fight every year or so for a few years, a movie now and then, the world as a stage.

Once again, we may have a heavyweight champion who feels he does not have to be what we want him to be, and this ultimately, will be a profound disappointment to those who expect him to sink or save us.

Ali, at twenty-nine, is everything that he was at twenty-two, deepened and broadened like his chest, but basically, the same: He is a better fighter, a more polished entertainer, a smoother preacher, and a shrewder judge of character. But he is also more egocentric, manipulative, demanding, and protective of his interests, when he finds out where they lie.

I remember once, tooling through Harlem in a black limousine with the dual speakers blaring, as Ali spoke in dreamy cadences of the great housing developments that would rise under his hands, with malls and parks and day-care centers, with boys and girls arm in arm an example to the world of money properly spent. He had won the title only four months before, the trouble that lay ahead was only a cloud; such a vision seemed within grasp.

Sometimes I've thought about that vision, and how it was best left locked in the mind's attic with other rainy-day diversions. But it came to me last fall in Atlanta that afternoon before his return to the ring. The certified public accountant rose to leave, and Ali pointed to him and said, "There's my Jewish brains. Get those few brains around you, the best in the world. This man's the most important factor in my life. You're gonna have to come back to interview me about my corporations, my businesses, my financial dealings. Right now, we're putting some money in apartment houses, and…"

[March, 1971]

Please note that this piece has been edited for this volume and does not appear in its entirety.

EGO

NORMAN MAILER

It is the great word of the twentieth century. If there is a single word our century has added to the potentiality of language, it is ego. Everything we have done in this century, from monumental feats to nightmares of human destruction, has been a function of that extraordinary state of the psyche which gives us authority to declare we are sure of ourselves when we are not.

Muhammad Ali beings with the most unsettling ego of all. Having commanded the stage, he never pretends to step back and relinquish his place to other actors—like a six-foot parrot, he keeps screaming at you that he is the center of the stage. "Come here and get me, fool," he says. "You can't, 'cause you don't know who I am. You don't know *where* I am. I'm human intelligence and you don't even know if I'm good or evil." This has been his essential message to America all these years. It is intolerable to our American mentality that the figure who is probably most prominent to us after the President is simply not comprehensible, for he could be a demon or a saint. Or both! Richard Nixon, at least, appears comprehensible. We can hate him or we can vote for him, but at least we disagree with each other about him. What kills us about a.k.a. Cassius Clay is that the disagreement is inside us. He is *fascinating*—attraction and repulsion must be in the same package. So, he is obsessive. The more we don't want to think about him, the more we are obliged to. There is a reason for it. He is America's Greatest Ego. He is also, as I am going to try to show, the swiftest embodiment of human intelligence we have had yet, he is the very spirit of the twentieth century, he is the prince of mass man and the media. Now, perhaps temporarily, he is the fallen prince. But there still may be one holocaust of an urge to understand him, or try to, for obsession is a disease. Twenty little obsessions are twenty leeches on the mind, and one big obsession can become one big operation if we refuse to live with it. If Muhammad Ali defeats Frazier in the return bout, then he'll become the national obsession and we'll elect him President yet—you may indeed have to vote for any man who could defeat a fighter as great as Joe Frazier and still be Muhammad Ali. That's a combination!

Ego is driving a point through to a conclusion you are obliged to reach without knowing too much about the ground you cross between. You suffer for a larger point. Every good prizefighter must have a large ego, then, because he is trying to demolish a man he doesn't know too much about, he is unfeeling—which is the ground floor of ego; and he is full of techniques—which are the wings of ego. What separates the noble ego of the prizefighters from the lesser ego of authors is that the fighter goes through experiences in the ring which are occasionally immense, incommunicable except to fighters who have been as good, or to women who have gone through every minute of an anguish-filled birth, experiences which are finally mysterious. Like men who climb mountains, it is an exercise of ego which becomes something like soul—just as technology may have begun to have transcended itself when we reached to the moon. So, two great fighters in a great fight travel down subterranean rivers of exhaustion and cross mountain peaks of agony, stare at the light of their own death in the eye of the man they are fighting, travel into the crossroads of the most excruciating choice of karma as they get up from the floor against all the appeal of the sweet swooning catacombs of oblivion— it is just that we do not see them this way, because they are not primarily men of words, and this is the century of words, numbers, and symbols. Enough.

We have come to the point. There are languages other than words, languages of symbol and languages of nature. There are languages of the body. And prizefighting is one of them. There is no attempting to comprehend a prizefighter unless we are willing to recognize that he speaks with a command of the body which is as detached, subtle and comprehensive in its intelligence as any exercise of mind by such social engineers as Herman Kahn or Henry Kissinger. Of course, a man like Herman Kahn is by report gifted with a bulk of three hundred pounds. He does not move around with a light foot. So many a good average prizefighter, just a little punchy, does not speak with any particular éclat. That doesn't mean he is incapable of expressing himself with wit, style, and an esthetic flair for surprise when he boxes with his body, any more than Kahn's obesity would keep us from recognizing that his mind can work with strength. Boxing is a dialogue between bodies. Ignorant men, usually black, and usually next to illiterate, address one another in a set of *conversational* exchanges which go deep into the heart of each other's matter. It is just that they converse with their physiques. Boxing is a rapid debate between two sets of intelligence. It takes place rapidly because it is conducted with the body rather than the mind. If this seems extreme, let us look for a connection. Picasso could never do arithmetic when he was young because the number seven looked to him like a nose upside down. So to learn arithmetic would slow him up. He was a future painter—his intelligence resided somewhere in the coordination of the body and the mind. He was not going to cut off his body from his mind by learning numbers. But most of us do. We have minds which work fairly well and bodies which sometimes don't. But if we are white and want to be comfortable we put our emphasis on learning to talk with the mind. Ghetto cultures, black, Puerto Rican, and Chicano cultures having less expectation of comfort tend to stick with the wit their bodies provide. They speak to each other with their bodies, they signal with their clothes. They talk with many a silent telepathic intelligence. And doubtless feel the frustration of being unable to express the subtleties of their states in words, just as the average middle-class white will feel unable to carry out his dreams of glory by the uses of his body. If black people are also beginning to speak our mixture of formal English and jargon-polluted American with real force, so white corporate America is getting more sexual and more athletic. Yet to begin to talk about Ali and Frazier, their psyches, their styles, their honor, their character, their greatness, and their flaws, we have to recognize that there is no way to comprehend them as men like ourselves—we can only guess at their insides by a real jump of our imagination into the science Ali invented—he was the first psychologist of the body.

Okay. There are fighters who are men's men. Rocky Marciano was one of them. Oscar Bonavena and Jerry Quarry and George Chuvalo and Gene Fuller and Carmen Basilio, to name a few, have faces which would give a Marine sergeant pause in a bar fight. They look like they could take you out with the knob of bone they have left for a nose. They are all, incidentally, white fighters. They have a code—it is to fight until they are licked, and if they have to take a punch for every punch they give, well, they figure they can win. Their ego and their body intelligence are both connected to the same source of juice—it is male pride. They are substances close to rock. They work on clumsy skills to hone them finer, knowing if they can obtain parity, blow for blow with any opponent, they will win. They have more guts. Up to a far-gone point, pain is their pleasure, for their character in combat is their strength to trade pain for pain, loss of faculty for loss of faculty.

One can cite black fighters like them. Henry Hank and Reuben Carter, Emile Griffith, and Benny Paret. Joe Frazier would be the best of them. But black fighters tend to be complex. They have veins of unsuspected strength and streaks when they feel as spooked as wild horses. Any fight promoter in the world knew he had a good fight if Fullmer went against Basilio, it was a proposition as certain as the wages for the week. But black fighters were art/ ists, they were relatively moody, they were full of the surprises of Patterson or Liston, the virtuosities of Archie Moore and Sugar Ray, the speed, savagery, and curious lack of substance in Jimmy Ellis, the vertiginous neuroses of gi/ ants like Buster Mathis. Even Joe Louis, recognized by a majority in the years of his own championship as the greatest heavyweight of all time, was surpris/ ingly inconsistent with minor fighters like Buddy Baer. Part of the unpredict/ ability of their performances was due to the fact that all but Moore and Robinson were heavyweights. Indeed, white champions in the top division were equally out of form from fight to fight. It can, in fact, be said that heavy/ weights are always the most lunatic of prizefighters. The closer a heavyweight comes to the championship, the more natural it is for him to be a little bit in/ sane, secretly insane, for the heavyweight champion of the world is either the toughest man in the world or he is not, but there is a real possibility he is. It is like being the big toe of God. You have nothing to measure yourself by. Lightweights, welterweights, middleweights can all be exceptionally good, fantastically talented—they are still very much in their place. The best light/ weight in the world knows that an unranked middleweight can defeat him on most nights, and the best middleweight in the world will kill him every night. He knows that the biggest strongman in a tough bar could handle him by sitting on him, since the power to punch seems to increase quickly with weight. A fighter who weighs two/forty will punch more than twice as hard as a fighter who weighs one/twenty. The figures have no real basis, of course, they are only there to indicate the law of the ring: a good big man beats a good little man. So the notion of prizefighters as hardworking craftsmen is most likely to be true in the light and middle divisions. Since they are fighters who know their limitations, they are likely to strive for excellence in their category. The better they get, the closer they have come to sanity, at least if we are ready to assume that the average fighter is a buried artist, which is to say a *body* artist with an extreme amount of violence in him. Obviously the better and more successful they get, the more they have been able to transmute violence into craft, discipline, even body art. That is human alchemy. We respect them and they deserve to be respected.

But the heavyweights never have such simple sanity. If they become champions they begin to have inner lives like Hemingway or Dostoyevsky, Tolstoy or Faulkner, Joyce or Melville or Conrad or Lawrence or Proust. Hemingway is the example above all. Because he wished to be the greatest writer in the history of literature and still be a hero with all the body arts age would yet grant him, he was alone and he knew it. So are heavyweight champions alone. Dempsey was alone and Tunney could never explain himself and Sharkey could never believe himself nor Schmeling nor Braddock, and Carnera was sad and Baer an indecipherable clown; great heavyweights like Louis had the loneliness of the ages in their silence, and men like Marciano were mystified by a power which seemed to have been granted them. With the advent, however, of the great modern black heavyweights, Patterson, Liston, then Clay and Frazier, perhaps the loneliness gave way to what it had been protecting itself against—a surrealistic situation unstable beyond belief. Being a black heavyweight champion in the second half of the twentieth century (with black revolutions opening all over the world) was now not unlike being Jack Johnson, Malcolm X, and Frank Costello all in one. Going down the aisle and into the ring in Chicago was conceivably more frightening for Sonny Liston than facing Patterson that night—he was raw as uncoated wire with his sense of retribution awaiting him for years of prison pleasures and underworld jobs. Pools of paranoia must have reached him like different washes of color from different sides of the arena. He was a man who had barely learned to read and write—he had none of the impacted and mediocre misinformation of all the world of daily dull reading to clot the antenna of his senses—so he was keen to every hatred against him. He knew killers were waiting in that mob, they always were, he had been on speaking terms with just such subjects himself—now he dared to be king—any assassin could strike for his revenge upon acts Liston had long forgot; no wonder Liston was in fear going into the ring, and happier once within it.

And Patterson was exhausted before the fight began. Lonely as a monk for years, his daily gym work the stuff of his meditation, he was the first of the black fighters to be considered, then used, as a political force. He was one of the liberal elite, an Eleanor Roosevelt darling, he was political mileage for the NAACP. Violent, conceivably to the point of murder if he had not been a

fighter, he was a gentleman in public, more, he was a man of the nicest, quietest, most private good manners. But monastic by inclination. Now, all but
uneducated, he was appealed to by political blacks to win the Liston fight for
the image of the Negro. Responsibility sat upon him like a comic cutback in
a silent film where we return now and again to one poor man who has been
left to hold a beam across his shoulders. There he stands, hardly able to move.
At the end of the film he collapses. That was the weight put on Patterson.
The responsibility to beat Liston was too great to bear. Patterson, a fighter of
incorruptible honesty, was knocked out by punches hardly anybody saw. He
fell in open air as if seized by a stroke. The age of surrealistic battles had begun. In the second fight with Liston, Patterson, obviously more afraid of a
repetition of the first nightmare than anything else, simply charged his opponent with his hands low and was knocked down three times and out in the
first round. The age of body psychology had begun and Clay was there to
conceive it.

A kid as wild and dapper and jaybird as the president of a downhome
college fraternity, bowtie, brownandwhite shoes, sweet, happygolucky,
raucous, he descended on Vegas for the second PattersonListon fight. He was
like a beautiful boy surrounded by doting aunts. The classiestlooking middleaged Negro ladies were always flanking him in Vegas as if to set up a female field of repulsion against any evil black magnetic forces in the offing.
And from the sanctuary of his ability to move around crap tables like a kitten
on the frisk, he taunted black majestic kingsize Liston before the fight and after the fight. "You're so ugly," he would jeer, crap table safely between them,
"that I don't know how you can get any uglier."

"Why don't you sit on my knee and I'll feed you your orange juice," Liston would rumble back.

"Don't insult me, or you'll be sorry. 'Cause you're just an ugly slow bear."

They would pretend to rush at one another. Smaller men would hold
them back without effort. They were building the gate for the next fight. And
Liston was secretly fond of Clay. He would chuckle when he talked about
him. It was years since Liston had failed to knock out his opponent in the first
round. His charisma was majestic with menace. One held one's breath when
near him. He looked forward with obvious amusement to the happy seconds
when he would take Clay apart and see the expression on that silly face. In
Miami he trained for a threeround fight. In the famous fifth round when

Clay came out with the caustic in his eyes and could not see, he waved his gloves at Liston, a look of abject horror on his face, as if to say, "Your youn, ger brother is now an old blind beggar. Do not strike him." And did it with a peculiar authority. For Clay looked like a ghost with his eyes closed, tears streaming, his extended gloves waving in front of him like a widow's entreat, ies. Liston drew back in doubt, in bewilderment, conceivably in concern for his new great reputation as an ex,bully; yes, Liston reacted like a gentleman, and Clay was home free. His eyes watered out the caustic, his sight came back. He cut Liston up in the sixth. He left him beaten and exhausted. Lis, ton did not stand up for the bell to the seventh. Maybe Clay had even defeated him earlier that day at the weigh,in when he had harangued and screamed and shouted and whistled and stuck his tongue out at Liston. The Champ had been bewildered. No one had been able ever to stare him in the eyes these last four years. Now a boy was screaming at him, a boy reported to belong to Black Muslims, no, stronger than that, a boy favored by Malcolm X who was braver by reputation than the brave, for he could stop a bullet any day. Liston, afraid only, as he put it, of crazy men, was afraid of the Muslims for he could not contend with their allegiance to one another in prison, their puritanism, their discipline, their martial ranks. The combination was too complex, too unfamiliar. Now, their boy, in a pain of terror or in a mania of courage, was screaming at him at the weigh,in. Liston sat down and shook his head, and looked at the press, now become his friend, and wound his fingers in circles around his ear, as if saying, whitey to whitey, "That black boy is nuts." So Clay made Liston Tom it, and when Liston missed the first jab he threw in the fight by a foot and a half, one knew the night would not be ordinary in the offing.

For their return bout in Boston, Liston trained as he had never before. Clay got a hernia. Liston trained again. Hard training as a fighter grows older seems to speak of the dull deaths of the brightest cells in all the favorite organs; old fighters react to training like beautiful women to washing floors. But Liston did it twice, once for Clay's hernia, and again for their actual fight in Maine, and the second time he trained, he aged as a fighter, for he had a sparring partner, Amos Lincoln, who was one of the better heavyweights in the country. They had wars with one another every afternoon in the gym. By the day before the fight, Liston was as relaxed and sleepy and dopey as a man in a steambath. He had fought his heart out in training, had done it under constant pressure from Clay who keep telling the world that Liston was old and slow and could not possibly win. And their fight created a scandal, for Liston ran into a short punch in the first round and was counted out, unable to hear the count. The referee and timekeeper missed signals with one another while Clay stood over fallen Liston screaming, "Get up and fight!" It was no night for the fight game, and a tragedy for Clay since he had trained for a long and arduous fight. He had developed his technique for a major encounter with Liston and was left with a horde of unanswered questions including the one he could never admit—which was whether there had been the magic of a real knockout in his punch or if Liston had made—for what variety of reasons!—a conscious decision to stay on the floor. It did him no good.

He had taken all the lessons of his curious life and the outrageously deep comprehension he had of the motivations of his own people—indeed, one could even approach the beginnings of a Psychology of the Blacks by studying his encounters with fighters who were black—and had elaborated that into a technique for boxing which was almost without compare. A most cultivated technique. For he was no child of the slums. His mother was a gracious pale-skinned lady, his father a bitter wit pride-oriented on the family name of Clay—they were descendants of Henry Clay, the orator, on the white side of the family, nothing less, and Cassius began boxing at twelve in a police gym, and from the beginning was a phenomenon of style and the absence of pain, for he knew how to use his physical endowment. Tall, relatively light, with an exceptionally long reach even for his size, he developed defensive skills which made the best use of his body. Working apparently on the premise that there was something obscene about being hit, he boxed with his head back and drew it further back when attacked, like a kid who is shy of punches in a street fight, but because he had a waist which was more supple than the average fighter's neck, he was able to box with his arms low, surveying the fighter in front of him, avoiding punches by the speed of his feet, the reflexes of his waist, the long spoiling deployment of his arms which were always tipping other fighters off balance. Added to this was his psychological comprehension of the vanity and confusion of other fighters. A man in the ring is a performer as well as a gladiator. Elaborating his technique from the age of twelve, Clay knew how to work on the vanity of other performers, knew how to make them feel ridiculous and so force them into crucial mistakes, knew how to set such a tone from the first round—later he was to know how to begin it a year before he would even meet the man. Clay knew that a fighter who had been put in psychological knots before he got near the ring had already lost half, three-quarters, no, all of the fight could be lost before the first punch. That was the psychology of the body.

Now, add his curious ability as a puncher. Clay punched with a greater variety of mixed intensities than anyone around, he played with punches, was tender with them, laid them on as delicately as you put a postage stamp on an envelope, then cracked them in like a riding crop across your face, stuck a cruel jab like a baseball bat held head on into your mouth, next waltzed you in a clinch with a tender arm around your neck, winged away out of reach on flying legs, dug a hook with the full swing of a baseball bat hard into your ribs, hard pokes of a jab into the face, a mocking soft flurry of pillows and gloves, a mean forearm cutting you off from coming up on him, a cruel wres-tling of your neck in a clinch, then elusive again, gloves snake-licking your face like a whip. By the time Clay had defeated Liston once and was training for the second fight, by the time Clay, now champion and renamed Muham-mad Ali, and bigger, grown up quickly and not so mysteriously (after the po-tent ego-soups and marrows of his trip through Muslim Africa) into a Black Prince, Potentate of his people, new Poombah of Polemic, yes, by this time, Clay—we will find it more natural to call him Ali from here on out (for the Prince will behave much like a young god)—yes, Muhammad Ali, Heavy-weight Champion of the World, having come back with an amazing com-mitment to be leader of his people, proceeded to go into training for the second Liston fight with a commitment and then a genius of comprehension for the true intricacies of the Science of Sock. He alternated the best of spar-ring partners and the most ordinary, worked rounds of dazzling speed with Jimmy Ellis—later, of course, to be champion himself before Frazier knocked him out—rounds which displayed the high esthetic of boxing at its best, then lay against the ropes with other sparring partners, hands at his sides as if it were the eleventh or thirteenth round of an excruciating and exhaust-ing fight with Liston where Ali was now so tired he could not hold his hands up, could just manage to take punches to the stomach, rolling with them, smothering them with his stomach, absorbing them with backward moves, sliding along the ropes, steering his sparring partner with passive but off-setting moves of his limp arms. For a minute, for two minutes, the sparring partner—Shotgun Sheldon was his name—would bomb away on Ali's stomach much as if Liston were tearing him apart in later rounds, and Ali weaving languidly, sliding his neck for the occasional overhead punch to his face, bouncing from the rope into the punches, bouncing back away from punches, as if his torso had become one huge boxing glove to absorb punish-ment, had penetrated through into some further conception of pain, as if pain were not pain if you accepted it with a relaxed heart, yes, Ali let himself be bombarded on the ropes by the powerful bull-like swings of Shotgun Sheldon, the expression on his face as remote, and as searching for the last routes into the nerves of each punch going in as a man hanging on a subway strap will search into the meaning of the market quotations he has just read on the activities of a curious stock. So Ali relaxed on the ropes and took punches to the belly with a faint disdain, as if, curious punches, they did not go deep enough and after a minute of this, or two minutes, having offered his body like the hide of a drum for a mad drummer's solo, he would snap out of his communion with himself and flash a tattoo of light and slashing punches, mocking as the lights on water, he would dazzle his sparring part-ner, who, arm-weary and punched out, would look at him with eyes of love, complete was his admiration.

Training session over, Ali would lecture the press, instruct them—look-ing beyond his Liston defense to what he would do to Patterson, mocking Patterson, calling him a rabbit, a white man's rabbit, knowing he was put-ting a new beam on Patterson's shoulders, an outrageously helpless and heavy beam of rage, fear, hopeless anger, and secret black admiration for the all-out force of Ali's effrontery. Patterson's back gave way in the early rounds, and he fought twisted and in pain, half crippled like a man with a sacroiliac, for eleven brave and most miserable rounds before the referee would call it and Ali, breaking up with his first wife then, was unpleasant in the ring that night, his face ugly and contemptuous, himself well on the way to becoming America's most unpopular major American. That, too, was part of the art—to get a public to the point of hating him so much the burden on the other fighter approached the metaphysical—which is where Ali wanted it. White fighters with faces like rock embedded in cement would trade punch for punch. Ali liked to get the boxing where it belongs—he would trade metaphysic for metaphysic with anyone.

Ali had them psyched. He cut through moribund coruscated dirty business corridors, cut through cigar smoke and bushwah, hypocrisy and well-aimed kicks to the back of the neck, but through crooked politicians and patriotic pus, cut like a laser, point of the point, light and impersonal, cut to the heart of the rottenest meat in boxing, and boxing was always the buried South Vietnam of America, buried for fifty years in our hide before we went there, yes, Ali cut through the flag-dragooned salutes of drunken dawns and said, "I got no fight with those Vietcongs," and they cut him down, thrust him into the three and a half years of his martyrdom. Where he grew. Grew to have a little fat around his middle and a little of the complacent muscle of the clam to his world-ego. And grew sharper in the mind as well, and deepened and broadened physically. Looked no longer like a boy, but a sullen man, almost heavy, with the beginnings of a huge expanse across his shoulders. And developed the patience to survive, the wisdom to contemplate future nights in jail, grew to cultivate the suspension of belief and the avoidance of disbelief—what a rack for a young man! As the years of hope for reinstatement, or avoidance of prison, came up and waned in him, Ali walked the tightrope between bitterness and apathy, and had enough left to beat Quarry and beat Bonavena, beat Quarry in the flurry of a missed hundred punches, ho! how his timing was off! beat him with a calculated whip, snake-lick whip, to the corrugated sponge of dead flesh over Quarry's Irish eyes—they stopped it after the third on cuts—then knocked out Bonavena, the indestructible, never stopped before, by working the art of crazy mixing in the punches he threw at the rugged—some of the punches Ali threw that night would not have hurt a little boy—the punch he let go in the fifteenth came in like a wrecking ball from outer space. Bonavena went sprawling across the ring. He was a house coming down.

He did not train for Frazier as perhaps he had to. He worked, he ran three miles a day when he could have run five, he boxed some days and let a day and perhaps another day go, he was relaxed, he was confident, he basked in the undemanding winter sun of Miami, and skipped his rope in a gym crowded with fighters, stuffed now with working fighters looking to be seen, Ali comfortable and relaxed like the greatest of movie stars, he played a young fighter working out in a corner on the heavy bag—for of course every eye was on him—and afterward doing sit-ups in the back room and having his stomach rubbed with liniment, he would talk to reporters. He was filled with confidence there was no black fighter he did not comprehend to the root of the valve in the hard-pumping heart, and yes, Frazier, he assured everybody, would be easier than they realized. Like a little boy who had grown up to take on a mountain of responsibility he spoke in the deep relaxation of the wise, and teased two of the reporters who were present and fat. "You want to drink a lot of water," he said, "good cold water instead of all that liquor rot-your-gut," and gave the smile of a man who had been able to intoxicate himself on water (although he was, by repute, a fiend for soft sweet drinks), "and fruit and good clean vegetables you want to eat and chicken and steak. You lose weight then," he advised out of kind secret smiling thoughts, and went on to talk of the impact of the fight upon the world. "Yes," he said, "you just think of a stadium with a million people, ten million people, you could get them all in to watch they would all pay to see it live, but then you think of the hundreds of millions and the billions who are going to see this fight, and if you could sit them all down in one place, and fly a jet plane over them, why that plane would have to fly for an hour before it would reach the end of all the people who will see this fight. It's the greatest event in the history of the world, and you take a man like Frazier, a good fighter, but a simple hard-working fellow, he's not built for this kind of pressure, the eyes," Ali said softly, "of that many people upon him. There's an experience to pressure which I have had, fighting a man like Liston in Miami the first time, which he has not. He will cave in under the pressure. No, I do not see any way a man like Frazier can whup me, he can't reach me, my arms are too long, and if he does get in and knock me down I'll never make the mistake of Quarry and Foster or Ellis of rushing back at him, I'll stay away until my head clears, then I begin to pop him again, pop! pop!" a few jabs, "no there is no way this man can beat me, this fight will be easier than you think."

There was one way in which boxing was still like a street fight and that was in the need to be confident you would win. A man walking out of a bar to fight with another man is seeking to compose his head into the confidence that he will certainly triumph—it is the most mysterious faculty of the ego. For that confidence is a sedative against the pain of punches and yet is the sanction to punch your own best. The logic of the spirit would suggest that you win only if you deserve to win: the logic of the ego lays down the axiom that if you don't think you will win, you don't deserve to. And, in fact, usu-

ally don't; it is as if not believing you will win opens you to the guilt that per/
haps you have not the right, you are too guilty.

So training camps are small factories for the production of one rare psy/
chological item—an ego able to bear huge pain and administer drastic pun/
ishment. The flow of Ali's ego poured over the rock of every distraction, it
was an ego like the flow of a river of constant energy fed by a hundred tribu/
taries of black love and the love of the white left. The construction of the ego
of Joe Frazier was of another variety. His manager, Yancey "Yank" Dur/
ham, a canny foxy light/skinned Negro with a dignified mien, a gray head of
hair, gray mustache and a small but conservative worthy's paunch, plus the
quick/witted look of eyes which could spot from a half/mile away any man
coming toward him with a criminal thought, was indeed the face of a con/
summate jeweler who had worked for years upon a diamond in the rough un/
til he was now and at last a diamond, hard as the transmutation of black
carbon from the black earth into the brilliant sky/blue shadow of the rarest
shining rock. What a fighter was Frazier, what a diamond of an ego had he,
and what a manager was Durham. Let us look.

Sooner or later, fight metaphors, like fight managers, go sentimental. They
go military. But there is no choice here. Frazier was the human equivalent
of a war machine. He had tremendous firepower. He had a great left hook, a
left hook frightening even to watch when it missed, for it seemed to whistle; he
had a powerful right. He could knock a man out with either hand—not all
fighters can, not even very good fighters. Usually, however, he clubbed oppo/
nents to death, took a punch, gave a punch, took three punches, gave two,
took a punch, gave a punch, high speed all the way, always working, pushing
his body and arms, short for a heavyweight, up through the middle, bombing
through on force, reminiscent of Jimmy Brown knocking down tacklers,
Frazier kept on coming, hard and fast, a hang/in, hang/on, go/and/get/him,
got/him, got/him, slip and punch, take a punch, wing a punch, whap a
punch, never was Frazier happier than with his heart up on the line against
some other man's heart, let the bullets fly—his heart was there to stand up at
the last. Sooner or later, the others almost all fell down. Undefeated like Ali,
winner of twenty/three out of twenty/six fights by knockout, he was a human
force, certainly the greatest heavyweight force to come along since Rocky

Marciano. (If those two men had ever met, it would have been like two Mack trucks hitting each other head-on, then backing up to hit each other again— they would have kept it up until the wheels were off the axles and the engines off the chassis.) But this would be a different kind of fight. Ali would run, Ali would keep hitting Frazier with long jabs, quick hooks and rights while backing up, backing up, staying out of reach unless Frazier could take the punishment and get in. That was where the military problem began. For getting in against the punishment he would take was a question of morale, and there was a unique situation in this fight—Frazier had become the white man's fighter, Mr. Charley was rooting for Frazier, and that meant blacks were boycotting him in their heart. That could be poison to Frazier's morale, for he was twice as black as Clay and half as handsome, he had the rugged decent life-worked face of a man who had labored in the pits all his life, he looked like the deserving modest son of one of those Negro cleaning women of a bygone age who worked from six in the morning to midnight every day, raised a family, endured and occasionally elicited the exasperated admiration of white ladies who would kindly remark, "That woman deserves something better in her life." Frazier had the mien of the son, one of many, of such a woman, and he was the hardest-working fighter in training many a man had ever seen, he was conceivably the hardest-working man alive in the world, and as he went through his regimen, first boxing four rounds with a sparring partner, Kenny Norton, a talented heavyweight from the coast with an almost unbeaten record, then working on the heavy bag, then the light bag, then skipping rope, ten to twelve rounds of sparring and exercise on a light day, Frazier went on with the doggedness, the concentration, and the pumped-up fury of a man who has had so little in his life that he can endure torments to get everything, he pushed the total of his energy and force into an absolute abstract exercise of will so it did not matter if he fought a sparring partner or the heavy bag, he lunged at each equally as if the exhaustions of his own heart and the clangor of his lungs were his only enemies, and the head of a fighter or the leather of the bag as it rolled against his own head was nothing but some abstract thunk of material, not a thing, not a man, but thunk! thunk! something of an obstacle, thunk! thunk! thunk! to beat into thunk! oblivion. And his breath came in rips and sobs as he smashed into the bag as if it were real, just that heavy big torso-sized bag hanging from its chain but he attacked it as if it were a bear, as if it were a great fighter and they were in the mortal embrace of a killing set of exchanges of punches in the middle of the eighth round, and rounds of exercise later, skipping rope to an inhumanly fast beat for this late round in the training day, sweat pouring like jets of blood from an artery, he kept swinging his rope, muttering, "Two‑million‑dollars‑and‑change, two‑million‑dollars‑and‑change," railroad train chugging into the terminals of exhaustion.

That was one half of the strategy to isolate Frazier from Ali, hard work and thinking of thunking on inanimate Clay; the other half was up to Durham who was running front relations with the blacks of North Philly who wandered into the gym, paid their dollar, and were ready to heckle on Frazier. In the four rounds he boxed with Norton, Frazier did not look too good for a while. It was ten days before the fight and he was in a bad mood when he came in, for the word was through the gym that they had discovered one of his favorite sparring partners, just fired that morning, was a Black Muslim and had been calling Ali every night with reports, that was the rumor, and Frazier, sullen and cold at the start, was bopped and tapped, then walloped by Norton moving fast with the big training gloves in imitation of Ali, and Frazier looked very easy to hit until the middle of the third round when Norton, proud of his something like twenty wins and one loss, beginning to get some ideas himself about how to fight champions, came driving in to mix it with Frazier, have it out man to man and caught a right which dropped him, left him looking limp with that half‑silly smile sparring partners get when they have been hit too hard to justify any experience or any money they are going to take away. Up till then the crowd had been with Norton. There at one end of the Cloverlay gym, a street‑level storefront room which could have been used originally by an automobile dealer, there on that empty, immaculate Lysol‑soaked floor, designed when Frazier was there for only Frazier and his partners to train (as opposed to Miami where Ali would rub elbows with the people) here the people were at one end, the end off the street, and they jeered whenever Norton hit Frazier, they laughed when Norton made him look silly, they called out, "Drop the mother," until Durham held up a gentlemanly but admonishing finger in request for silence. Afterward, however, training completed, Durham approached them to answer questions, rolled with their sallies, jived the people back, subtly enlisted their sympathy for Frazier by saying, "When I fight Clay, I'm going to get him somewhere in the middle rounds," until the blacks quipping back said angrily, "You ain't fighting him, Frazier is."

"Why you call him Clay?" another asked. "He Ali."

"His name is Cassius Clay to me," said Durham.

"What you say against his religion?"

"I don't say nothing about his religion and he doesn't say anything about mine. I'm a Baptist."

"You going to make money on this?"

"Of course," said Durham, "I got to make money. You don't think I work up this sweat for nothing."

Upstairs, dressed, and sucking an orange, sweat still pouring, gloom of excessive fatigue upon him, Frazier was sitting through his two-hundredth or two-thousandth interview for this fight, reluctant indeed to give it at all. "Some get it, some don't," he had said for refusal, but relented when a white friend who had done roadwork with him interceded, so he sat there now against a leather sofa, dark blue suit, dark T-shirt, mopping his brow with a pink-red towel, and spoke dispiritedly of being ready too early for the fight. He was waking up an hour too early for roadwork each morning now. "I'd go back to sleep but it doesn't feel good when I do run."

"I guess the air is better that hour of the morning."

He nodded sadly. "There's a limit to how good the air in Philly can get."

"Where'd you begin to sing?" was a question asked.

"I sang in church first," he replied, but it was not the day to talk about singing. The loneliness of hitting the bag still seemed upon him as if in his exhaustion now, and in the thoughts of that small insomnia which woke him an hour too early every day was something of the loneliness of all blacks who work very hard and are isolated from fun and must wonder in the just-awakened night how large and pervasive was the curse of a people. "The countdown's begun," said Frazier, "I get impatient about now."

For the fight, Ali was wearing red velvet trunks, Frazier had green. Before they began, even before they were called together by the referee for instructions, Ali went dancing around the ring and glided past Frazier with a sweet little-boy smile, as if to say, "You're my new playmate. We're going to have fun." Ali was laughing. Frazier was having nothing of this and turned his neck to embargo him away. Ali, having alerted the crowd by this big first move, came prancing in again. When Frazier looked ready to block him, Ali went around, evading a contact, gave another sweet smile, shook his head at the lack of high spirit. "Poor Frazier," he seemed to say.

The referee gave his instructions. The bell rang. The first fifteen seconds of a fight can be the fight. It is equivalent to the first kiss in a love affair. The fighters each missed the other. Ali blocked Frazier's first punches easily, but Ali then missed Frazier's head. That head was bobbing as fast as a third fist. Frazier would come rushing in, head moving like a fist, fists bobbing, too, his head working above and below his forearm, he was trying to get through Ali's jab, get through fast and sear Ali early with the terror of a long fight and punches harder than he had ever taken to the stomach, and Ali in turn, backing up, and throwing fast punches, aimed just a trifle, and was therefore a trifle too slow, but it was obvious Ali was trying to shiver Frazier's synapses from the start, set waves of depression stirring which would reach his heart in later rounds and make him slow, deaden nerve, deaden nerve went Ali's jab flicking a snake tongue, whooeet! whooeet! but Frazier's head was bobbing too fast, he was moving faster than he had ever moved before in that bobbing nonstop never-a-backward step of his, slogging and bouncing forward, that huge left hook flaunting the air with the confidence it was enough of a club to split a tree, and Ali, having missed his jabs, stepped nimbly inside the hook and wrestled Frazier in the clinch. Ali looked stronger here. So by the first forty-five seconds of the fight, they had each surprised the other profoundly. Frazier was fast enough to slip through Ali's punches, and Ali was strong enough to handle him in the clinches. A pattern had begun. Because Ali was missing often, Frazier was in under his shots like a police dog's muzzle on your arm, Ali could not slide from side to side, he was boxed in, then obliged to go backward, and would end on the ropes again and again with Frazier belaboring him. Yet Frazier could not reach him. Like a prestidigitator Ali would tie the other's punches into odd knots, not even blocking them yet on his elbows or his arms, rather throwing his own punches as defensive moves, for even as they missed, he would brush Frazier to the side with his forearm, or hold him off, or clinch and wrestle a little of the will out of Frazier's neck. Once or twice in the round a long left hook by Frazier just touched the surface of Ali's chin, and Ali waved his head in placid contempt to the billions watching as if to say, "This man has not been able to hurt me at all."

The first round set a pattern for the fight. Ali won it and would win the next. His jab was landing from time to time and rights and lefts of no great consequence. Frazier was hardly reaching him at all. Yet it looked like Frazier had established that he was fast enough to get in on Ali and so drive him to the ropes and to the corners, and that spoke of a fight which would be determined by the man in better condition, in better physical condition rather than in better psychic condition, the kind of fight Ali could hardly want for his strength was in his pauses, his nature passed along the curve of every dialectic, he liked, in short, to fight in flurries, and then move out, move away, assess, take his time, fight again. Frazier would not let him. Frazier moved in with the snarl of a wolf, his teeth seemed to show through his mouthpiece, he made Ali work. Ali won the first two rounds but it was obvious he could not continue to win if he had to work all the way. And in the third round Frazier began to get to him, caught Ali with a powerful blow to the face at the bell. That was the first moment where it was clear to all that Frazier had won a round. Then he won the next. Ali looked tired and a little depressed. He was moving less and less and calling upon a skill not seen since the fight with Chuvalo when he had showed his old ability, worked on all those years ago with Shotgun Sheldon, to lie on the ropes and take a beating to the stomach. He had exhausted Chuvalo by welcoming attacks on the stomach but Frazier was too incommensurable a force to allow such total attack. So Ali lay on the ropes and wrestled him off, and moved his arms and waist, blocking punches, slipping punches, countering with punches—it began to look as if the fight would be written on the ropes, but Ali was getting very tired. At the beginning of the fifth round, he got up slowly from his stool, very slowly. Frazier was beginning to feel that the fight was his. He moved in on Ali jeering, his hands at his side in mimicry of Ali, a street fighter mocking his opponent, and Ali tapped him with long light jabs to which Frazier stuck out his mouthpiece, a jeer of derision as if to suggest that the mouthpiece was all Ali would reach all night.

There is an extortion of the will beyond any of our measure in the exhaustion which comes upon a fighter in early rounds when he is already too tired to lift his arms or take advantage of openings there before him, yet the fight is not a third over, there are all those rounds to go, contractions of torture, the lungs screaming into the dungeons of the soul, washing the throat with a hot bile that once belonged to the liver, the legs are going dead, the

arms move but their motion is limp, one is straining into another will, breathing into the breath of another will as agonized as one's own. As the fight
moved through the fifth, the sixth, and the seventh, then into the eighth, it was
obvious that Ali was into the longest night of his career, and yet with that
skill, that research into the pits of every miserable contingency in boxing, he
came up with odd somnambulistic variations, holding Frazier off, riding
around Frazier with his arm about his neck, almost entreating Frazier with
his arms extended, and Frazier leaning on him, each of them slowed to a pit-
a-pat of light punches back and forth until one of them was goaded up from
exhaustion to whip and stick, then hook and hammer and into the belly and
out, and out of the clinch and both looking exhausted, and then Frazier,
mouth bared again like a wolf, going in and Ali waltzing him, trying him,
tapping him lightly as if he were a speed bag, just little flicks, until Frazier,
like an exhausted horse finally feeling the crop, would push up into a trot and
try to run up the hill. It was indeed as if they were both running up a hill. As
if Frazier's offensive was so great and so great was Ali's defense that the fight
could only be decided by who could take the steepest pitch of the hill. So Frazier, driving, driving, trying to drive the heart out of Ali, put the pitch of that
hill up and up until they were ascending an unendurable slope. And moved
like somnambulists slowly working and rubbing one another, almost embracing, next to locked in the slow moves of lovers after the act until, reaching into the stores of energy reaching them from cells never before so used,
one man or the other would work up a contractive spasm of skills and throw
punches at the other in the straining slow-motion hypnosis of a deepening
act. And so the first eight rounds went by. The two judges scored six for Frazier, two for Ali. The referee had it even. Some of the press had Ali ahead—
it was not easy to score. For if it were an alley fight, Frazier would win. Clay
was by now hardly more than the heavy bag to Frazier. Frazier was dealing
with a man, not a demon. He was not respectful of that man. But still! It was
Ali who was landing the majority of punches. They were light, they were
usually weary, but some had snap, some were quick, he was landing two
punches to Frazier's one. Yet Frazier's were hardest. And Ali often looked as
tender as if he were making love. It was as if he could now feel the whole absence of that real second fight with Liston, that fight for which he had trained
so long and so hard, the fight which might have rolled over his laurels from
the greatest artist of pugilism to the greatest brawler of them all—maybe he

had been prepared on that night to beat Liston at his own, be more of a slug-ger, more of a man crude to crude than Liston. Yes, Ali had never been a street fighter and never a whorehouse knock-it-down stud, no, it was more as if a man with the exquisite reflexes of Nureyev had learned to throw a knockout punch with either hand and so had become champion of the world without knowing if he was the man of all men or the most delicate of the del-icate with special privilege endowed by God. Now with Frazier, he was in a sweat bath (a mud-pile, a knee, elbow, and death-thumping chute of a pit) having in this late year the fight he had sorely needed for his true greatness as a fighter six and seven years ago, and so whether ahead, behind, or even, terror sat in the rooting instinct of all those who were for Ali for it was obviously Frazier's fight to win, and what if Ali, weaknesses of character now flicker-ing to the surface in a hundred little moves, should enter the vale of prizefight-ing's deepest humiliation, should fall out half conscious on the floor and not want to get up. What a death to his followers.

The ninth began. Frazier mounted his largest body attack of the night. It was preparations-for-Liston-with-Shotgun-Sheldon, it was the virtuosity of the gym all over again, and Ali, like a catcher handling a fastball pitcher, took Frazier's punches, one steamer, another steamer, wing! went a screamer, a steamer, warded them, blocked them, slithered them, winced from them, absorbed them, took them in and blew them out and came off the ropes and was Ali the Magnificent for the next minute and thirty seconds. The fight turned. The troops of Ali's second corps of energy had arrived, the energy for which he had been waiting long agonizing heart-sore vomit-mean rounds. Now he jabbed Frazier, he snake-licked his face with jabs faster than he had thrown before, he anticipated each attempt of Frazier at counterattack and threw it back, he danced on his toes for the first time in rounds, he popped in rights, he hurt him with hooks, it was his biggest round of the night, it was the best round yet of the fight, and Frazier full of energy and hordes of sud-den punishment was beginning to move into that odd petulant concentration on other rituals beside the punches, tappings of the gloves, stares of the eye, that species of mouthpiece-chewing which is the prelude to fun-strut in the knees, then Queer Street, then waggle on out, drop like a steer.

But in the eleventh, that story also broke. Frazier caught him, caught him again and again, and Ali was near to knocked out and swayed and slid on Queer Street himself, then spent the rest of the eleventh and the longest round of the twelfth working another bottom of Hell, holding off Frazier who came on and on, sobbing, wild, a wild honor of a beast, man of will reduced to the common denominator of the will of all of us back in that land of the animal where the idea of man as a tool-wielding beast was first conceived. Frazier looked to get Ali forever in the eleventh and the twelfth, and Ali, his legs slapped and slashed on the thighs between each round by Angelo Dundee, came out for the thirteenth and incredibly was dancing. Everybody's story switched again. For if Ali won this round, the fourteenth and the fifteenth, who could know if he could not win the fight? . . . He won the first half of the thirteenth, then spent the second half on the ropes with Frazier. They were now like crazy death-march-maddened mateys coming up the hill and on to home, and yet Ali won the fourteenth, Ali looked good, he came out dancing for the fifteenth, while Frazier, his own armies of energy finally caught up, his courage ready to spit into the eye of any devil black or white who would steal the work of his life, had equal madness to steal the bolt from Ali. So Frazier reached out to snatch the magic punch from the air, the punch with which Ali topped Bonavena, and found it and thunked Ali a hell and hit Ali a heaven of a shot which dumped Muhammad into fifty thousand newspaper photographs—Ali on the floor! Great Ali on the floor was out there flat singing to the sirens in the mistiest fogs of Queer Street (same look of death and widowhood on his far-gone face as one had seen in the fifth blind round with Liston) yet Ali got up, Ali came sliding through the last two minutes and thirty-five seconds of his heathen holocaust in some last exercise of the will, some iron fundament of the ego not to be knocked out, and it was then as if the spirit of Harlem finally spoke and came to rescue and the ghosts of the dead in Vietnam, something held him up before arm-weary triumphant near-crazy Frazier who had just hit him the hardest punch ever thrown in his life and they went down to the last few seconds of a great fight, Ali still standing and Frazier had won.

The world was talking instantly of a rematch. For Ali had shown America what we all had hoped was secretly true. He was a man. He could bear moral and physical torture and he could stand. And if he could beat Frazier in the rematch we would have at last a national hero who was hero of the world as well, and who could bear to wait for the next fight? Joe Frazier, still the champion, and a great champion, said to the press, "Fellows, have a heart—I got to live a little. I've been working for ten long years." And Ali, through the agency of alter-ego Bundini, said—for Ali was now in the hos-pital to check on the possible fracture of a jaw—Ali was reported to have said, "Get the gun ready—we're going to set traps." Oh, wow. Could America wait for something so great as the Second Ali-Frazier?

[March, 1971]

Please note that this piece has been edited for this volume and does not appear in its entirety.

THE DISINTEGRATION OF A FOLK HERO

PETE HAMILL

In the sixties, we still believed in princes, and for a few brief years, one of the gaudiest American princes of all was a heavyweight prizefighter who called himself Muhammad Ali. He might have been the best heavyweight who ever lived, a man with an astonishing range of skills, with fast hands and beautiful legs, a fighter who made a brutal sport contain the illusion of beauty. His fights resembled some bloody offshoot of ballet, choreographed in some dark region of his mind, a place where violence and control and courage met to forge a champion. Ten times he climbed through those red velvet ropes to fight for the heavyweight championship of the world. Ten times he won, and each time he was better.

And then quite suddenly, in the winter of 1967, it was over. The boy who had started life as Cassius Clay in Louisville, Kentucky, found that the world was a far more complicated place than the boxing ring. He had, quite simply, broken too many rules on the way to becoming a man. At the beginning, he had charmed people with his atrocious poetry, with the predictions he always made before his fights, with his sometimes humorous insolence. He seemed to understand early that boxing was a form of show business, and he was not afraid to break the old molds, the way the Beatles had done in music and El Cordobes in bullfighting. He was not going to be a "God-is-on-our-side" champion in the style of Joe Louis, nor would he ever display the shy grace of a Floyd Patterson. The boy who was then Cassius Clay decided early to risk arrogance.

While he was selling tickets, the boxing establishment did not care. On the morning after he won the championship from the feared Sonny Liston, they started to care very much. That morning Cassius Clay announced that he had changed his name to Muhammad Ali and had become a Black Muslim. From that moment on, the laughter went out of it for Muhammad Ali, and he lived the rest of the decade in a swirl of controversy. He announced

123

that he would not serve in the United States Army, on religious grounds, adding, "I got nothing against them Vietcongs." He showed up at his draft board after being classified 1-A, but refused to take the symbolic step forward. Within minutes, he had been stripped of his title by some of the jingoist politicians who run athletic commissions, and the next step forward took him into three and a half years of exile.

When he came back after almost forty-three months away, to finally confront the man he thought of as a usurper, there was no question about the degrees of talent in Muhammad Ali and Joe Frazier. Four years before, the stocky, hard-fisted Frazier would not have been a problem; he is a fighter who comes on in a straight line, possessed of all the tactical imagination of a locomotive. The young Ali would have danced around him, spearing him with the left hand, moving, always moving, making Frazier miss, chopping him up, and ultimately, knocking him out. It would have been a contest between a manual laborer with honest skills and an artist at the exuberant peak of his powers.

But Ali had lost three of the best years of his life, as he scuffled around the country, making speeches at college campuses and Muslim mosques, followed by a retinue of lawyers, hangers-on, and acolytes. He appeared in an off-Broadway play, espoused his views on a hundred television shows, did everything, in fact, except what he did best.

Last year, the ice-jam broke; Ali won the right in court to practice his trade at the same time that black legislators managed to get him licensed in Atlanta, Georgia. He made his first comeback fight against Jerry Quarry, a good California heavyweight; in the first round it looked as if he had never been away; then, almost imperceptibly, he began to slow down; the fight ended in the third round with Quarry badly cut, but the doubts were there. In his next fight, against a clumsy Argentine, Oscar Bonavena, the doubts were confirmed.

The great skills, the magic and the gaud, seemed to have deserted him, as the lunging Bonavena pushed and pulled him across fourteen sloppy rounds. Then the fifteenth Ali pulled the fight out with a series of crushing left hooks; Bonavena went down three times and the fight was over. But for the first time in his career, Ali looked like just another heavyweight prizefighter.

On the night of March eighth, in a New York charged with the dark electricity of a big fight, Ali stepped into the ring with Joe Frazier. It was the biggest fight in the history of boxing, the single most spectacular (in the true sense of that word) event in sports history. Madison Square Garden was jammed with celebrities, politicians, gangsters, blondes, peacocks from Harlem, gamblers, tap-outs, high-rollers, and frauds. They came to cheer Ali or root for his demolition, but none of that really mattered to the fighters. They were in that ring for $2,500,000 each, for matters of honor, and to fight.

In the end, Frazier won because he was a better fighter across the tough, grueling fifteen rounds of combat. The skills Ali once possessed seemed gone forever; his punches were not accurate and were occasionally even flabby. There was nothing wrong with his will or his courage, but his body simply did not have enough left in it to perform in the old way. He was hurt badly in the eleventh round, and knocked on his back in the fifteenth round. He survived both rounds, but when the fight was over the old glittering style was gone, the glib, almost arrogant confidence shaken.

He had not disgraced himself, of course, because Joe Frazier is a very good fighter, certainly the best fighter Ali had ever fought. But Ali had come along at a point in time when people needed heroes; in the ghettos, young black kids imitated his swaggering style; they love his boldness and his arrogance, and when he challenged the government on a matter of principle, it was as if he had done it for all of them. He could have left America, as Jack Johnson did fifty years before, as Eldridge Cleaver and others have done more recently. But he knew that was somehow too easy; the fight, if it was to be made, had to be made in America. He made it here, and became a prince, and in the end, when the title he loved so much was finally taken from him in the ring, there was nothing to feel but sadness and a certain regret. But we knew we had spent some time in the company of a man of honor.

[May, 1971]

MUHAMMAD ALI AND THE FLY

IRA BERKOW

A couple of flies did midair imitations of the Ali shuffle as the original, Muhammad Ali himself, sat in the motel lobby talking with a companion. One fly alighted on the right knee of Ali.

"See that fly? Mind that fly," said Ali, his conversational tone interrupted by his whisper. His large left hand began to creep out. His eyes were fixed on the fly.

"You gotta know how to do it," he said, barely moving his lips. "The fly is facing me and he can only fly forward. Now, I come forward and turn my hand back-handed. It's like a left jab."

Ali struck. Then he brought his fist in front of the man seated next to him. "Watch this," said Ali. He slowly opened his hand. Ali looked up wide-eyed. "Thought I had him," he said. "My timing's off."

Ali was in training for a fight with Jimmy Ellis. This was shortly after the announcement that the Supreme Court had overturned his conviction for refusing the draft.

"It's hard to train now," he said. "I got bigger things on my mind, bigger things than just beatin' up somebody. Fighting's not the thing any more for me. I see myself fighting for another year, at most. I'll have one more fight with Joe Frazier.

"Then I got obligations to keep. I want to help clean up black people. I want to help respect black women. I want to help the wine-heads in the alleys. I want to help the little black kids in the ghettos. I want to help in narcotics programs. I want to serve the honorable Elijah Muhammad (the head of the Black Muslim religion, of which Ali is a minister, though temporarily suspended).

"Fighting is just two brutes beatin' on each other. A man goes through certain stages in his life. Fightin' was a joy to me at one time, now it's work.

I don't even like for anybody to see me doing roadwork. But I remember when I first turned pro in 1960, I was in Florida and I was going to write the name Floyd Patterson on my jacket. To trick the people, to make them think I was the champ when I was runnin' alongside the highway. I wanted to show off."

Ali was suspended by Elijah Muhammad because Ali continued as a fighter, a profession supposedly anathema to the religion. But Ali has been a boxer since he was a boy in Louisville. And he needs money to pay alimony to his first wife and also to pay the astronomical legal fees which have piled up in the last four years as he fought his draft case.

Ali swiped at another fly. Missed. He tried again. Missed. And again. Same result. One more. Nothing.

"You've missed five times," said the companion.

Ali looked embarrassed. "Five?" he repeated.

"These flies keep flying 'round me," he said. "They must know I'm not all I used to be. They must see the little gray hairs that been growin' in my head lately.

"If Ellis is as quick as these flies, I'm in trouble."

A man approached and asked for Ali's autograph for two boys. "Their mother has trouble making them clean their room," the man said.

Ali wrote: "To Timmy and Rickie. From Muhammad Ali. Clean that room or I will seal your doom." Ali smiled at his spontaneous doggerel, the man laughed, thanked him.

The implied threat to the boys was in keeping with his easy wit, his breezy charm, the bluster that too many people have taken too seriously over the years. His still-smooth face and, now, subdued yet animated ways seem to belie his vicious profession. And when he refused to enter the draft, saying, "I ain't got no quarrel with them Vietcong," many held that he was being hypocritical. A fighter is a fighter, they held, whether in the ring or in the rice paddies.

A fly again landed on his knee. Ali suddenly grew still. He slowly reached out to snatch the fly. Jabbed. Had it! "My timing's back!" cried Ali. "See, at least I'm not *too* old."

He dropped the fly to the carpet. The fly didn't move.

"He's staggered," said Ali, proudly, bending down. "That's a science, y'know. To stagger the fly and not to kill him. You get him in your hand, but you don't squeeze."

Ali flicked the fly with his index finger. "Go on, fly, fly away. I don't want to kill him. Let him live like us."

The fly flew off.

[July, 1971]

MUHAMMAD ALI, MAY HIS TRIBE INCREASE

ROGER KAHN

Muhammad Ali had been rambling, talking, moving through one week's mix of cities on the endless road show of his life. Chicago. Phoenix. Los Angeles. Spar an exhibition. Wander ghetto streets. Talk to convicted felons. Now he had come to New York to speak a sermon.

It was a difficult thing for the newspapermen to grasp. Ali does not issue advance bulletins: "Attention news desks. Prepare for a major economic, theologic boxing story." Spontaneity is the Ali style and impulse is a muse that enchants him. So no one had been forewarned. No one was ready.

Scores of sportswriters arrived to share breakfast with Ali in the Baroque Room of the Plaza Hotel, expecting, I suppose, one more of Ali's unique prefight shows. I'll fight him now. I'll take my jacket off and whip him. I got to whip this man. He called me nigguh! The trappings of black anger, a put-on to sell tickets. But maybe, just maybe, part of that anger has been real.

The Baroque Room is the sort of velvet hall where surgeons from Bronxville give away firstborn daughters in marriage. The chandeliers and carpeting bespeak quiet, insistent materialism. "Don't ever say we're rich, my dear. Say, rather, that we have a little money." And here, among reporters looking for fight notes, in a setting at once sedate and WASP, Muhammad preached a simple, spellbinding, eloquent black socialism.

He had earned enough money, Ali said. He owned seven cars, including a Greyhound Scenicruiser. He personally had plenty of land. His wife and children did not lack for things. Right now, he could produce two or two and a half million in cash. From here on, then, he was going to fight for nothing. Well, not quite for nothing. He had to cover the expenses of his training camp and he had to pay his taxes. But after that, everything he earned would go into ghettos, to start a bakery here, open a restaurant there, to buy buses for Black Muslim schools and shoes for barefoot children. Ali's voice rose in pitch and volume. He challenged other successful blacks to do the same.

Don't give everything away, but give as much as you can to your brothers. The whites won't do it for you. "This come on me sudden," Ali said with soft intensity, in a glare of television lights. "This idea—Ali, you got enough. You got no right to more. It come on me so sudden that it must have come from God."

Riding home from the Plaza, I imagined how the *New York Times* would play this extraordinary story. A gray headline on page one: ALI PLEDGES FUTURE PURSES TO BLACK POOR. Underneath a straight news story, supplemented by sidebars. What can Ali expect to gross over the next four years? (Twenty-five million dollars possibly.) What does Internal Revenue say about giving away your income? (The IRS allows charitable deductions of up to fifty percent of your gross.) Ali had thrown down a challenge to other prosperous blacks. I imagined the *Times* assigning a young reporter (a young, female, black reporter) to get reactions. How would Jesse Jackson, Frank Robinson, Jim Brown, Diana Ross respond?

As far as I can tell, this story had no precedent, and newspapers are not pliant to new events. The *Times* buried Ali's antipoverty campaign in the sports section, among paragraphs about his puffery for his next fight. The *Daily News* denigrated the impact that Ali's cash would make on the wasteland of America's ghettos.

Christ, I thought, here is someone who wants to give away a fortune. Here is a man who cannot read without the most painful pauses between words making a stirring and even profound speech. Here is a black millionaire, socialist and populist and revivalist and most of all idealist. Yes. Mostly that. Idealist. And in a society that forever confuses value and net worth, this aging, baby-faced champion, this dreamer finely tuned to reality, throws out a mighty blow with his checkbook. What do the papers report? Ali to concentrate on body blows in Wepner bout. I shrug and say, I guess I better go and get the story myself.

In eastern Pennsylvania, near a village called Deer Lake, a nameless mountain rises. White barns painted with Dutch hex signs stand in the lowlands, along with a red clapboard Lutheran church with a belfry that leans leeward. Roadside signs advertise a mink ranch and the Dusselfink Motel. Ali has bought the top of that mountain—no sign advertises his lair—and there he has built a gymnasium, a dining hall, and a home. Each is a log replica styled along the lines of eighteenth-century cabins. He is, Ali says proudly, the first black champion to "own his training camp, not to have to rent it from some white man."

A twisting blacktop leads to Muhammad's Mountain. Granite boulders bound with parking areas and walks. Each boulder is painted with a fighter's name: Jack Johnson, Kid Gavilan, Rocky Marciano. The names are what Ali calls his boxing idols and Gene Kilroy, a black-haired white Pennsylvanian who is Ali's business manager, suggests, "People say he's vain, but you'll notice there isn't any boulder painted with the name Muhammad Ali."

Ali was going to spar five rounds with a strong heavyweight named Roy Williams and when he came out of his dressing room, wearing gray sweatpants, one was struck first with his size. Except for Jess Willard and Primo Carnera, Ali is the biggest of heavyweight champions. He is bigger than Dempsey, bigger than Louis, bigger than Liston. But he moves with such fluidity, one forgets his bulk.

Under fluorescent lights, his oiled bronze torso glistened. The gymnasium walls were bright with the covers of fifty magazines, portraits of Ali across the decade of his ascendancy. He moved before a mirror and skipping, dancing, threw fierce punches against the air. He stands six feet three and, with a layer of gruel showing at the middle, he weighs two-thirty. He is thirty-three now and though he runs four to five miles a day, the bulge keeps battling him. He prefers to fight at about two-fifteen.

Unlike many champions, Ali charges no admission to his camp. (Of course, you have to find that unmarked blacktop up the mountain.) About two dozen of us sat around the ring and Ali worked hard with Williams, scuffling and talking.

He is so brilliant a boxer that he deliberately takes missteps to keep the sparring interesting. He came in elbows high, the midriff naked, crying through the mouthpiece, "C'mon. Git me. Take your shot." Williams pounded hard body punches into Ali's gut with the cushiony sixteen-ounce gloves one wears to spar. Ali kept coming in, the big eyes focused on Williams, without expression.

Ali danced toward the ropes and moved himself into a corner: "Come on," Ali said. "Come git me. I'll show him I'm the champ. Take a shot. Come on git me. It's hard to be heavyweight champion. Hard to be champ."

The round ended. Ali stood in his corner and removed his mouthpiece. "I played with him this round," he announced. "He's finished now. He knows I'm champion. They all want to git the champion. But they can't do it. He'll know I'm champion. He's finished now."

More sparring. Ali moving, bouncing off the ropes, countering rather than leading, that quick left darting like a lizard's tongue. Williams could hit and twice he landed hard rights to Ali's cheek. Ali was moving, working, talking. "You hit me, but your power's gone. Let's show the people some, thing. But you can't. Your power's gone." He kept moving, countering, dancing, and talking, always talking so that the sparring, which can be dull, became a show.

They fought the last round without mouthpieces, Ali proclaiming, "I'm gonna hit him now. He's gonna fall." They bulled one another about the ring, and Williams fell against the ropes. Ali feinted a left at the body and Williams's right arm dropped. His jaw was bare. But for all the words, Ali was sparring, not fighting. He did not throw his own right. Instead, he bounced away, crying, "Come on. Your power's gone. Come on."

After the workout, Ali stood in a corner declaiming: "This nigguh can rumble. This nigguh's good. Excuse me, white folks, for saying nigguh all the time." He inhaled. "The next champ is at Ali's camp." Someone handed him a comb. "I comb my hair after I work to keep my image up." He climbed over the ropes and paused before a mirror. "I always check my fea, tures when I come out of the ring." Then hustler, Barnum, entertainer and champion, Muhammad Ali retreated to his dressing room and closed the door.

Inside, I found him lying on a leather couch. He wore a white robe and he was puffing. Sweat beaded his forehead.

"Tired?"

He nodded slowly. The public performance was over. The private, or semiprivate effort lay ahead. Ali likes a retinue. Someone checked his robe, as he stirred his legs, covering him against the possibility of a *Playgirl* centerfold. Someone else glanced over my shoulder from time to time, monitoring my notepad. You do not really converse with Muhammad Ali. He knows about what he wants to say and where he wants to be quoted and questions distract him no more than do weak jabs.

"Had you thought about giving all that money away for a while?" I began.

"What I say in New York? That came sudden. But I been thinking before and an idea was coming slowly. Cleveland. You been to Cleveland? They need a day-care center. They need it bad. Gary, Indiana. You been there? They got a black mayor, but there's no restaurant in the whole town where a black man can go with his daughters and know that it's safe and nice, with chandeliers and good carpets where there's no drinking. I want that restaurant opened and I know where. A man had it and he went broke and the first thing we do when we take over, for fifty or a hundred thousand, is pull out the bar. But you know, since New York, I found out it's not that simple." Candor had seized him. "I didn't know this, but you can't give everything away. You got to set up foundations, charitable foundations, the government says."

"Are the Muslims a charitable foundation?"

"Not fully. But I want to talk to you about the human heart." His voice had been tight and somewhat hoarse. Now it opened into a lyric sound.

"There is nothin' no greater than the human heart. Nothin'. There's the golden heart and gold is beautiful an' the silver heart, and silver's more useful and the heart of iron. Strong, but it can melt. And the heart of rock, which must be broke, and the paper heart, that flies with the winds, like a kite flies, but that's all right so long as the string is strong. There's many more hearts and each is different, and each is a miracle. What can compare with the human heart?" He smiled slightly. "I didn't just make that up. I use that when I speak to students.

"I talk at colleges and I can't read much, and can you imagine what's in my own heart when there's thousands and thousands trying to touch me and listening to what I have to say. In Egypt Nasser offered me his own daughter in marriage and I coulda lived there by the Nile. But I asked the Honorable Elijah Muhammad, and he said no, marry one of your own and I did. I got lots of beautiful homes and the Italian government has expressed serious interest in rebuilding the Colosseum so I can fight George Foreman there, but if that don't work, I'm going to fight him outdoors in Egypt, right beside the pyramids. And they're talking about a guarantee of eight and a half million dollars."

"So the times are pretty good," someone said.

"No," Ali said. "Couple of nigguhs like me make a few bucks. All the rest?" He shook his head and told more tales from the ghettos.

His crystal sense of the irrationality and the cruelty of this society would win approval from Herbert Marcuse. Perhaps that was why I felt so startled later when Gene Kilroy told me that Ali—"a great man," Kilroy calls him—had graduated from high school in a class of one hundred fifty-seven, and finished one hundred fifty-seventh.

[June, 1975]

PLAYBOY INTERVIEW: MUHAMMAD ALI

Playboy: The last time we interviewed you, eleven years ago, you were still Cassius Clay. What would the old Cassius be doing today?

Ali: Cassius Clay would now be training in Paris, France, because French promoters would've offered me—like they've done—free rooms in a hotel on some beach. If not, I'd probably be in Jamaica, training in a plush hotel. When I see a lady now, I do my best to try to teach her about the Honorable Elijah Muhammad so I can help her. Cassius Clay would carry her to some hotel room and use her.

If I was Cassius Clay today, I'd be just like Floyd Patterson. I'd probably have a white wife and I wouldn't represent black people in no way. Or I'd be like Charley Pride, the folk singer. Nothin' bad about him—he's a good fella and I met his black wife, but Charley stays out of controversy. It's not only him, because I could name Wilt Chamberlain and others who just don't get involved in struggle or racial issues—it might jeopardize their position. I'd be that kind of man.

If I was Cassius Clay *tonight,* I'd probably be staying in a big hotel in New York City, and I might say, "Well, I got time to have a little fun. I'm going out to a big *discotheque* full of white girls and I'll find the prettiest one there and spend the night with her."

Playboy: What's the physical sensation of really being nailed by hitters like Foreman and Frazier?

Ali: Take a stiff tree branch in your hand and hit it against the floor and you'll feel your hand go *boinggggggg.* Well, getting tagged is the same kind of jar on your whole body, and you need at least ten or twenty seconds to make that go away. You get hit again before that, you got another *boinggggggg.*

Playboy: After you're hit that hard, does your body do what you want it to do?

Ali: No, because your mind controls your body and the moment you're tagged, you can't think. You're just numb and you don't know where you're at. There's no *pain,* just that jarring feeling. But I automatically know what to do when that happens to me, sort of like a sprinkler system going off when a fire starts up. When I get stunned. I'm not really conscious of exactly where I'm at or what's happening, but I always tell myself that I'm to dance, run, tie my man up, or hold my head way down. I tell myself all that when I'm conscious, and when I get tagged, I automatically do it. I get hit, but all great fighters get hit—Sugar Ray got hit, Joe Louis got hit, and Rocky Marciano got hit. But they had something other fighters didn't have: the ability to hold on until they cleared up. I got that ability, too, and I had to use it once in each of the Frazier fights. That's one reason I'm a great defensive fighter. The other is my Rope-a-Dope defense—and when I fought Foreman, he was the dope.

Playboy: If you prepared that tactic for your fight with Foreman in Zaire, then why was Angelo Dundee, your trainer, so shocked when you suddenly went to the ropes?

Ali: Well, I didn't really *plan* it. After the first round, I felt myself getting too tired for the pace of that fight, but George wasn't gonna get tired, 'cause he was just cutting the ring off on me. I stayed out of the way, but I figured that after seven or eight rounds of dancing like that, I'd be really tired. Then, when I'd go to the ropes, my resistance would be low and George would get one through to me. So while I was still fresh, I decided to go to the ropes and try to get George tired.

Playboy: What was your original Foreman fight plan?

Ali: To dance every round. I had it in mind to do what I did when I was twenty-two but I got tired, so I had to change my strategy. George didn't change his strategy, 'cause he can't do nothin' but attack—that's the *only* thing he knows. All he wants to do is get his man in the corner, so in the second round, I gave him what he wanted. He couldn't do *nothin'!*

Playboy: Did Foreman seem puzzled when he had you cornered but couldn't land any punches?

Ali: Nope, he just figured he'd get me in the next round. When he didn't do it in the third, he thought he'd get me in the fourth. Then he thought it would be the fifth, and then the sixth. But in the sixth round, George was so *tired.* All of a sudden, he knew he'd threw everything he had at me and hadn't hurt me at all. And he just lost all his heart.

Playboy: How could you tell?

Ali: He stopped attacking the way he'd been doin'. He had shots to take and didn't take 'em, and then I purposely left him some openings and he wouldn't take *them.* George knew he'd been caught in my trap and there wasn't but one way he could get out of it: by knocking me out. He kept trying with his last hope, but he was too tired, and a man of his age and talent shouldn't get used up that quick. George was *dead* tired: He was throwing wild punches, missing, and falling over the ropes. So I started tellin' him how bad he looked: "Lookatcha, you're not a champ, you're a tramp. You're fightin' just like a sissy. C'mon and *show* me somethin', boy."

Playboy: You also called him all kinds of names before the fight: How does that help?

Ali: You mean when I called him the Mummy, 'cause he walks like one? Listen, if a guy loses his temper and gets angry, his judgment's off and he's not thinking as sharp as he should. But George wasn't angry. No, sir. George had this feeling that he was *supreme.* He believed what the press said—that he was unbeatable and that he'd whup me easy. The first three rounds, he still believed it. But when I started throwing punches at him in the fourth, George finally woke up and thought, "Man, I'm in trouble," He was *shocked.*

Playboy: Do you think Foreman was so confident of beating you that he didn't train properly?

Ali: No. George didn't take me lightly. He fought me harder than he fought Frazier or Norton. *Whoever* I fight comes at me harder, because if you beat Muhammad Ali, you'll be the big man, the legend. Beating me is like beating Joe Louis or being the man who shot Jesse James. George just didn't realize how hard I am to hit and how hard I *can* hit. He thought he was greater than me. Well, George is humble now. I did just what I told him I'd do when the ref was giving us instructions. There was George, trying to scare me with his serious look—he got that from his idol, Sonny Liston. And there I was, tellin' him. "Boy, you in *trouble!* You're gonna meet the greatest fighter of all time! We here now and there ain't no way for you to get out of this ring—I *gotcha!* You been readin' about me ever since you were a little boy and now you gonna see me in action. Chump, I'm gonna show you how great I am— I'm gonna eat you up. You don't stand a *chance!* You lose the crown tonight!"

Playboy: Foreman claims he was drugged before the fight. Did you see any evidence of that?

Ali: George is just a sore loser. The day after the fight, he actually said he was the true champion; he beat me. Then, when he got to Paris, he said the ropes had been too loose. Then, after the ropes were too loose, his next excuse was that the count was too fast. Then it was the canvas—he said it was too *soft.* Well, it was soft for me, too. Weeks after the fight, he finds out he was drugged? If he was drugged, he'd have knew it the next day. Somebody oughtta ask him just *how* he was drugged. Did somebody give him a needle? If it was dope, what *kind* of dope? *Excuses!* The truth is that the excuses started comin' as soon as George began to realize he *lost.* He couldn't take los-ing the championship.

Playboy: Won't it make him that much tougher an opponent when and if you fight him again?

Ali: Next fight is gonna be *easier.* George now knows he can be knocked out, so he'll be more on guard and attackin' less. But his only chance of winning is to charge and corner me and wham away and hope one or two shots get through my defense. But he's gun-shy of that, 'cause he tried it—threw every-thing he had—and all he got was tired. For him to go into that same old bam-bam-bam thing again will mentally destroy him, because the first thing he's gonna think is, "Uh-oh, I'm going to wear myself out again." So then he'll keep more to the center of the ring and do more boxing.

And that's just where I want him. Poppin' and jabbin' in the center of the ring is *my* thing, so now he's really beat. The only chance he has to whup me is to stay on me and keep me on the ropes—and he knows that's bad, 'cause the odds are he's not gonna hurt me and he's gonna tire himself out. But if he don't do that, he's in *more* trouble, 'cause I'll pop away at him with my left. In other words, Foreman's wrong if he do and wrong if he don't. The second time around, I'll beat him 'cause he has no confidence. The first fight, I beat him 'cause he thought he was a big indestructible lion—but George found out the facts of life when we had our rumble in the jungle.

Playboy: Did you like the idea of Zaire as the fight site?

Ali: I wanted my title back so bad I would've fought George in a telephone booth. World heavyweight champion, that's a big title. When you're the champ, whatever you say or do is news. George would go to Las Vegas and the newspapers are writin' about it. I turn on the television and there's George. It was Foreman this and Foreman that, and I was sitting here in my Pennsylvania training camp, thinkin', "dadgummit, I really had somethin'. People looked up to *me* that way." That really got me down and made me want to win that title *bad.*

Now that I got it back, every day is a sunshiny day: I wake up and I know I'm the heavyweight champion of the world. Whatever restaurant I walk into whatever park I go to, whatever school I visit, people are sayin', "The *champ's* here!" When I get on a plane, a man is always sayin' to his little boy. "Son, there goes the heavyweight champion of the world." Wherever I go, the tab is picked up, people want to see me and the TV wants me for interviews. I can eat all the ice cream, cake, pudding, and pie I want to and still get $100,000 for an exhibition. That's what it means to be champ, and as long as I keep winning, it'll keep happenin'. So before I fight, I think, "Whuppin' this man means everything. So many good things are gonna happen if I win I can't even imagine what they'll *be!*"

When I first won the championship from Sonny Liston, I was riding high and I didn't realize what I had. Now, the second time around, I appreciate the title, and I would've gone anywhere in the world to get it back. To be honest, when I first heard the fight would be in Africa, I just hoped it would go off right, being in a country that was supposed to be so undeveloped. Then, when we went down to Zaire, I saw they'd built a new stadium with lights and that everything would be ready, and I started getting used to the idea and liking it. And the more I thought about it, the more it grew on me how *great* it would be to win back my title in Africa. Being in Zaire opened my eyes.

Playboy: In what way?

Ali: I saw black people running their own country. I saw a black President of a humble black people who have a modern country. There are good roads throughout Zaire and Kinshasa has a nice downtown section that reminds you of a city in the States. Buildings, restaurants, stores, shopping centers—I could name you a thousand things I saw that made me feel good. When I was in training there before the fight, I'd sit on the riverbank and watch the boats going by and see the 747 jumbo jets flying overhead, and I'd know there were black pilots and black stewardesses in 'em, and it just seemed so nice. In Zaire, *everything* was black—from the train drivers and hotel owners to the teachers in the schools and the pictures on the money. It was just like any other society, except it was all black, and because I'm black oriented and a Muslim, I was *home* there. I'm not home *here*. I'm trying to make it home, but it's not.

Playboy: Why not?

Ali: Because black people in America will never be free so long as they're on the white man's land. Look, birds want to be free, tigers want to be free, everything wants to be free. We can't be free until we get our own land and our own country in North America. When we separate from America and take maybe ten states, then we'll be free. Free to make our own laws, set our own taxes, have our own courts, our own judges, our own schoolrooms, our own currency, our own passports. And if not here in America, the Honorable Elijah Muhammad said the white man should supply us with the means to let us go back somewhere in Africa and build up our own country. America, rich as it is, was made rich partly through the black man's labor. It can afford to supply us for twenty-five years with the means to make our own nation work, and we'll build it up, too. We can't be free if we can't control our own land. I own this training camp, but it ain't really *my* land, not when some

A young Cassius Clay sports a U.S. Olympic team jacket at a workout in 1960.

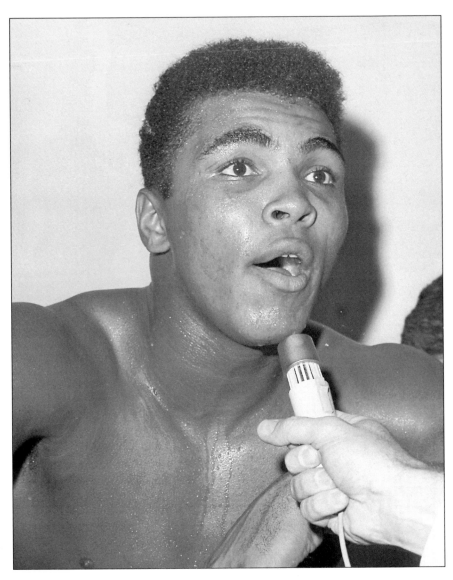

Cassius Clay talks to journalists at the Los Angeles Sports Arena after his heavy-weight title elimination bout with Archie Moore, whom he knocked out in the fourth round, November, 1962.

Heavyweight boxing champion Cassius Clay in training camp in Miami, Florida, February, 1964.

Cassius Clay gets advice from trainers Angelo Dundee (left) and Drew Brown as he continues his "psychological warfare" against champ Sonny Liston in 1964.

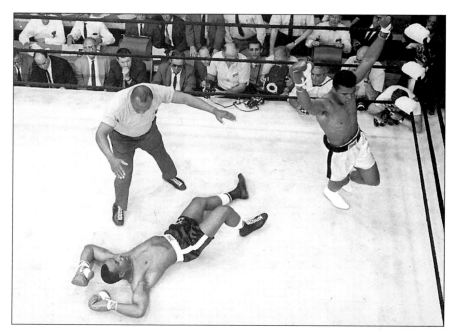

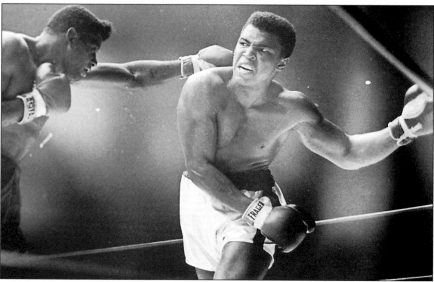

Top: Cassius Clay in the ring with Sonny Liston on the mat during the first round of their May, 1965 title bout. Clay retained his title by a knockout.
Bottom: Cassius Clay ducks under a long left jab by former champion Floyd Patter⁄ son during the sixth round of their title bout in November, 1965.

Cassius Clay jumping rope at the gym in 1967.

Muhammad Ali addresses a Black Muslim annual convention in 1968 as Elijah Muhammad looks on.

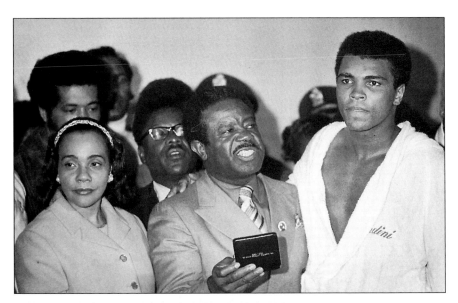

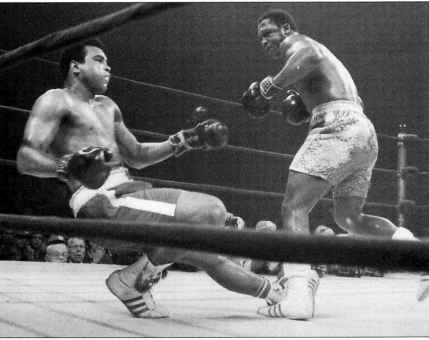

Top: Coretta Scott King and Ralph Abernathy with Ali in 1970.
Bottom: Muhammad Ali takes a vicious left hook from heavyweight champion Joe Frazier in the fifteenth round of their March, 1971 title fight.

Heavyweight champion Muhammad Ali shows off the $15,000 diamond-studded belt he was awarded in January, 1975 when he was named "Professional Athlete of the Year."

Ali with his eighteen-month-old son Dustin in 1978.

Top: After signing for a 1976 title bout to be held at New York's Yankee Stadium, Ali and challenger Ken Norton play tag on the field in "street" shoes.

Bottom: In 1986, Muhammad Ali and Joe DiMaggio after receiving Ellis Island Medals of Honor, given to distinguished members of various U.S. nationalities.

Muhammad Ali gets a kiss from his daughter May May after donating his boxing robe, a gift from Elvis Presley, to the Hard Rock Cafe in 1988.

Ali at ringside for the Tyson-Spinks 1988 heavyweight title bout in Atlantic City.

Muhammad Ali throws a mock punch to the cameras before watching the
Leonard-Duran fight in 1989.

1960 Olympic gold medalist Muhammad Ali lights the flame at the opening ceremony at the 1996 Olympic Games in Atlanta, Georgia.

Muhammad Ali with President Bill Clinton at the 1996 Olympic Games in Atlanta, Georgia.

white lady comes up and gives me a $4,000 tax bill to pay if I want to stay here. If I thought the taxes I paid was really going to benefit my people, I wouldn't mind paying up. But that ain't what's happening. Black people need to have their own nation.

Playboy: Since it's unlikely they'll get one carved out of—or paid for by—the U.S., are you pessimistic about America's future race relations?

Ali: America don't *have* no future! America's going to be destroyed! Allah's going to divinely chastise America! Violence, crimes, earthquakes—there's gonna be all *kinds* of trouble. America's going to pay for all its lynchings and killings of slaves and what it's done to black people. America's day is over—and if it doesn't do justice to the black man and separate, it gonna *burn!* I'm not the leader, so I can't tell you how the separation will take place or whether it will happen in my lifetime or not, but I believe there's a divine force that will make it happen. I wish *I* could make it happen, but I can't—Allah will. It took the white men five hundred years after they got here to get this country the way they want it, it took a lot of time and work, and it's gonna take *us* time and work. And if it takes a thousand years, well, the world is millions of years old; and a thousand years can be regarded as a day in the history of the world; so according to time, it's just around the corner.

And it'll happen, because it's right that black people should have their own nation. God bless the child that has his own—Christians teach that. Well, we don't have *nothin'* that's our own. If white men decide to close their grocery stores tomorrow, black people will starve to death. We're *tired* of being slaves and never having nothing. We're *tired* of being servants and waiting till we die and go to heaven before we get anything. We want something while we're living. The Honorable Elijah Muhammad has passed on physically, but his message is still with us: Muslims will never be satisfied with integration and all the little jobs and promises black people get. We want our own nation. We're twenty-five million black people—there's a lot of Negroes in America, you know? Man, there's only about ten million people in Cuba, and when they tell America to stay out, America *stays* out. They're just a few million, but they got their own nation and can get away with it. Nigerians and Ghanians have *their* own country. When I rode through Zaire and looked at their little flag and watched them doing their little dances, hey, it was *their* own country. But we're a whole nation of slaves still in bondage to white people. We worked three hundred years to make this country rich and fought for it in the Japanese war, the German war, the Korean war—in all the wars—and we *still* don't have nothing! So now, since they don't need cot-ton pickers 'cause machines can do it, and since we're walkin' the streets and multiplying, and there are no jobs for us—why *not* separate? Why *not* say, "Okay, slave, we don't need you no more for picking cotton"?

Playboy: Elijah Muhammad preached that all white men are blue-eyed dev-ils. Do you believe that?

Ali: We know that every individual white ain't devil-hearted, and we got *black* people who are devils—the worst devils I've run into can be my own kind. When I think about white people, it's like there's a thousand rattle-snakes outside my door and maybe a hundred of them want to help me. But they all look alike, so should I open my door and hope that the hundred who want to help will keep the other nine hundred off me, when only one bite will kill me? What I'm sayin' is that if there's a thousand rattlesnakes out there and a hundred of them mean good—I'm still gonna shut my door. I'm gonna say, "I'm sorry, you nice one hundred snakes, but *you don't really matter.*"

Yeah, every Negro can say, "Oh, here's a white man who means right." But if that's true, where are the twenty-five million whites standing next to the twenty-five million blacks? Why can't you even get a hundred of them to-gether who are ready to stand up and fight and maybe even die for black free-dom? Hey, we'd *look* if you did that.

Playboy: Didn't white freedom riders of the sixties—at least four of whom were murdered—demonstrate that many whites were ready to risk their lives for black civil rights?

Ali: Look, we been told there's gonna be whites who help blacks. And we also know there's gonna be whites who'll escape Allah's judgment, who won't be killed when Allah destroys this country—mainly some Jewish peo-ple who really mean right and do right. But we look at the situation as a whole. We *have* to. Okay, think about a white student who's got long hair and who wants minority people to have something and so he's against the slave white rule. Well, other whites will beat his behind and maybe even kill him, because they don't want him helping us. But that doesn't change what happens to the black man. If white boys get beat up, am I supposed to say, "Oh, some white folks are good. Let's forget our whole movement and integrate and join up in America"?

Yes, a lot of these white students get hurt 'cause they want to help save their country. But listen, your great-granddaddy told my great-granddaddy that when *my* granddaddy got grown, things would be better. Then your grandaddy told my grandaddy that when *my* daddy was born, things would get better. Your daddy told my daddy that when I got grown, things would be better. But they ain't. Are you tellin' me that when *my* children get grown, things'll be better for black people in this country?

Playboy: No, we're just trying to find out how you honestly feel about whites.

Ali: White people are good thinkers, man, but they're crazy. Whoever makes the commercials shown on Johnny Carson's TV show and whoever makes all them movies, well, they're smart, they're planners, and they can rule the world. Mostly 'cause they always got a story to tell. Is Martin Luther King marching and causing trouble? Okay, we'll let the blacks use the public toilets, but let's make 'em fight six months for it, and while they're fighting, we'll make another plan. They wanna come in the supermarket next week? Okay, let's make 'em fight two years for that. Meanwhile, we're still trying to get into schools in *Boston,* of all places. I'm telling you, the same men who write movies *must* be writing these plans. It's like, okay, the airlines will give jobs to a few black pilots and black stewardesses—but by the time they're finally hired, white folks are on the moon in *spaceships.*

So black folks stay far behind, *so* far behind that it's a shame. Think of how rich America is: The government spends more than $300 billion a year to run this country and, meanwhile, black people ain't even got money to go to the hospital. For a man who's alive, a man like Muhammad Ali, who's listened to the wisest black man in America, the Honorable Elijah Muhammad, the only thing to want is freedom in our own nation. Ain't *nothing* you can tell me or show me to match what I'm saying. The only thing the white man can offer me is a job in America—he ain't gonna offer me no flag, no hospitals, no land, no freedom. But once a man knows what freedom is, he's not satisfied even being the President of your country. And as Allah is my witness, I'd die today to prove it. If I could be President of the U.S. tomorrow and do what I can to help my people or be in an allblack country of twentyfive million Negroes and my job would be to put garbage in the truck, I'd be a garbageman. And if that included not just me but also my children and all my seed from now till forever, I'd still rather have the lowest job in a black society than the highest in a white society. If we got our own country, I'd empty trash ahead of being President of the U.S.—or being Muhammad Ali, the champion.

Playboy: You've earned nearly $10 million in fight purses in the past two years alone. Would you really part with all your wealth so easily?

Ali: I'd do it in a minute. Last week, I was out taking a ride and I thought, "I'm driving this RollsRoyce and I got another one in the garage that I hardly ever use that cost $40,000. I got a Scenicruiser Greyhound bus that sleeps fourteen and cost $120,000 and another bus that cost $42,000— $162,000 just in mobile homes. My training camp cost $350,000 and I just spent $300,000 remodeling my house in Chicago. I got all that and a lot more."

Well, I was driving down the street and I saw a little black man wrapped in an old coat standing on a corner with his wife and little boy, waiting for a bus to come along—and there I am in my RollsRoyce. The little boy had holes in his shoes and I started thinkin' that if he was *my* little boy, I'd break into tears. And I started crying.

Sure, I know I got it made while the masses of black people are catchin' hell, but as long as they ain't free, *I* ain't free. You think I need to hire all the people I do to help me get in shape? Listen, I can go down to Miami Beach with my cook and my sparring partners and get three hotel rooms and live it up—and I'd save money. I spent $850,000 training for George Foreman, most of it employing the few black people I could. In two months of training for Chuck Wepner, I spent $30,000. I wasn't doing it for me. See, once you become a Muslim, you want for your brother what you want for yourself. For instance, Kid Gavilan was a black boxing champion who had trouble in Cuba after he retired and he wound up in Miami working in a park. News paper reporters used to write stories about it that would embarrass Kid Gav ilan and when I heard what he was doing, I thought, "Kid Gavilan ain't gonna work in no *park*." So I found Kid Gavilan and now he works for me, and I pay him a lot better than what he made in the park. Why should I allow one of the world's greatest black fighters in history to end up workin' in a park? He's representing all of us. The Honorable Elijah Muhammad gave me that.

Man, I think white folks would actually be *frightened* if they could see a Muslim convention. Not frightened from fear of Muslims bothering you, only that you can see the end of white rule coming when you see fifty thousand Muslims together, all clean, all orderly, all dedicated. And the reason for that is because being a Muslim wakes you up to all kinds of things.

Playboy: Such as?

Ali: Black people in America never used to know that our religion was Islam or that Jesus was a black man—we always made him white. We never knew we were the original people. We thought black was bad luck. We never thought that Africans would own their own countries again and that they were our brothers. God is white, but we never knew that the proper name of God is Allah—and Allah ain't white. We never even knew our names, because in slavery we were named what our white masters were named. If our master's name was Robinson, we were Robinson's property. If they sold you to Jones, you were Jones's property. And if you were then auctioned off to Mr. Williams, you were Williams's property. So we got identified by our masters' names. Well, today there's no chains on us, yet we still got names like George *Washington,* but as we wake up, we want our own beautiful names back. If a black man and woman have their first son, name him somethin' pretty like Ahad, which means the beginning. A black woman whose name is Constance or Barbara, let her change her name to a black name. Like Rashida or Jamilla, Satina, Alissia. Those are black people's names you find in Africa and Asia.

Black people in America should have those names, too, and lemme show you why. If I say Mr. Chang Chong or Mr. Loo Chin, the name tells you to look for a Chinaman. If I say Mr. Castro or Mr. Gonzales, you look for a Cuban or a Spaniard. If I say Mr. Weinstein or Mr. Goldberg, you look for a Jew. If I say Mr. Morning Star or Mr. Rolling Thunder, you know it's an

Indian. If I say Mr. Mobutu or Mr. Kenyatta, you know it's an African. But if I say Mr. Green or Mr. Washington or Mr. Jones, the man could be white or black. See, you can identify everybody else by their names but us. And everybody *should* have their own names, which is what Elijah Muhammad taught us and which is what God taught him. I mean, did you ever hear of a white Englishman named Lumumba? Well, that's how black Americans feel about English names like Robinson. See how our teaching wakes you up? And not only are our names beautiful, they also have beautiful meanings.

Playboy: What does *your* name mean?

Ali: Muhammad means worthy of all praises, Ali means the most high. And a lot of brothers today are doing like me and giving up their old slave name and taking new first and last names, nice-soundin' ones like Hassan Sharif or Kareem Shabazz. Those *were* our names before we were brought over here and named after George Washington. It's important we get them back, too, because if black folks don't know God's name, which is Allah, or their own name, they're starting too far behind. So the first step is to get out of that old slave name and start you a new family name—every time I hear about another black family doin' that, I get happier and happier. And if you know truth when *you* hear it, then you know how joyful I am to be a Muslim.

Playboy: Will you assume a place in the Muslim movement when your boxing career is over?

Ali: Yes, sir. If I'm blessed to and they allow me, I'm gonna be a minister. I'm goin' to work with our new spiritual leader, brother Wallace D. Muhammad, son of Elijah Muhammad.

Playboy: How has Elijah Muhammad's death affected the Black Muslims?

Ali: Naturally, it was saddening, because it's bad to lose him physically, but if we should lose him in ourselves, that's worse. So we just have to keep pushing, and we now follow his son, who's taking up just where his father left off. And we're one hundred percent behind him. We were taught by Elijah Muhammad not to fear or grieve, and we don't.

Playboy: What difference did he make in your own life?

Ali: He was *my* Jesus, and I had love for both the man and what he repre-sented. Like Jesus Christ and all of God's prophets, he represented all good things and, having passed on, he is missed. But prophets never die spiritually, for their words and works live on. Elijah Muhammad was my savior, and ev-erything I have came from him—my thoughts, my efforts to help my people, how I eat, how I talk, my *name*.

Playboy: Do you think you could ever lose the faith?

Ali: I pray to Allah it don't happen, but it could. Every day, I say, "Surely I have turned myself to thee, O Allah, trying to be upright to him who has originated the heavens and the earth. Surely my prayers, my sacrifices, my life and my death are all for Allah, the lord of all the world." That's the begin-ning of a long prayer and I say it daily, and sometimes five times a day, to keep myself strong and on the right path. It's possible that I can lose faith, so I gotta pray, and to keep myself fired up. I gotta talk like I'm talkin' now. It's the kind of talk that keeps us Muslims together. And you can tell a bunch of Mus-lims: no violence, no hate, no cigarettes, no fightin', no stealin', all happy. It's a *miracle*. Most Negro places you be in, you see folks fussin' and cussin', eatin' pork chops and women runnin' around. You've seen the peace and unity of my training camp—it's all Elijah Muhammad's spirit and his teachings. Black people never acted like this before. If every one of us in camp was just like we were before we heard Elijah Muhammad, you wouldn't be able to see for all the smoke. You'd hear things like, "Hey, man, what's happenin', where's the *ladies?* What we gonna *drink* tonight? Let's get that music on and *party!*" And hey, this isn't an Islamic center. We're *happy* today. And we're better off than if we talked Christianity and said, "Jesus loves you, brother, Jesus died for your sins, accept Jesus Christ."

Playboy: You find something wrong with that?

Ali: Christianity is a good philosophy if you live it, but it's controlled by white people who preach it but don't practice it. They just organize it and use it any which way they want to. If the white man lived Christianity, it would be different; but I tell you, I think it's against *nature* for European people to live Christian lives. Their nations were founded on killing, on wars. France, Germany, the bunch of 'em—it's been one long war ever since they existed. And if they're not killing each other over there, they're shooting Indians over here. And if they're not after the Indians, they're after the reindeer and every other living thing they can kill, even elephants. It's always violence and war for Christians.

Muslims, though, live their religion—*we* ain't hypocrites. We submit entirely to Allah's will. We don't eat ham, bacon, or pork. We don't smoke. And everybody knows that we honor our women. You can see our sisters on the street from ten miles away, their white dresses dragging along the ground. Young women in this society parade their bodies in all them freak clothes—miniskirts and pants suits—but our women don't wear them. A woman who's got a beautiful body covers it up and humbles herself to Allah and also turns down all the modern conveniences. Nobody else do that but Muslim women. You hear about Catholic sisters—but they do a lot of screwing behind doors. Ain't nobody gonna believe a woman gonna go all her life and say, "I ain't never had a man," and is happy. She be *crazy.* That's against nature. And a priest saying he'd never touch a woman—that's against nature, too. What's he gonna do at night? Call upon the hand of the Lord?

Playboy: Catholic readers will no doubt provide you with an answer, but, meanwhile, perhaps you could tell us why restrictions on Muslim women are far more stringent than upon Muslim men.

Ali: Because they should be. Women are sex symbols.

Playboy: To whom?

Ali: To me.

Playboy: And aren't you a sex symbol to women?

Ali: Still, men don't walk around with their chests out. Anyway, I'd rather see a man with his breasts showing than a woman. Why should she walk around with half her titties out. There gotta be restrictions that way.

Playboy: But why should men formulate those restrictions?

Ali: Because in the Islamic world, the man's the boss and the woman stays in the background. She don't *want* to call the shots.

Playboy: We can almost hear women's liberation leaders saying, "Sisters, you've been brainwashed. You should control your *own* lives."

Ali: Not Muslim women—Christian women. Muslim women don't think like that. See, the reason we so powerful is that we don't let the white man control *our* women. They obey *us.* And when a Muslim girl becomes a woman, she don't *want* to walk around with her behind hanging out. Horses and dogs and mules walk around with their behinds out. Humans hide their behinds.

Playboy: Are Muslim women allowed to have careers or are they supposed to stay in the kitchen?

Ali: A lot of 'em got careers, working for and with their bothers, but you don't find 'em in no white man's office in downtown New York working be-hind secretarial desks. Too many black women been *used* in offices. And not even in bed—on the floor. We know it because we got office Negroes who've told us this. So we protect our women, 'cause women are the field that pro-duces our nation. And if you can't protect your women, you can't protect your nation. Man, I was in Chicago a couple of months ago and saw a white fella take a black woman into a motel room. He stayed with her two or three hours and then walked out—and a bunch of brothers saw it and didn't even *say* nothin'. They should have thrown rocks at his car or kicked down the door while he was in there screwing her—do *something* to let him know you don't like it. How can you be a man when another man can come get your woman or your daughter or your sister—and take her to a room and screw her—and, nigger, you don't even *protest?*

But nobody touches our women, white *or* black. Put a hand on a Muslim sister and you are to *die.* You may be a white or black man in an elevator with a Muslim sister and if you pat her on the behind, you're supposed to die right there.

Playboy: You're beginning to sound like a carbon copy of a white racist. Let's get it out front: Do you believe that lynching is the answer to interracial sex?

Ali: A black man *should* be killed if he's messing with a white woman. And white men have always done that. They lynched niggers for even looking at a white woman; they'd call it reckless eyeballing and bring out the rope. Rap- ing, patting, mischief, abusing, showing our women disrespect—a man should die for that. And not just white men—black men, too. We will kill you, and the brothers who don't kill you will get their behinds whipped and probably get killed themselves if they let it happen and don't do nothin' about it. Tell it to the President—*he* ain't gonna do nothin' about it. Tell it to the FBI: We'll kill anybody who tries to mess around with our women. Ain't *no- body* gonna bother them.

Playboy: And what if a Muslim woman wants to go out with non-Muslim blacks—or white men, for that matter?

Ali: Then *she* dies. Kill her, too.

Playboy: Are Muslim women your captives?

Ali: Hey, our women don't want no white men, period. Can you picture me, after what I been talking and thinking, wanting a white woman? Muslims think about three hundred years of slavery and lynching, and you think we want to *love* our slave masters? No *way* we think about that. And no, our women aren't captives. Muslim women who lose their faith are free to leave. I'm sure that if all the black men and women who started following Elijah Muhammad were still with us, we'd have an easy ten million followers. That many came through the doors but didn't stay. They free to go if they want to.

Playboy: If all the blacks in America became Muslims by the end of the year, what do you think would happen as a result?

Ali: President Ford would call our leaders to the White House and negotiate about what states he wants to give us or what country we want to be set up in.

Can you imagine twenty-five million Negroes all feeling the way I do? There'd be nothing you could do with them but let 'em go.

Playboy: "Let 'em go" doesn't mean handing over a group of states to Muslim religious leaders.

Ali: Maybe, maybe not. You could rope off Georgia, Alabama, Tennessee, Kentucky, we could go in there and live, and whites could have passports to come in, do business, and leave. Or a mass exodus from America. I wish I can see it before I die. Let me ask *you* something.

Playboy: Shoot.

Ali: You think I'm as pretty as I used to be? I was *so* pretty. Somebody took some pictures of me and they're in an envelope here, so let me stop talking for a few seconds, 'cause I want you to take a look at 'em. . . .

Hey, I'm *still* pretty! What a wonderful face! Don't I look *good* in these pictures? I can see I gotta stay in shape if I want to stay pretty, but that's so *hard*. I've been fighting for twenty-one years and just *thinkin'* about it makes me tired. I ain't twenty-two anymore—I'm thirty-three and I can't fight like I did eight or ten years ago. Maybe for a little while, but I can't keep it up. I used to get in a ring and dance and jump and hop around for the whole fifteen rounds. Now I can only do that for five or six, and then I have to slow down and rest for the next two or three rounds. I might jump around again in the eleventh and twelfth rounds, or I might even go the whole rest of the fight like I used to, but I have to work much more to be able to do it now. Weight is harder to get off and it takes more out of me to lose it. That means getting out every day and running a couple of miles, coming into the gym and punching the bags four days a week, and eatin' the right foods. But I like to eat the *wrong* foods. I'll go to a coffee shop and order a stack of pancakes with strawberry preserves, blueberry preserves, whipped cream, and butter, and then hit them hot pancakes with that good maple syrup and then drink a cold glass of milk. At dinnertime, I'll pull into a McDonald's and order two big double cheeseburgers and a chocolate milkshake—and the next day I weigh ten pounds more. Some people can eat and not gain weight, but if I just *look* at food, my belly gets bigger. That's why, when I'm training, about all I eat is broiled steaks, chicken, and fish, fresh vegetables and salads. I don't even get to *see* them other things I like.

Playboy: Are there parts of training you enjoy?

Ali: Except for getting' up at five or six in the morning and runnin' for two miles, it's all work. But I don't train like other boxers. For instance, I let my sparring partners try to beat up on me about eighty percent of the time. I go on the defense and take a couple of hits to the head and the body, which is good: You gotta condition your body and brain to take those shots, 'cause you're gonna get hit hard a couple of times in every fight. Meanwhile, I'm not gonna beat up on my sparring partners, because what's the pleasure in that? Besides, if I kill myself punching at them, it'll take too much out of me. When you're fightin' as much as I have lately, you're supposed to be boxin' and doin' something every day, but I can't dance and move every day like I should, because my body won't let me. So I have to stall my way through.

Playboy: Have you always been so easy on yourself in training?

Ali: That's not being easy, it's being smart. I pace my training the way I do my fights—just enough to let me win. When I boxed tough but unranked fighters like Jurgen Blin, Rudi Lubbers, Mac Foster, and Al "Blue" Lewis, I hardly trained, but I was in shape enough to beat them. You got to realize that after I fought Joe Frazier—who took a lot out of me—for the second time, I had had fifteen fights. If I had trained for all fifteen the way I trained for Frazier, I wouldn't be here today, 'cause I'd have killed myself. So instead of being all worn out for that second fight, I was able to come back and beat Frazier. The second time with Norton, I almost killed myself training, but that turned out to be right, because I had something left at the end of that fight. For George Foreman, I *did* kill myself. But I didn't have to do that for Chuck Wepner, Ron Lyle, or Joe Bugner, because they're not the same quality. So nobody should worry about how I train or tell me to train differently, for I'm the master of my craft. The main thing is to watch my performance on fight night, that's the only thing that counts. When the money is on the table and my title is on the line, I always come through.

Playboy: How much longer do you intend to defend your title?

Ali: I'd like to give up the championship and retire today, but there's too many things I've got to do. We're taught that every Muslim has a burden to do as much as he can to help black people. Well, my burden is real big, for I'm the heavyweight champion and the most famous black man on the whole planet, so I got to do a whole lot. That's why I just bought a shopping center in a black part of Cleveland, Ohio, for $500,000. It's got room for forty stores and we'll rent them out for just enough money to pay the upkeep and taxes—I'm not looking to make a quarter off it. That's gonna create jobs for black people. I'm also buying an A&P supermarket in Atlanta that will employ 150 black people. Then I'm going down to Miami, Florida, which doesn't have one nice, plush restaurant for black people; I'm goin' to get one built. You know, there used to be a sign along Miami Beach that said, "No Jews Allowed." Well, the Jews got mad, united, and bought up the whole damn beach. That's what *we* got to start doin'—uniting and pooling our money—and I hope to get black celebrities and millionaires behind me, because the Muslim movement is the onliest one that's really going to get our people together. I may be just one little black man with a talent for fightin', but I'm going to perform miracles: When black people with money see what I can do with my pennies, they'll begin to see what can be done with their millions.

My big contribution is goin' to come after the next Foreman fight. I might get $10 million for fighting George again, and out of that I'll give the government its $5 million in tax, I'll put aside $1 million for myself and spread the other $4 million around. With that kind of money, we can make a lot of this country's black neighborhoods bloom, which will show that Allah is surely with me and my Muslim brothers. For we *can* change things. Look at our restaurants and buildings along Lenox Avenue in Harlem and you know we're not just *jivin'*. The $4 million I'll invest in my people after the Foreman fight will be the start of making every ghetto in America beautiful, and you'll be able to see where *that* money went. The government says it spends billions in the ghettos—but *we* can't see where the money goes.

People might read all this and say it's easy to talk but I'm not just talkin'. You watch: I'm goin' to spend the next five years of my life takin' my fight money and settin' up businesses for the brothers to operate. That's the *only* reason why I'll hold on to my title.

Playboy: Since you've already told us that age has been steadily eroding your skills, what makes you think you'll still be champion when you're thirty-eight?

Ali: Hey, Jersey Joe Walcott *won* his title when he was thirty-seven. Sugar Ray Robinson fought till he was in his forties, and Archie Moore went until he was fifty-one.

Playboy: At which point you took him apart with ease. Would you want to wind up your career the same way?

Ali: Archie didn't end up hurt and he's still intelligent—in spite of thinking Foreman could beat me. Going five more years don't mean going till I'm fifty-one, and I can do it just by slowing down my style. You also got to remember I spent three and a half years in exile, when they took away my title because I wouldn't be drafted. That's three and a half years less of tusslin', trainin', and fightin'; and if not for all that rest, I don't think I'd be in the same shape I am today. Because of my age, I don't have all of those three and a half years coming to me, but I have *some* of them.

Playboy: Was that period of enforced idleness a bitter part of your life?

Ali: I wasn't bitter at *all*. I had a good time speaking at colleges and meeting the students—whites, blacks, and all kinds, but mainly whites, who supported me a hundred percent. They were as much against the Vietnam War as I was.

In the meantime, I was enjoying everything I was doin'. As a speaker, I was makin' $1,500 and $2,500 at every stop, and I was averaging $5,000 a week, so I had money in my pocket. I was also puttin' pressure on the boxing authorities. I'd walk into fight arenas where contenders for my title were boxing and I'd interrupt everything, because I wanted to show everybody that I was still the Man. The people would jump up and cheer for me and the word soon got out that the authorities would have to reckon with me. When I won the Supreme Court decision and they had to let me go back to work, a lot of people came around saying, "Why don't you sue the boxing commission for unjustly taking your title away?" Well, they only did what they thought was right and there was no need for me to try to punish them for that. It's just too bad they didn't recognize that I was sincere in doing what *I* thought was right at the time.

Playboy: Did you receive a lot of hate mail during those years?

Ali: Only about one out of every three hundred letters. And I kinda liked those, so I put 'em all away in a box. When I'm ninety years old, they'll be something to show my great-grandson. I'll tell him, "Boy, here's a letter your great-granddaddy got when he fought the draft way back when they had wars." Anyway, there's good and bad in every race. People got their own opinions and they free to talk.

Playboy: Considering your feelings about white America, did it surprise you that so many whites agreed with your stand against the draft?

Ali: Yes, it did. I figured it would be worse and that I'd meet with a lot more hostility, but that didn't happen. See, that war wasn't like World War II or like America being attacked. I actually had a lot going for me at the time: The country was halfway against it, the youth was against it, and the world was saying to America, "Get out." And there I was, among people who are slaves and who are oppressed by whites. I also had a platform, because the Muslim religion and the Koran preaches against such wars. I would've caught much more hell if America was in a declared war and I didn't go.

Playboy: Would you have served if America had been in a declared war?

Ali: The way I feel, if America was attacked and some foreign force was prowling the streets and shooting, naturally I'd fight. I'm on the side of America, not them, because I'm fighting for myself, my children, and my people. Whatever foreigners would come in, if they saw some black people with rifles, I'm sure they'd start shooting. So, yeah, I'd fight if America was attacked.

Playboy: When you returned to the ring in 1970, most boxing observers felt you'd lost a good deal of your speed and timing. Did you think so?

Ali: Nope, I thought I was about the same, maybe even better. My first bout when I came back was with Jerry Quarry, who I'd fought before. It was the strangest thing, but when I watched films of the first Quarry fight, I looked fast; yet when I looked at the second Quarry fight I was *superfast*. Then, after I lost to Frazier, I studied the films and even though I wasn't in great shape and clowned a lot, look at how *sharp* I was, how much I *hit* Joe. Anyway, you saw what Foreman did to Frazier and then what I did to Foreman, so what could I have lost by resting for three and a half years? Couldn't be much, could it? That's why I can stay champ for a long time, and if I fight just twice a year, my title can't be taken away. And those'll be big, big fights worth at least $5 million apiece. That's $10 million a year for five years, which means I'll split $50 million with the government. I'll wind up with $25 million after taxes. Whew!

Playboy: That kind of money wasn't around when you began boxing professionally. Are you ever astonished by the fact that you can make $5 million in the course of an hour?

Ali: No, and when I leave boxing, there will never be that kind of money for fighters again. I can get $5 million or $7.5 million a fight because I got a world audience. The people who are puttin' up that money are the richest people in the world—black oilmen. It was a rich black man who paid me and George Foreman, and he did it because he wanted some publicity for his little country, and he got it. For fifteen years after the white Belgians had to get out of there, no one—including me—ever heard of Zaire. No one knew it was a country of more than twenty-two million people, but now we do.

I just got offered $7.5 million to fight Foreman in Djakarta, Indonesia, by a black oilman who wants to promote *his* country. How to do it? Call Muhammad Ali over and have him fight for the title and the *world* will read about where he's fighting. But after I'm out of boxing and the title goes back to a fighter like a George Foreman or any good American, title fights won't travel no further than America and England. And that'll be the end of the big, big money.

Playboy: Do you think you'll miss boxing when you finally retire?

Ali: No, because I realize you got to get old. Buildings get old, people get old, and we're all goin' to die. See the fat I have around my stomach? Ten years ago, it would come off in two weeks, but not anymore. I can't exactly *feel* myself getting old, but I ain't like I was ten years ago, so time equips me to face the facts of life. When I get to be fifty, I won't really miss boxing at all, because I'll know I can't do it anymore.

But when I quit, I sure ain't goin' out like the old-time fighters. You ain't gonna hear it said about me that when I was champ I bought me a Cadillac, had me a couple of white girls on my arm, and that when I retired I went broke. You'll *never* read articles about me that say, "Poor Muhammad Ali, he made so much money and now he's working in a car wash." No, sir.

Playboy: Will you continue to associate yourself with boxing after you retire?

Ali: I don't think so. I'm the champion right now and I can't even find time for training because of other things. I talk to senators like John Tunney of California, and black bourgeois congressmen who like to act so *big,* and black doctors and lawyers who have white friends and who no longer want to be black—and who act like they're too good for any of the brothers. I can always say to them, "Why do you-all act like this? I don't act like that, and *you* can't get no bigger than Muhammad *Ali.*"

That's the truth, too. I was over in Ireland and had dinner with Jack Lynch, the prime minister. I was in Cairo and stayed at Sadat's palace for two days. I wined and dined with King Faisal of Saudi Arabia. I might not've been that happy around all of those leaders, but people who look up to them see *them* looking up to *me.* Now when I bring my program down, they'll listen. See, you got to have something going in front for you. A smart fella might go down the street, but if people look at him and think, "Oh, just an ordinary fella," he won't get things done. But when a guy in a Rolls-Royce drives up and says, "Hey, I want to make a deal," people with talk money with him. Same thing with me. My money and my title give me influence.

And I also have something to say. You notice that when we talk, eighty-five percent of our conversation is away from boxing? Interview some other fighters and see what *they* can talk about: nothing. We couldn't talk this long—you couldn't *listen* this long—if we just talked boxing.

Playboy: Agreed; but let's stick with that fifteen percent a bit longer. Many people believe that after you retire, boxing will disappear in America. Do you believe that?

Ali: Boxing will never die. There will always be boxing in schools and clubs, and the fight crowd will always follow the pros. And every once in a while, a sensational fighter will come through.

Playboy: As sensational as yourself?

Ali: Physically, maybe, but not in the way I'm known worldwide. I just don't think another fighter will ever be followed by people in every country on the planet. You can go to Japan, China, all the European, African, Arab, and South American countries and, man, they know me. I can't name a country where they *don't* know me. If another fighter's goin' to be that big, he's goin' to have to be a Muslim, or else he won't get to nations like Indonesia, Lebanon, Iran, Saudi Arabia, Pakistan, Syria, Egypt, and Turkey—those are all countries that don't usually follow boxing. He might even have to be named Muhammad, because Muhammad is the most common name in the world. There are more Muhammads than there are Williamses, Joneses, Ecksteins, Smiths, or anything else on earth. And he's also gonna have to say the name Allah a lot, can't say God. I know that God is the Supreme Being, but Allah is the name used most on the planet. More people pray to Allah than to Jehovah, Jesus, or just plain Lord, 'cause there are about eleven Muslims in the world to every nonMuslim.

But he's got to have the personality, too, because just being a Muslim champ won't make it. My corn, the gimmicks, the acting I do—it'll take a whole lot for another fighter to ever be as popular as Muhammad Ali.

Playboy: You once said that you act all the time. Where does your act begin and where does it end?

Ali: The acting begins when I'm working. Before a fight, I'll try to have something funny to say every day and I'll talk ten miles a minute. Like before the Chuck Wepner fight, I was tellin' reporters all *kinds* of things.

Playboy: Care to give us a small sampling?

Ali: All right: "If Chuck Wepner becomes the only white man ever to beat the arrogant Muhammad Ali, he will be America's greatest hero! He will make White Tornado commercials and go on *Gunsmoke,* but for him this fight is really *Mission: Impossible!* Wepner has a strong will—and if the will is great, the will can overpower the skill! I understand Wepner had a meeting with the Ku Klux Klan and they told him to *whup* this nigger!"

That's acting, and it ends when I get into the ring. There are no pleasures in a fight, but some of my fights have been a pleasure to win—especially the second Norton and Frazier fights and the Foreman fight. I was left for dead before the second Norton fight, because my jaw had been broken the first time out. One loss to Frazier and *Sports Illustrated* ran a headline on its cover saying END OF THE ALI LEGEND. And I was also left for dead against Foreman, who was supposed to be the toughest champ of all time. You know, I once read something that said, "He who is not courageous enough to take risks will accomplish nothing in life." Well, boxing is a risk and life is a gamble, and I got to take both.

Playboy: People close to you say that in the past year you've grown visibly weary of boxing. Is that true?

Ali: Well, I started fighting in 1954, when I was just twelve, so it's been a long time for me. But there's always a new fight to look forward to, a new publicity stunt, a new *reason* to fight. Now I'm fighting for this charities thing, and it helps me get ready. When I think of all the money and the jobs winning means, I'll run those two miles on mornings when I'd rather sleep.

Playboy: With the possible exceptions of a few of our politicians, you're probably the most publicized American of this century. What kinds of problems does fame on such a grand scale create?

Ali: None. It's a blessing if you use publicity for the right thing, and I use it to help my brothers and to promote truth around the world. It's still an honor for me to talk to TV reporters who come all the way from Germany and

Australia just to interview me. And when we're talking, I don't see a man from Germany. I see millions of Germans. The reporter will go back home and show his film to his entire nation, which keeps me popular and sells fight tickets, which is how I earn my living—and also how I can keep buying up buildings for my people. That's why talkin' so much don't bother me, but I'll be bothered when the reporters quit coming around, because on that day I'll realize I'm not newsworthy anymore, and that's when it all ends. So I enjoy it while it's happening.

Playboy: Do you enjoy being mobbed by autograph seekers as well?

Ali: Most of the time, it's okay with me, because service to others is the rent I pay for my room on earth. See, when you become spiritual and religious, you realize that you're not big and great, only Allah is. You can't hurt people's feelings just because you're up there. When I was younger, Sugar Ray Robinson did that to me, and I didn't like it at all.

Playboy: What happened?

Ali: I was on my way to fight in the Rome Olympics, and I stopped by a nightclub in Harlem, because Sugar Ray—my idol, *everybody's* idol—was there. I'd watched all his fight films and I just wanted to see him and touch him. I wanted outside for him to leave that club and I was hoping he'd talk to me and maybe give me his autograph. But he didn't do it and I was so *hurt*. If Sugar Ray only knew how much I loved him and how long I'd been following him, maybe he wouldn't have done that.

Man, I'll *never* forget how bad I felt when he turned me down. Sugar Ray said, "Hello kid, how ya' doin'? I ain't got time," and then got into his car and took off. I said to myself right then, "If I ever get great and famous and people want my autograph enough to wait all day to see me, I'm sure goin' to treat 'em different."

Playboy: Still, aren't there times when living in the public eye becomes slightly unbearable?

Ali: Yeah, and when that happens, I get into my bus, stock up on food, and take my wife and four children and drive somewhere near the ocean and just rest for four or five days.

My real pleasure is having no appointments, but that hardly ever happens. There's always people I gotta talk to, business deals I gotta think about, telephones that are always ringing, and roadwork and time in the gym that I gotta take care of. There's always *something* I have to do, but I guess we're all busy in our own ways. I'm sure President Ford has a bigger job than all of us. Like any big man—a spiritual leader like Wallace D. Muhammad, a politician, a president of a college—he's in prison. Same thing with me, because I'm a heavyweight champion who represents not only boxing but many, many other things that boxers can't even speak of. Therefore, I always have a deskful of stuff, piles and piles of letters and projects that no other boxer would be literate enough to even imagine handling. The times when it all gets me down, I just want to get away—from the commercials and TV and college appearances and airline flights and friends asking for loans and people begging for money that they need. I don't like to do it, but I wind up ducking: "When the phone rings, tell 'em I'm not here." It never lets up, so if I can just get away for a day every once in a while, I'm happy. Yet I don't let that stuff get me *too* bothered, because I have only one cause—the Islamic cause—and my mission is to spread the works and faith that Elijah Muhammad taught me.

Playboy: For a man who's become more and more of a missionary, boxing must occasionally seem like a particularly brutal and inappropriate way to make a living. Did you ever consider a career in any other sport?

Ali: About the onliest other sport I ever thought about was football, but I didn't like it, because there was no personal publicity in it: you have to wear too much equipment and people can't see you. Folks sitting back in the bleachers can't hardly pick you out of a field of twenty-two men and a bunch of other guys shufflin' in and out, but in a boxing ring there's only two men. I made my decision about sports when I was a twelve-year-old kid, and I went with boxing because fighters can make more money than other athletes and the sport isn't cut off by a season, like football. And I've never regretted that decision, 'cause when you're the greatest at what you're doing, how can you question it?

Playboy: Does your claim of being the greatest mean that you think you could have beaten every heavyweight champion in modern ring history?

Ali: I can't really say. Rocky Marciano, Jack Johnson, Joe Louis, Jack Dempsey, Joe Walcott, Ezzard Charles—they *all* would have given me trouble. I can't know if I would've beaten them all, but I do know this: I'm the most talked-about, the most publicized, the most famous, and the most colorful fighter in history. And I'm the fastest heavyweight—with feet and hands—who ever lived. Besides all that, I'm the onliest poet laureate boxing's ever had. One other thing, too: If you look at pictures of all the former champions you know in a flash that I'm the best-looking champion in history. It all adds up to being the greatest, don't it?

Playboy: Do you think you'll be remembered that way?

Ali: I don't know, but I'll tell you how I'd *like* to be remembered: as a black man who won the heavyweight title and who was humorous and who treated everyone right. As a man who never looked down on those who looked up to him and who helped as many of his people as he could—financial and also in their fight for freedom, justice, and equality. As a man who wouldn't hurt his people's dignity by doing anything that would embarrass them. As a man who tried to unite his people through the faith of Islam that he found when he listened to the Honorable Elijah Muhammad. And if all that's asking too much, then I guess I'd settle for being remembered only as a great boxing champion who became a preacher and a champion of his people.

And I wouldn't even mind if folks forgot how pretty I was.

[November, 1975]

Please note that this piece has been edited for this volume and does not appear in its entirety.

MUHAMMAD ALI

GARRY WILLS

Muhammad Ali is the supreme marksman. Time after time he touches the target, so fast it is hard to count the blows. He washes his opponent's face in leather, raising a fleshy foam and red general swelling. Though he is very large, even for a heavyweight, his punch has been clocked, frame-by-frame, and found swifter than that of Sugar Ray Robinson, the fastest middleweight in anyone's memory. Ali does not, like many fighters, do speed-bag drills to show off in his camp—his punch is faster than the bag can show. There is an irreducible minimum of bounce-back time required between punches at the bag. But not in punches to the head. Ali disdains the dull but often necessary work of slowing men down with fatiguing blows to the ribs, midsection, and arms. Those fighting him know that almost every punch will go to the head, and guard accordingly—it is the equivalent of passing on every play in football, and never using the run. Certain fighters can take a tremendous amount of head punishment, so long as you leave their breathing apparatus alone. Ali does not adjust to this advantage. He just takes it as a greater challenge to his ability to hit even so impassive a head as Frazier's often enough and hard enough to chop him down.

Speed is nothing without accuracy, of course—and accuracy is the thing that sets Ali apart. Even Joe Frazier has an irregular little bobbing motion of his head that makes him hard to hit. But you would never know it from the Manila fight. Ali's accuracy is a technical accomplishment grounded in a moral one, in courage. The best rifle in the world is no good without the marksman's eye. Ali carries his head high and partly exposed, so he can see everything all the time. Even the coolest fighter flinches, closes his eyes, ducks his head while being punched (or a split second before). But Ali more than any other heavyweight keeps both eyes open and on his man all the time. He whips his head back just enough to escape a punch without losing sight of his man. His head seems to float above the fight, looking down on it. Occasionally a barrage will reach up to him, and he swerves away, but with that wide-eyed whinnying expression, as much of measurement as of wonder. He has the best eyes in boxing.

And his eyes are his principal defensive tool. The conventional supposition is that a stand-up "classical" boxer must depend on his legs to protect him—must stay on the move, circling away from the other man's strong hand, not letting him "set" for the big punch. That kind of mobility a Sugar Ray Robinson could retain through most of his career. And Cassius Clay had it as a light heavyweight winning his gold medal in the 1960 Olympics. He even had it as a very young heavyweight (twenty-two when he won the professional championship). But no man his size, having reached his mid-thirties, can dance all night with Joe Frazier. Ali has accepted the extra weight of his later years, conditioned it to take any amount of body punches, and set about protecting his eyes. He does this just by slight moves of his head—and mainly moves backward or to the side, so his vision is not blocked. He almost never ducks. He does not pay the price most fighters have to, of evading *this* punch by losing sight of the *next* one, momentarily. Ali's terrific speed and reflexes are not in his feet any more, but in his neck—guided by those undeflectable eyes. (Archie Moore, too, survived what seemed forever on his cool—by perpetual little defensive motions directed from a tranquil observation post.)

There is a quality of sheer concentration in Ali that would tire him if he attempted to sustain it through a long fight—a laser beam burning backward into its own generator. The effort of sighting, of throwing those fast punches, of hitting the target, is too much for him. He rests against the ropes, covering up his head and letting the other fighter punch himself out against his sides. In the thirteenth round of the Manila fight, Ali's quick flurry, that late in the evening, almost had Frazier out. But Ali could punch no more for a while. His foot slipped, and then he lounged around the ring, gathering resources. Rather than punch slower and slower through the night, Ali likes to deal out his lightnings in little packets, then save up for the next barrage. This loses him points on the scorecard, but he likes that too. He is in love with risk. He takes unnecessary chances.

He has everything—speed, size, strength, looks, charm, defiance. His very childishness takes the edge off the outrageous things he does—as was the case with Babe Ruth. Oddly enough, heavyweight champions often look less than imposing. They tend to be spindly-legged like Dempsey or Jack Johnson; stump-legged like Marciano or Frazier; apearmed like Liston; bony-framed like Patterson. But Ali looks as if Praxiteles had sculpted him from caramel. To get such balanced limbs, one normally has to go to smaller men, like middleweight Randy Turpin. Ali's body seems almost too symmetrical to be functional. He could earn an epinikion from Pindar any day. He is a superb athlete. I wonder why that is not enough.

It isn't, of course. Modern Pindars sing the weirdest songs about Ali. They cluster around him, trying to probe nonexistent mysteries. There is Mailer, under the impression that he is interviewing the Heart of Darkness. (What did Heart have to say today? "Being a fighter enables me to attain certain ends." Heavy.) Even Wilfrid Sheed asks Ali to recite the Muslim catechism. This buzzing of the literary gents around Ali calls to mind Nathanael West's description of Faye Greener:

> None of them really heard her. They were all too busy watching her smile, laugh, shiver, whisper, grow indignant, cross and uncross her legs, stick out her tongue, widen and narrow her eyes, toss her head so that her platinum hair splashed against the red plush of the chair back. The strange thing about her gestures and expressions was that they didn't really illustrate what she was saying. They were almost pure. It was as though her body recognized how foolish her words were and tried to excite her hearers into being uncritical. It worked that night; no one even thought of laughing at her. The only move they made was to narrow their circle about her.

Sheer physical beauty, of unusual degree, seems to become different in *kind,* to call for *complementary* significances. That can be bewildering to the beauty's possessor, who feels his or her power over others and recognizes that they want such power to include something *more.* More than mere animal glow. The magnetic "star" tries to supply this something extra—wit, say; getting primed with one-liners like Marilyn Monroe's answer to "What do you sleep in?" "Chanel Number Five." Or Muhammad Ali's "Float like a butterfly, sting like a bee." (I am surprised, with all these literary gents around, that no one has recalled James Whistler's graphic "signature"—a butterfly with a bee's sting added.) When the wit does not work, the star might try pro, fundity—attend Actors Studio, marry Arthur Miller, read Dostoevski.

Ali cannot read books—he is barely able to make out newspaper head, lines; but he had his gingerly affair with various causes in the sixties. His Russian novels became the emerging nations. The surest thing of all is to try religion—become a convert to one of Hollywood's theological extrava, gances. The star feels destined anyway; holds special powers. It is in the star's stars. Superstitions like astrology fill up any gaps in the stricter theology adopted. Ali, of course, had the best religion ever fashioned for a star—one that combined a high regard for money with black militance and Vietnam pacifisim. For his draft,dodging he was punished by Spiro Agnew's Wash, ington, just as Ingrid Bergman had been by Louis B. Mayer's Hollywood. It added a note of suffering to Ali's brashness, and made him a Cause some, where down the line from boycotting grapes. By the end of the sixties, Ali was the intellectuals' catnip.

For some reason, people don't want fighters just to be fighters. They have to stand for an era, for the color of hope, for a metaphysics of the spirit. Virtue (Floyd Patterson) meets vice (Sonny Liston). Poor Jerry Quarry was, for a while, the voice of the new ethnics. Joe Louis, we were brought up to believe, dropped the first American bombs of World War II on Schmeling's head. It is as if the *art* were not enough to redeem boxing's violence, all that cruelty in, flicted on the face—so we prefer to think the loser is being destroyed for some deeply ideological reason. Get the Nazi. Smash the traitor. Beat Whitey. This tendency, quite as degrading as it is silly, reached a new low in Manila, where people cheered for Frazier in the name of family life (Ali's current "fox" was more conspicuous at this fight than at others). Ali had finally to take a rap not analogous to Ingrid Bergman's, but identical with it. Our stars have to keep themselves pure. They are our own stars, and no one wants to read dirty jokes in his horoscope.

If all else fails, in our quest to have our heroes escape the confines of a merely physical luster, we can fall back on Hollywood's ultimate con—the claim that a starlet is really *bright* because she has the brains to recognize how *dumb* she is. This ploy turns publicity agents into scholastic disputants, and the star goes readily along:

Had any other girl been so affected, he would have thought her intolerable. Faye's affectations, however, were so completely artificial that he found them charming. Being with her was like being backstage during an amateurish, ridiculous play. From in front, the stupid lines and grotesque situations would have made him squirm with annoyance, but because he saw the perspiring stagehands and the wires that held up the tawdry summerhouse with its tangle of paper flowers, he accepted everything and was anxious for it to succeed. . . . Faye did have some critical ability, almost enough to recognize the ridiculous. He had often seen her laugh at herself.

That is roughly the Wilfrid Sheed Thesis on Ali. The poor fellow may have a short attention span and low IQ; but he is on to his own hype, and graciously shares this awareness with us: "He grins a lot off camera, sheepishly, with an 'ain't I a devil? isn't this just too much?' quality. As if he wants *us* to be in on the joke on *them*: the basic principle of dramatic irony, whether he knows it or not." Marilyn, too, was always committing Ironies, according to her press agent. "He is, though he says so himself, a humble man: it is one of the weird secrets of his success. Once you notice it, his wildest boasts never bother you again." Sheed has gone backstage during Faye Greener's act, and seen the grips at work; so the lines no longer mean what they say for him.

The other Sheed Thesis is that fame on Ali's scale is a universal currency, convertible to any other kind of power or influence, good or bad. And he fears Ali's influence will be bad in time, out of mere quest for novelty, when he has worn out whatever good influence he cares to exercise. It is a more sophisticated version of the Ingrid Bergman problem—what if the children find out what Joan of Arc is *really* doing with her time? Sheed forgets how far Ali had dropped from view by the third year of his "exile." When he is not fighting, the magic drains from him. Then the doggerel is just doggerel. Ali will be a celebrity as long as he lives—like the Duke of Windsor. But he only *rules* from the ring. He has nothing, really, to say, except with his fists. Yet how eloquent they are.

[October, 1975]

HYPERBOLE'S CHILD

A. B. GIAMATTI

It suddenly became clear to me, sitting in Madison Square Garden on September 29, watching the preliminary bouts to the Ali-Shavers fight, that the basis of sport is work. Running, jumping, lifting, pushing, bending, pulling, planting the legs, and using the back—these exertions are essential to physical labor and to athletic competition. The closeness of a given game to the rituals and effort of work invests the game with dignity; without that proximity to labor, the game would be merely a release from work instead of a refinement of it. The radical difference between work and game, however, occurs when limits or rules are imposed on this labor, patterns which acknowledge that this new work, this sport is not a matter of life and death. Whereas that work, the work of your back and arms, in field or mill, on ship or in forest, was crucial to your survival, and to the survival of those dependent on you, this work is different; it is delimited, separate, independent, a refinement of reality but distinct. This work is fully as serious and difficult as real work, but this unreal work is not coextensive with life. This work of sport, usually but not always at some predetermined point, will have an end. It will be over, not to begin again with the sun. This work, unlike that real work, does not sustain life in any immediate and practical way, such as providing food; but this unreal serious work does sustain life in the sense that it makes life bearable. It allows all of us to go back renewed to whatever real work we do, perhaps to go back for a moment redeemed. I have often thought that the worldwide appeal of soccer lies in part in its unabashed emphasis on penetrating the other's territory; partly in its wonderfully seamless and continuous quality, where no quarter is given, no pause taken, but like the tides men come and go; but mostly in its denial of the use of the hands. For the millions who work with their hands, there can be no greater relief than to escape the daily focus on those instruments of labor, and no greater confirmation of the centrality of hands to life than their denial in this sport.

These notions formed while I waited for the Ali-Shavers fight. I had been watching the undercard, and admiring the way Alfredo Evangelista of Uruguay would get his back into his punches, like a man digging a hole, and how the sheer expenditure of effort had forced Pedro Soto to fight Evangelista's fight until, in the eighth round, Soto was so badly punished by the patient, awkward digging of Evangelista that the referee stopped the bout. At this moment of victory, which is also a moment of reunion, as the men finish work and leave together, the crowd's attention was diverted from Soto and Evangelista by the presence of Ali, who suddenly appeared in the back of the garden and roared through the aisles shaking his finger, surrounded by about ten of his entourage. The crowd responded with delight—"A-li, A-li, A-li," they chanted; and when they turned from that spectacle, Evangelista and Soto were gone. If for most athletes and spectators sport is work conceived in some special way as play, for Muhammad Ali sport is work conceived as theater.

Ali has theatricalized his work in that, rather than continuing to serve his work as a worker, or slave, he has made what he does serve him as a setting. Ali has extended himself and boxing, the sport most like work, in the direction of theater by emphasizing the other being that lives beside the worker in every athlete, the actor. In the athlete worker and actor meet, the expenditure of energy and the power to give shape come together. Of course, workers "perform" tasks and actors work hard; the spectrum worker-athlete-actor is not a broad one and the three points are distinguished by emphasis more than anything else. As the athlete resembles the worker in the way he exerts his body, and in the way he catches the deep rhythms in work, so the athlete resembles the actor in the way he uses the body to express what I can only call an inner vision. Both athlete and actor release energy in order to restrain it and in restraining it, to give shape to a new idea. Both are judged effective or ineffective (that is what "good" or "bad" means in these two professions) by how well they execute what is set them; and for both athlete and actor execution depends not on inspiration or luck or the weather, inner or outer, but on coordination, economy of gesture, timing, good coaching.

It is Ali who has brought to the surface the actor in every athlete more successfully and obsessively than anyone else. Ali is in many ways profoundly bored, and he knows only one craft. In order to remain interested in what he must do, Ali has allowed the performer to erupt unchecked, burying the worker in him, the skilled artisan with extraordinary hands and legs and specific, worldly ambitions, under the sulfurous, scalding lava of his improvisations. Improvisation is the only way he has found to order the endless days: the monologizing, poeticizing, and prophesying, all that grimacing and exhorting and praying, is the style of a man who is not sure even he knows when his acts are simply acting, but who does know he does not care.

And when a fight is in view, and training is required, a regimen guaranteed to exacerbate boredom with brutal fatigue, Ali goes deeper into his protean reserves and whole dramas emerge. There is often the heroic beast fable—Ali will slay a dragon in the form of a Bear, a Rabbit, a Gorilla, or, lately, an Acorn. As time goes on, other subplots emerge. Howard Cosell once regularly took a part; occasionally whole countries, like Zaire, are cast. In recent years the press has been less and less willing to be the megaphone to this sideshow, but the press has no choice but to be megaphone when the source of news insists on defining himself as a barker. So we are treated to sermons, doggerel, parables, myths, even creations from whole cloth: JIMMY ELLIS, SPARRING PARTNER, KNOCKS DOWN CHAMP TWICE TODAY. That particular story, out of Ali's Pennsylvania training camp some eight days before the bout, is a good example of the problems Ali poses and the problem he has.

Perhaps only a headline announcing the pope's intention to remarry would be as immediately unconvincing as the news that Ellis knocked Ali down twice in one round. The gloves used in sparring sessions weigh sixteen ounces apiece. Then there is the fact that these two know each other well, having met more than twenty years ago in Louisville when they were both young teenagers. Ali and Ellis cannot surprise each other and while Ellis would work for a man he could knock down, Ali would not hire a man who might even try it. Even once. But *twice!* Such an idea staggers the imagination.

Why put out the story then? In part because where the rest of us were born under a star, Ali was born under a rhetorical figure, hyperbole, defined by the great Quintilian as "an elegant straining of the truth." Surely Ali was also impelled by a realization that the advance sale for September 29 was slow; and he was propelled by that instinct of his to hype the gate, to work his own crowd (as he would do as Soto and Evangelista finished work), to shill for himself, to be both the show and the man who hustled them into the tent. If there is one born every minute, Ali wants to be the midwife. But does that deep instinct justify putting out such a palpably transparent story as the one about being knocked down twice? No, that instinct does not justify straining the truth quite so inelegantly. An even deeper need justifies the story, the need to pump up once again the white man's hope to see the black champion beaten.

Here we engage Ali's deepest game, the only work he does with a will. While you are being encouraged to think he can be beaten, you are being allowed to understand that the form the encouragement takes is fraudulent. Your ability to see through the con undermines your belief in his vulnerability (he can't be beaten if he says he can) and reaffirms your faith in his theatrical mastery (knocked down twice, my foot! What a showman). You are now his. Ali has transformed all the potential spectators, the fight crowd, into something far different, an audience; he has enticed the naive, titillated the devoted, amused the jaded, outraged the mass; he has had it out with his opponent now in the press and on television for at least two weeks, his sense of pace impeccable, the whole spectacle building to the grand final number, the climax just before the last curtain, the weigh-in; and, most important, he has managed to legitimize race as an issue in the fight by making it part of the show, or, for those so inclined, the whole show. One so inclined is Ali, and the last scene is played.

At the weigh-in, the state lends whatever moral and legal credibility it has to the ritual of assessing the fighters' weight and physical fitness. They are always found to be fit. (Examinations and X rays conducted on September 28 could find no injuries, indeed no trace of trauma, resulting from the two knockdowns suffered by the champion during training.) And after the tape and scales, Ali takes over, and tears a passion to tatters, splitting the ears of the groundlings in the press, o'erdoing Termagant and out-heroding Herod, now the player, now the Prince, doing all the parts and, at the weigh-in on September 28, ranting at length about the theatrical nature of his ranting, exposing the structure of his illusion, the old actor getting himself worked up for the part, doing what Elvis Presley could no longer do, getting into the circle, recapturing the energy and interest to go out on stage by pretending to have it—all of this working precisely to the extent that all the hangers-on and reporters and onlookers and cuties and commission people and cameramen and friends and spies and flunkies and acolytes, who have seen it dozens of times, get pulled in, and begin to laugh and nudge and shake their heads and stamp their feet as if it were the first time; and yet, if you listen rather than acquiesce, at the center of this whirlwind of words and gestures and postures and poses the chosen epithet of the chosen opponent is chanted and honed and, finally, hurled like a knife at the man it signifies. The real fight is now almost over, as Ali turns on his opponent all the power of the opponent, turning the man's physical characteristics, his background, his class, his worth as a man against him. Ali deflects the opponent's strength from Ali, and now the opponent is left, in the weeks or hours remaining (for this process does not start at the weigh-in), to fight himself, to fight his ugliness or his awkwardness or his lack of education or, in the most savage blow of all, to fight his race. If the man is white, he is not allowed to be the White Hope. Ali bestows this duty as if it were a dukedom, and then watches while the opponent tries to figure out whether to hoist this load, and, if he will, how to gain a purchase on it, and, once it is up, where to take it. It is too easy.

With black fighters there is more sport, though the press here draws a line and the public does not, evidently, get the full force of Ali's treatment of black opponents. But the technique is clear. In calling Frazier a gorilla, or Shavers "shiftless," Ali simply unleashes the power of traditional racist epithets. He thus sets his black opponent to battling two chimeras, both now identified with himself. The opponent must confront his main sense of himself, his strength, his identity as a black man, as if it were a weakness; he must struggle with, rather than use, the source of his power, because this black champion has turned their race into a vicious insult. Lest the opponent miss the point to the burden that he alone now carries, Ali will during the fight clarify his status for him as he did for Shavers by calling him throughout the fight, according to reports, "nigger." It is a technique as simple, and decent, as rubbing your glove's laces on an opponent's swollen eye.

But while Ali has a black opponent fighting his blackness, he also has the other man fighting his whiteness. Everyone who fights Ali must be the white hope. The gate demands it, and hyperbole's child would have it no other way. Every opponent is the champion of that vast, hostile white mass that, since February 28, 1964, when Ali announced that he had a few months before joined the Nation of Islam, and especially since his refusal in Houston on April 28, 1967, to be inducted into the army, has wanted to see him knocked out. So, at least, Ali believes; and so believed the elegantly dressed, affable black man who sat behind me at the Ali-Shavers bout, and who laughingly insisted for fifteen rounds that I had come to see Ali beaten by my fighter, Shavers. But I believe that the act at Houston and the announcement about the Nation of Islam were themselves not the causes of an attitude, but the results of an even older attitude of Ali's. For those acts of 1967 and 1964 were acts of separation, of secession from black and white America's traditional assumptions about how to behave, and were themselves responses to the conviction, held by the boy who by his account in *My Own Story* felt a "deep kinship" with Emmett Till, that they wanted him out, and that he would dance inside and sting them before they could put him down and put him out.

Ali's boredom with training and fighting only masks a fear, a fear of being peripheral, a terror of being out, and that fear accounts for his need to be at the center of something, a stage, a ring, a Nation, a cosmic racial drama. His fear of being marginal accounts for the savagery of his desire to get in, to land the first blow, and for the outlandish intensity of his acting center stage, before the bell has ever rung or the lights have dimmed. Ali's sense of racial antagonism forces him to scorn his black opponents for being black, while at the same time smearing Frazier, Norton, Shavers with whiteface, grotesquely deforming the other's face in every way while trumpeting the beauty of his own, that clean-shaven, smooth, unblemished face so unlike the scarred, roughened laborers' faces his mocks. His is an extraordinary series of performances, culminating in the weigh-in, each scene contributing, as do rounds, to that overall accumulation of episode and pace and shaped energy we call a starring role. He has, particularly in the last year or so as preparation gets more and more difficult, set up the actual fight as an anticlimax to the weeks before it. And certainly the bout on the evening of September 29 was an anticlimax; for, regardless of what you saw on television, where close-ups on intense faces covered a great deal of standing, leaning, peek-a-booing, clowning, missing, waiting, the Shavers-Ali fight was a good fight only once you had accepted how much less good a fighter Ali has become.

The real struggle goes on earlier, when Ali transforms the coming fight into a ghastly minstrel show, he never more black than when the other end man is daubed in white, the other never blacker than when Ali sneers at his color, the races locked together, at one and at odds, the whole a parody of race relations in every city street and union and school and firehouse and subway and unemployed black waking hour in America, the prizefight finally only a skirmish in the larger race war, this little battle masquerading as a show starring Muhammad Ali and a cast of everyone else.

Ali has known from the beginning what every good athlete learns: Make him play your game, fight your fight, and you will beat him every time. But Ali has also learned a lesson kept from most athletes precisely by the pleasure of their work, a pleasure now beneath Ali, a pleasure in work insufficiently exhilarating to one who has the art born in him, the art of filling a scene: And that subtler lesson is that while you can only beat him if he fights your fight, you can destroy him if he acts in your play. If, like Othello, he will accept the role you set for him, you will master him as you master all scenes. And if you can make him play nigger and white racist all at once, surely you are the greatest and he is yours. This is, after all, an old drama and an old style, learned from the white slave-masters; they were the ones who based their play on others' brutal work and who forced the others to enact roles simply to survive. Ali, with his incredible gifts of body and mind, has brought the central drama of his people's history in America to a bright, gaudy life, for everyone to see. He has brought the patterns of work, play, and acting that commingle in slaves and athletes to the surface, and he has refined his techniques for communicating, through the media, what those old patterns mean.

Sitting in Madison Square Garden on September 29, I did not think Ali beat Shavers, even giving Ali all the even rounds, I scored the fight for Shavers, 8–7. I do not think Ali beat Shavers this September any more than many think he beat Ken Norton in September of 1976, or beat Jimmy Young in the spring of 1976. I also do not believe that Ali, at this point, really cares what anyone thinks, or cares what really happened. The fights in the ring, vastly remunerative, full of effort and clowning, are only incidental to the real battle. I believe he will participate in the ring fights longer than he should because he cannot stop until he has fought down the need, compounded of fear and fury, to act out completely what, in his view, it is to be black in America, to be always living at the margin, on the edge, in a position where, despite the pain of your work and the beauty of your play, a man may announce with superb casualness at any given moment that you have been counted out.

[December, 1977]

EX-FIGHTER'S NOTES ON THE CHAMPION

JOSE TORRES

It happened to all of them. It happened to Joe Louis, Sugar Ray Robinson, and Willie Pep. It happened to Archie Moore, Rocky Graziano, and Carlos Ortiz. I know; it happened to me. Call it age. Call it growing old. Call it the erosion of time. I call it getting bored, losing interest and desire. But whatever it is, you find that the legs no longer take you where you want to go. Punches once easily evaded by a quarter of an inch now make contact. Openings appear but there is no swiftness in your punches to take advantage of them. Joe Louis put it best "I knew I was getting old," he said, "when I had to think about throwing the right hand."

But, at what age is a fighter old? At twenty-eight? At thirty-two? At thirty-six? The truth is that old age in boxing has yet to be clearly defined. I have seen fighters—good, talented fighters—get old at twenty-five. In the complex business of pugilism it is not unusual to see even young champions suddenly look fifty years old in the ring. One such fighter was former lightweight champion Armando "Mando" Ramos. Born in 1948, he was a world champion at twenty-one. He beat Davey Moore in November 1969 in a spectacular exhibition displayed only by great champions. A year later, "Mando" lost his crown to Ismael Laguna. He tried desperately to regain the championship but the magic moment was gone. He finally retired in 1975 after suffering five consecutive KOs. He was only twenty-seven. But two years before Ramos was already a beat-up washed-up fighter—at twenty-five. He had gotten very old—in his head. Why? Why do some champs have tremendous consistency and longevity, no matter what their age? And why is it that some don't? Why is it that other fighters who display great talent and potential fail to reach the top? Why was Ali such an exciting performer at thirty or thirty-two, and not at thirty-four, or now, at thirty-six?

The answer to these questions is certainly hidden among the many enigmas that have always surrounded the world of boxing. But I am convinced that in Ali's case he is mainly haunted by the "getting old" myth. Once he entered his thirties he began to show decadence—inside his head. Opponents did not make him old. He has done this to himself.

Watch Muhammad Ali today, watch him closely and you'll see how his ring performances of the last few years display a man obsessed with the search for youth. "I'm not as fast," he often boasts, "and I'm not punching with the same speed as before." An attack on his own youth? "But I stand firmer and can punch harder." Justification for his age?

Then watch him in the gym. Unhampered by the pressure of actual competition, he performs in the gym as he did in the days when he was still Cassius Clay. He moves constantly, punches with speed and accuracy, eludes punches with the facility of a bee, and punches like one. And when he lays against the ropes it is purely by choice. He's simply practicing an act he has mastered: deceit.

It is in actual competition that Muhammad Ali drifts toward the ropes, bends his six-three, 225-pound frame partially forward with his elbows protecting his body, gloves too close to the cheeks, guarding his face. And he stays in that position for long periods of time, every ounce of energy dedicated to defense. He laughs, talks, mocks the few punches that penetrate his barricade. And he doesn't bother to throw punches. It's an old boxing habit.

We usually do this when we feel tired, frustrated, discouraged, or hurt. The ropes offer us a false sense of protection. So we rest against them to weather a continuous attack, or we use them to take breathers.

But when I used to see my opponents move to the ropes it was an exhilarating moment, one I always hoped for. There it was: a motionless target inviting me (although the opponent was usually forced into the position) to dish it out, to play the game of discovering the vulnerable places for my punches. As the attacker, I always found punching territory. There was always enough time available for me to look for the open spaces. Against the ropes the recipient was always at a disadvantage. Muhammad Ali does it differently.

When we first heard of Muhammad Ali, he was the fastest heavyweight we had ever seen. He was a constant mover as he floated like a butterfly and his punches were swift, as he stung like a bee. But once he hit thirty, his mind apparently told him he was getting old. Boxers that age are not supposed to be fast. So Ali's consistency began to fade. Like most other fighters that age, Ali ran for cover. In the ring that cover is the "protective" ropes. But, unlike his peers, Ali put his creative pugilistic mind to work, making this protective tactic into an act of deception.

Once again he conned all of us, this time by making us believe that when he retreats toward the ropes, he's actually executing the latest and most important scientific boxing discovery: The Rope-a-Dope. The old, classic art of using the ropes as a hiding place, an act often provoked more by psychological demand than by physical necessity, becomes suddenly the Rope-a-Dope. I call it the Ali-Bull. One more act in the long repertoire of Ali's mental tricks.

By the time he fought George Foreman in Africa, Ali apparently felt himself losing something. But he was still confident about his ability to conjure magic. So he patented the Rope-a-Dope. It is now one of his major devices. No one else can use it. At least, not like him. As a true, experienced peddler, Ali is selling his product, and doing quite well with it.

He has sold this newest creation to everyone connected with the boxing world, including, among others, champions Joe Frazier and George Foreman, top fighters like Ken Norton and Jimmy Young; and, among his latest clients, Earnie Shavers. The job Ali has done to promote his Rope-a-Dope technique must make the most successful Madison Avenue mind-manipulator envious.

But unlike Madison Avenue propagandists, Ali must test his product himself. He has to confront the potential buyer and show it works. For a while he did pretty well. But of late, the selling of the Ali-Bull is getting harder and harder. The most recent clients seem to be losing confidence in the product. Some are becoming downright reluctant. Others may soon decide to buy no more. Worse, Ali himself seems to be losing confidence in his ability sell his Ali-Bull. He has become a dull salesman. He appears to be steadily losing will and determination. To me he merely looks bored.

The obvious deterioration could be seen in the inconsistency of his last few fights. I think the problem is in his head, which produces boredom that in turn affects his physical performance; we see slow moves, dullness in his punches, poor reflexes. He is probably one more victim of a condition that behavioral experts call psychosomatic. The mind tells the body a lie and the body simply obeys it as truth. Ali's head is telling him that he is getting old, that he is tired, that he is slower and his physical mechanism is faithfully complying. And in one more of the many paradoxes of Ali's conduct, this condition clashes with Ali's magic. The magic whose major power resides in Ali's extraordinary ability to deceive his rivals. For the truth is—and here is the paradox—that the more Ali declines physically, the more he must use his Ali-Bull gimmick. His spirit and ego could be badly hurt in the process, which is the worst thing that could happen to Ali. It would be a tragic irony if Ali winds up a victim of his own deceptions and tricks. He could actually deceive himself.

I don't mean that a couple of losses by Ali will produce a punch-drunk fighter, but Ali's latest pattern will almost certainly lead to additional punishment. He could even go down, or be knocked out, as have so many other champions before him. But no one can tell me that as a result he will end up walking our streets, evading invisible mosquitoes, or throwing punches at unseen opponents.

So it bothered me immensely to see a boxing man like Madison Square Garden matchmaker Teddy Brenner call a dramatic press conference after the Shavers bout to tell the world that Ali should retire, that he wouldn't encourage Ali to ever fight again, not even in Madison Square Garden. "I don't want Ali coming to me one day saying, Wha . . . What . . . my . . . my . . . na . . . name?" Brenner said in the most disparaging statement I've ever heard concerning the greatest heavyweight boxing has produced.

It was a melodramatic appeal to the emotional state of the boxing people after the exciting Ali-Shavers match, in which Ali received several solid shots to head and body. Brenner tried to perpetuate the myth so effectively shown in fight films by good actors who play punch-drunk fighters. That myth is almost entirely false. In my twenty-three years in boxing I have never met a single punch-drunk fighter. If I want to see one I have to go to a movie house. Or maybe go to Brenner, if we take his basis for the retirement of Ali, then we must question his effort to make the Earnie Shavers–Joe Frazier match. Here is Brenner "upset" by Ali's victory because he took a few punches and then taking a former champion who was forced into retirement after receiving savage beatings, and making him fight Shavers.

The truth is that Ali, in *all* his professional career, has not gotten hit as many punches as those received by Frazier in his two fights with former champion George Foreman. Frazier was unmercifully pummeled by Foreman in such a fashion that the entire boxing community screamed for Frazier's retirement. Brenner didn't. It should make you wonder why he now wants Ali out of the business.

Even now when he seems not to care much about his profession—what once was an avocation is now a vocation; what once was fun is now a duty; what once was his most enjoyable diversion is now a moral obligation—Ali is not suffering heavy punishment. True, all this has dropped his perfor-mance-percentage to what I would estimate is about fifty-five percent. But Ali is still too clever to get seriously hurt this late in the game. He is too clever and durable. Ali, the first important heavyweight in history to become an anti-establishment figure, was able to masterfully transform his social, politi-cal, and religious beliefs into a personal force to be applied effectively in the ring. Thanks, in part, to Malcolm X.

The social and religious consciousness of Muhammad Ali was awakened and partially developed by the late Malcolm X. It was Malcolm X who first went to the upcoming heavyweight contender, saw his intellectual potential, and proceeded to make his persuasive pitch. Ali, whose brother, Rudolph, was already a Muslim, bought Malcolm's philosophy.

At the time, Malcolm was the most loyal supporter of Elijah Muham-mad, the Messenger of God and leader of the Muslims, and was expanding and strengthening the Black Muslim discipline around the country. In a way, Malcolm was saying that a well-organized Muslim structure could serve as the major force for black revolution in America. Once a dangerous criminal ("so vicious a convict," Malcolm once said of himself, "other convicts called me Satan"), Malcolm X became respected and powerful, and the most con-troversial black man in America. So powerful indeed as to worry his mentor, Elijah Muhammad, about his own absolute control of the growing Black Muslim organization. A break between the two men followed, not long after Ali's conversion, and Malcolm formed a splinter of the Black Muslims in America. Not much later, Malcolm was shot down in a Manhattan Muslim mosque and two Elijah Muhammad followers were later convicted of the slaying.

But he had planted the seed in Muhammad Ali's head. Ali was to be-come the greatest heavyweight in the game and the best known Black Muslim in the world. Malcolm told Ali about blue-eyed white devils. In those early days, Ali spoke of his dislike for the white man. Later he mitigated his tone. "Who said I hate the white man?" he once said to me in Miami. "I don't hate

the white man, I *know* the white man." These days Ali no longer philoso-
phizes about his dislike for the white man. He is older, more mature, and now
admits to the fact that he has white friends. In fact, in the many years I've
known Ali, I never could detect genuine hate in his eyes for *anyone.* I don't
think he really knows how to hate.

His own complex nature and circumstances of his life have also produced
Ali's obvious contradictions. He seems to be an example of that phenomenon of understanding and agreeing intellectually with a situation and not being able to accept it emotionally. I'm almost convinced that Ali was more
impressed with Malcolm's theoretical ideas than he was with Elijah's prag-
matism, but when the two Black Muslim leaders broke ranks, Ali stuck to
the most successful of the two: the Honorable Elijah Muhammad.

However, none of these intellectual transitions seems to have affected Ali's
boxing behavior. For example, his entourage is basically the same. And no
one, with the exception of his masseur, Luis Sarria, and Ferdie Pacheco, the
brilliant Cuban doctor who is Ali's personal physician, acts rationally and
conventionally in Ali's presence.

Angelo Dundee, for example, the only true boxing man in the camp, does
not tell Ali what to do. If he does, Ali pays no attention anyway. "You give
Ali no direct order," Dundee once told me. "So if he, for example, is not using the left jab at all, when he comes to the corner, I tell him: "That was a very
good jab. Keep using it. Very good man." Next round you see Ali using the
jab. That's the way I communicate my orders."

And luckily, Dundee was there when Ali was confronted with his moment of truth; that most frightening moment when the will of the fighter
faces its maximum test; when a sudden decision must be made; shall I continue or not? That's basically the question one asks. For Ali, that moment
came the night of February 25, 1964, in Miami Beach, when he dethroned
Sonny Liston. Fifth round ends. Ali comes back to the corner rubbing his
eyes and vigorously complaining of having a blinding substance in his eyes.
"Cut-off the gloves!" he demands of Dundee. "Stop the fight! I am blind.
Stop it!" Dundee pays no attention and delays reaction until the bell rings.
Dundee proceeds to push Ali to the middle of the ring as the referee readies
himself to stop the fight. The rest is history. Ali went on to win the fight in the
next round, when Liston didn't answer the bell for the seventh round.

Ali remembers, I'm sure, but there was not much about it in his autobiography *The Greatest.* It deals with this moment as something inconsequential in Ali's boxing career. In fact, talking with someone from Ali's camp, I brought up this subject and the person, who asked me not to quote him, said: "The book was as interesting as Ali when it was finished. But it was chopped up to pieces by the Muslim censors. The final book needed the approval of Herbert, and he wouldn't have anything in it he thought too embarrassing or too detrimental to the puritanical foundation of the Nation of Islam." I thought it was understandable, but it also affected the sensational sales many people expected the book to have. I, for one, thought that the censorship was unfair to me as a reader.

Although the manner in which Ali's book was treated could not get my enthusiastic applause, I must admit that the Ali–Black Muslim association has been one of tremendous successful complimentation for both parties. For I'm convinced that it has been this fraternization, which has been mostly responsible for Ali's unequaled determination, will, and confidence, qualities that separate champions from all others. And I think that Ali's magic was certainly inspired by his beliefs in the Nation of Islam.

We should not be surprised if Ali gives us a few more years of singular performance by recovering the skills he seems to be losing to the myths of boxing. One of these myths is age.

Ali, and this surprises me, has not been able to deal properly with the classical nemesis of all athletes: The Over-Thirty-Year-Old Syndrome. Only a few have been able to ignore this notion: Jersey Joe Walcott, who became heavyweight champ at thirty-eight, Carmen Basillo, welterweight champ after thirty; Sugar Ray Robinson, who, for a long time, was as good after thirty as he was before; Tony Zale, who stunned the fans when he was thirty-three; and the classical Archie Moore, who more than any other fighter showed the world that old age has not been permanently defined in the boxing business.

Obviously, these men have not been able to dispel the idea that once an athlete gets to be thirty, he is through as a performer. But it is still the unwritten law by which every athlete is judged. Ali, so far, is no exception.

Perhaps Ali need not surrender to this arbitrary myth. He's so superior to his heavyweight contemporaries that his fifty-five percent ring performance excels the hundred percent of his nearest opposition. And that can easily influence any boxing champion not to try his maximum best. Too often, the best is not really necessary. In the case of Ali, he simply depends on his magic to do whatever is required to produce victory. No more.

But many Ali watchers are beginning to worry. They don't know when Ali's prodigious magic will finally run out. Ali himself doesn't know. But it can be reasonably said that Ali has the capacity and potential to overcome the psychological forces that are today limiting his performance.

He might do it, or he might not. Until then we must adjust ourselves to watching Ali getting hit more and more. We may even see him on the canvas a few times! But once his ego tells him enough, he will stop fighting, or he'll change.

If he changes then we could be once more amazed by the rejuvenation of the man who has given boxing more shocking surprises and experiences than any other in boxing history. True connoisseurs of my business will once again take their hats off for the greatest man ever to enter a boxing ring. If not now, then someday, somewhere, somehow, someone will surpass Ali. But for now we must conclude that in the most important way, the future of Muhammad Ali is up to Muhammad Ali. Not to anyone else. Only one thing is certain: No champion is a champion forever. It happens to all of them. I know. It happened to me.

[February, 1978]

LAST TANGO IN VEGAS

HUNTER S. THOMPSON

WILD RAVINGS OF AN AUTOGRAPH HOUND. . . .
A THREAT OF PUBLIC MADNESS. . . . THE PANTYHOSE
PRESS CONFERENCE

I waited until I was sure the Muhammad Ali party was well off the plane and up the ramp before I finally stood and moved up the aisle, fixing the stewardess at the door with a blind stare from behind two mirror lenses so dark that I could barely see to walk—but not so dark that I failed to notice a touch of mockery in her smile as I nodded and stepped past her. "Good-bye, sir." she chirped. "I hope you got an interesting story."

You nasty little bitch! I hope your next flight crashes in a cannibal country. . . . But I kept this thought to myself as I laughed bitterly and stomped up the empty tunnel to a bank of pay phones in the concourse. It was New York's La Guardia airport, around eight-thirty on a warm Sunday night in the first week of March, and I had just flown in from Chicago—supposedly "with the Muhammad Ali party." But things had not worked out that way and my temper was hovering dangerously on the far edge of control as I listened to the sound of nobody answering the phone in Hal Conrad's West Side apartment. . . . *That swine! That treacherous lying bastard!*

We were almost to the ten-ring limit, that point where I knew I'd start pounding on things unless I hung up very quickly before we got to eleven . . . when suddenly a voice sounding almost as angry as I felt came booming over the line. "Yeah, yeah, what is it?" Conrad snapped. "I'm in a hell of a hurry. Jesus! I was just about into the elevator when I had to come back and answer this goddamn—"

"YOU CRAZY BASTARD!" I screamed, cutting into his gravelly mumbling as I slammed my hand down on the tin counter and saw a woman using the phone next to me jump like a rat had just run up her leg.

"It's *me*, Harold!" I shouted. "I'm out here at La Guardia and my whole

183

story's fucked and just as soon as I find all my baggage I'm going to get a cab and track you down and slit your goddamn throat!"

"*Wait* a minute!" he said. "What the hell is wrong? Where's Ali? Not with *you?*"

"Are you kidding?" I snarled. "That crazy bastard didn't even know who I *was* when I met him in Chicago. I made a GODDAMN FOOL OF MYSELF, Harold! He looked at me like I was some kind of *autograph hound!*"

"No!" said Conrad. "I told him all about you—that you were a good friend of mine and you'd be on the flight with him from Chicago. He was *expecting* you."

"Bullshit!" I yelled. "You told me he'd be traveling alone, too. . . . So I stayed up all night and busted my ass to get a first-class seat on that Continental flight that I knew he'd be catching at O'Hare; then I got everything arranged with the flight crew between Denver and Chicago, making sure they blocked off the first two seats so we could sit together. . . . Jesus, Harold," I muttered, suddenly feeling very tired, "what kind of sick instinct would cause you to do a thing like this to me?"

"Where the hell is Ali?" Conrad shouted, ignoring my question. "I sent a car out to pick you up, *both* of you!"

"You mean *all* of us," I said. "His wife was with him, along with Pat Patterson and maybe a few others—I couldn't tell, but it wouldn't have made any difference; they *all* looked at me like I was weird; some kind of psycho trying to muscle into the act, babbling about sitting in Veronica's seat. . . ."

"That's impossible," Conrad snapped. "He knew—"

"Well, I guess he *forgot!*" I shouted, feeling my temper roving out on the edge again. "Are we talking about *brain damage,* Harold? Are you saying he *has no memory?*"

He hesitated just long enough to let me smile for the first time all day. "This could be an *ugly* story, Harold," I said. "Ali is so punch-drunk that his memory's all scrambled? Maybe they should lift his license, eh? Yeah, let's croak all this talk about comebacks, Dumbo. Your memory's fucked, you're on Queer Street—and by the way, Champ, what are your job prospects?"

"You son of a bitch," Conrad muttered. "Okay. To hell with all this bullshit. Just get a cab and meet us at the Plaza. I should have been there a half-hour ago."

"I thought you had us all booked in the Park Lane," I said.

"Get moving and don't worry about it," he croaked. "I'll meet you at the Plaza. Don't waste any time."

"WHAT?" I screamed. "What am I doing *right now?* I have a *Friday deadline,* Harold, and this is Sunday! You call me in the middle of the goddamn night in Colorado and tell me to get on the first plane to Chicago because Muhammad Ali has all of a sudden decided he wants to talk to me—after all that lame bullshit in Vegas—so I take the *insane* risk of dumping my whole story in a parachute bag and flying off on a two-thousand-mile freakout right in the middle of a deadline crunch to meet a man in Chicago who treats me like a wino when I finally get there. . . . And now you're talking to *me,* you pigfucker, about WASTING TIME?"

I was raving at the top of my lungs now, drawing stares from every direction—so I tried to calm down; no need to get busted for public madness in the airport, I thought; but I was also in New York with no story and no place to work and only five days away from a clearly impossible deadline, and now Conrad was telling me that my long overdue talk with Ali had once again "gone wrong."

"Just get in a cab and meet me at the Plaza," he was saying. "I'll pull this mess together, don't worry. . . ."

"Well . . ." I said. "I'm already here in New York and I definitely *want to see you,* Harold—so yeah, I'll be there. But"—I paused for a moment, fascinated by a scene that was suddenly running very vividly behind my eyeballs as I stood there at the pay phone in the concourse—"let me *tell* you what I'm going to do at noon tomorrow, if you *don't* pull this mess together."

"Not now," he said. "I have to get going—"

"Listen!" I yelled. "I want you to *understand* this, Harold, because it could do serious things to your image."

Silence.

"What I plan to do when I wake up in the Plaza at exactly eleven o'clock tomorrow morning," I said calmly, "is have a few Bloody Marys and then go down to the hotel drugstore and buy some of those sheer pantyhose, along with a black wig and some shades like yours, Harold. . . . Then I'll go back up to my room and call the *Daily News* to say they should have a photographer at the Plaza fountain exactly at noon for a press conference with Ali and ing wizard and executive spokesman for Muhammad Ali.

"And *then,* Harold," I continued, "exactly at noon I will leave my room in the Plaza, wearing nothing but a pair of sheer pantyhose and a wig and black shades . . . and I will take the elevator down to the lobby and *stroll* very casually outside and across the street and climb *into the Plaza fountain,* waving a bottle of Fernet Branca in one hand and a joint in the other . . . And I'll be SCREAMING, Harold, at anybody who gets in my way or even stops to stare."

"Bullshit!" he snapped. "You'll get yourself locked up."

"No," I said. "I'll get *you* locked up. When they grab me I'll say I'm Hal Conrad and all I wanted to do was get things organized for the upcoming Ali-Arum press conference—and then you'll have a new picture for your scrapbook, a front-page shot in the *News* of 'famous boxing wizard Harold Conrad.'"

I suddenly saw the whole scene in that movie behind my eyes. I would intimidate anybody in the elevator by raving and screeching at them about things like *"the broken spirit"* and *"fixers who steal clothes from the poor."* That, followed by an outburst of deranged weeping, would get me down to the lobby where I would quickly get a grip and start introducing myself to everybody within reach and inviting them all to the press conference in the fountain . . . and then, when I finally climbed into the water and took a real stance for the noon/lunch crowd, I could hear myself screeching, "Cast out VANITY! Look at me—I'm not VAIN! My name is Hal Conrad and I feel *wonderful!* I'm *proud* to wear pantyhose in the streets of New York—*and so is Muhammad Ali.* Yes! He'll be here in just a few moments, and he'll be dressed *just like me. And Bob Arum, too!*" I would shriek, "He's not ashamed to wear pantyhose."

The crowd would not be comfortable with this gig: there was not much doubt about that. A naked man in the streets is one thing, but the sight of the recently dethroned Heavyweight Champion for the World parading around in the fountain, wearing nothing but sheer pantyhose, was too weird to tolerate.

Boxing was bad enough as it was, and wrestling was worse; but not even a mob of New Yorkers could handle such a nasty spectacle as this. They would be ripping up the paving stones by the time the police arrived.

"Stop threatening me, you drunken freak," Conrad shouted. "Just get in a cab and meet me at the Plaza. I'll have everything under control by the time you get there—we'll go up to his room and talk *there.*"

I shrugged and hung up the phone. Why not? I thought. It was too late to catch a turnaround flight back to Colorado, so I might as well check into the Plaza and get rid of another credit card, along with another friend. Conrad was *trying;* I knew that—but I also knew that this time he was grasping at straws, because we both understood the deep and deceptively narrow-looking moat that eighteen years of celebrity forced Ali to dig between his "public" and his "private" personas.

It is more like a *ring* of moats than just one, and Ali has learned the subtle art of making each one seem like the last great leap between the intruder and himself. . . . But there is always *one more moat* to get across, and not many curious strangers have ever made it that far.

Some people will settle happily for a smile and joke in a hotel lobby, and others will insist on crossing two or even three of his moats before they feel comfortably "private" with The Champ . . . But very few people understand how many rings there really are:

My own quick guess would be Nine; but Ali's quick mind and his instinct for public relations can easily make the third moat *seem* like the ninth; and this world is full of sporting journalists who never realized where they were until the same "private thoughts" and "spontaneous bits of eloquence" they had worked so desperately to glean from The Champ in some rare flash of personal communication that none other would ever share, appeared word for word, in cold black type, under somebody else's byline.

This is not a man who *needs* hired pros and wizards to speak for him; but he has learned how to use them so skillfully that he can save himself for the rare moments of confrontation that *interest* him. . . . Which are few and far between, but anybody who has ever met Muhammad Ali on that level will never forget it. He has a very lonely sense of humor, and a sense of himself so firmly entrenched that it seems to hover, at times, in that nervous limbo between Egomania and genuine Invulnerability.

There is not much difference in his mind between a challenge *inside* the ring, with Joe Frazier, or in a TV studio with Dick Cavett. He honestly believes he can handle it all; and he has almost two decades of evidence to back him up, at this point; so it takes a rare sense of challenge to get him cranked up. He has coped with everything from the White Heavies of Louisville to Sonny Liston and the War of Vietnam; from the hostility of old/white draft boards to the sullen enigma of the Black Muslims; from the genuine menace

of Joe Frazier to the puzzling threat of Ken Norton . . . and he has beaten every person or thing that God or even Allah ever put in his way—except perhaps Joe Frazier and the Eternal Mystery of Women. . . .

And now, as my cab moved jerkily through the snow-black streets of
Brooklyn toward the Plaza Hotel, I was brooding on Conrad's deranged plot that I felt would almost certainly cause me another nightmare of
professional grief and personal humiliation. I felt like a rape victim on the
way to a discussion with the rapist on the Johnny Carson show. Not even Hal
Conrad's fine sense of reality could take me past Moat #5—which would
not be enough, because I'd made it clear from the start that I was not especially interested in anything short of at least #7 or 8.

Which struck me as far enough, for my purposes, because I understood
#9 well enough to know that if Muhammad was as smart as I thought he
was, I would never see or even smell that last moat.

THE TRUE MEANING OF GONZO. . . . DEATH TO THE WEIRD

"My way of joking is to tell the truth. That's the funniest joke in the world."
—Muhammad Ali

Indeed. . . . And that is also as fine a definition of "Gonzo Journalism" as
anything I've ever heard, for good or ill. But I was in no mood for joking
when my cab pulled up to the Plaza that night. I was half-drunk, fully
cranked, and pissed off at everything that moved. My only real plan was to
get past this ordeal that Conrad was supposedly organizing with Ali, then
retire in shame to my eighty-eight-dollar-a-night bed and deal with Conrad
tomorrow.

But this world does not work on "real plans"—mine or anyone else's—so
I was not especially surprised when a total stranger wearing a *serious* black
overcoat laid a hand on my shoulder as I was having my bags carried into the
Plaza:

"Doctor Thompson?" he said.

"What?" I spun away and glared at him just long enough to know there
was no point in denying it. . . . He had the look of a rich undertaker who had

once been the light-heavyweight karate champion of the Italian Navy; a *very quiet* presence that was far too heavy for a cop. . . . He was on *my* side.

And he seemed to understand my bad nervous condition; before I could ask anything, he was already picking up my bags and saying—with a smile as uncomfortable as my own: "We're going to the Park Lane; Mister Conrad is waiting for you. . . ."

I shrugged and followed him outside to the long black limo that was parked with the engine running so close to the front door of the Plaza that it was almost up on the sidewalk . . . and about three minutes later I was face-to-face with Hal Conrad in the lobby of the Park Lane Hotel, more baffled than ever and not even allowed enough time to sign in and get my luggage up to the room. . . .

"What took you so goddamn long?"

"I was masturbating in the limo," I said. "We took a spin out around Sheepshead Bay and I—"

"Sober up!" he snapped. "Ali's been *waiting* for you since ten o'clock."

"Balls," I said, as the door opened and he aimed me down the hall. "I'm tired of your bullshit, Harold—and where the hell is my luggage?"

"Fuck your luggage," he replied as we stopped in front of 904 and he knocked, saying, "Open up, it's *me.*"

The door swung open and there was Bundini, with a dilated grin on his face, reaching out to shake hands. "Welcome!" he said. "Come right in, Doc—make yourself at home."

I was still shaking hands with Bundini when I realized where I was— standing at the foot of a king-size bed where Muhammad Ali was laid back with the covers pulled up to his waist and his wife, Veronica, sitting next to him: They were both eyeing me with very different expressions than I'd seen on their faces in Chicago.

Muhammad leaned up to shake hands, grinning first at me and then at Conrad: "Is this *him?*" he asked. "You sure he's safe?"

Bundini and Conrad were laughing as I tried to hide my confusion at this sudden plunge into unreality by lighting two Dunhills at once, as I backed off and tried to get grounded . . . but my head was still whirling from this hurricane of changes and I heard myself saying, "What do you mean—*Is this him?* You bastard! I should have you *arrested* for what you did to me in Chicago!"

Ali fell back on the pillows and laughed. "I'm sorry, boss, but I just couldn't *recognize* you. I knew I was supposed to meet *somebody,* but—"

"Yeah!" I said. "That's what I was trying to *tell* you. What did you think I was *there* for—an autograph?"

Everybody in the room laughed this time, and I felt like I'd been shot out of a cannon and straight into somebody else's movie. I put my satchel down on the bureau across from the bed and reached in for a beer. . . . The pop-top came off with a hiss and a blast of brown foam that dripped on the rug as I tried to calm down.

"You *scared* me," Ali was saying. "You looked like some kind of bum— or a hippie."

"What?" I almost shouted. *"A bum? A hippie?"* I lit another cigarette or maybe two, not realizing or even thinking about the gross transgressions I was committing by smoking *and* drinking in the presence of The Champ. (Conrad told me later that *nobody* smokes or drinks in the same room with Muhamad Ali—and Jesus Christ! Not—of all places—in the sacred privacy of *his own bedroom at midnight,* where I had no business being in the first place.) . . . But I was mercifully and obviously ignorant of what I was doing. Smoking and drinking and tossing off crude bursts of language are not *second* nature to me, but *first*—and my mood, at that point, was still so mean and jangled that it took me about ten minutes of foulmouthed raving before I began to get a grip on myself.

Everybody else in the room was obviously relaxed and getting a wonderful boot out of this bizarre spectacle—which was *me;* and when the adrenaline finally burned off I realized that I'd backed so far away from the bed and into the bureau that I was actually *sitting* on the goddamn thing, with my legs crossed in front of me like some kind of wild-eyed, dope-addled budda (Buddah? Buddah? Budda? . . . Ah, fuck these wretched idols with unspellable names—let's use *Budda,* and to hell with Edwin Newman) . . . and suddenly I felt just fine.

And why not?

I was, after all, the undisputed heavyweight Gonzo champion of the world—and this giggling yoyo in the bed across the room from me was no longer the champion of *anything,* or at least nothing he could get a notary public to vouch for. . . . So I sat back on the bureau with my head against the mirror and I thought, "Well, shit—here I am, and it's definitely a weird place to be; but not *really,* and not half as weird as a lot of other places I've been. . . . Nice view, decent company, and no *real* worries at all in this tight group of friends who were obviously having a good time with each other as the conversation recovered from my flaky entrance and got back on the fast⁄break, bump⁄and⁄run track they were used to . . .

Conrad was sitting on the floor with his back to the big window that looks out on the savage, snow⁄covered wasteland of Central Park—and one look at his face told me that he was *finished working* for the night; he had worked a major miracle, smuggling a hyena into the house of mirrors, and now he was content to sit back and see what happened. . . .

Conrad was as happy as a serious smoker without a serious smoke could have been right then. . . . And so was I, for that matter, despite the crossfire of abuse and bent humor that I found myself caught in, between Bundini and the bed.

Ali was doing most of the talking: His mind seemed to be sort of wander⁄ing around and every once in a while taking a quick bite out of anything that caught his interest, like a good⁄humored wolverine. . . . There was no talk about boxing, as I recall.

There was a lot of talk about "drunkards," the sacred nature of "unsweet⁄ened grapefruit" and the madness of handling money—a subject I told him I'd long since mastered: "How many acres do you own?" I kept asking him whenever he started getting too high on his own riffs. "Not as many as me," I assured him. "I'm richer than Midas, and nine times as shrewd—whole val⁄leys and mountains of acres," I continued, keeping a very straight face: "Thousands of cattle, stallions, peacocks, wild boar, sloats . . ." And then the final twist: "You and Frazier just never learned how to handle money—but for twenty percent of the nut I can make you almost as rich as I am."

I could see that he didn't believe me. Ali is a hard man to con—but when he got on the subject of his tragic loss of "all privacy," I figured it was time for the drill.

"You really want a cure for your privacy problem?" I asked him, ripping the top out of anotherL Ballantine Ale.

He smiled wickedly. "Sure, boss—what you got?"

I slid off the bureau and moved toward the door, "Hang on," I told him. "I'll be right back."

Conrad was suddenly alert. "Where the hell are you going?" he snapped.

"To my room," I said. "I have the ultimate cure of Muhammad's privacy problem."

"What room?" he asked. "You don't even know where it is, do you?"

More laughter.

"It's 1011," Conrad said, "right upstairs—but hurry back," he added. "And if you run into Pat, we never heard of you."

Pat Patterson, Ali's fearfully diligent bodyguard, was known to be prowling the halls and putting a swift arm on anything human or otherwise that might disturb Ali's sleep. The rematch with [Leon] Spinks was already getting cranked up, and it was Patterson's job to make sure The Champ stayed deadly serious about his new training schedule.

"Don't worry," I said. "I just want to go up to the room and put on my pantyhose. I'll be a lot more comfortable."

The sound of raucous laughter followed me down the hall as I sprinted off toward the fire exist, knowing I would have to be fast or I'd never get back in that room—tonight or tomorrow.

But I knew what I wanted, and I knew where it was in my parachute bag: yes, a spectacularly hideous fullhead, realhair, seventyfivedollar moviestyle red devil mask—a thing so fiendishly *real* and ugly that I still wonder, in moments like these, what sort of twisted impulse caused me to even pack the goddamn thing, much less wear it through the halls of the Park Lane Hotel and back into Muhammad Ali's suite at this unholy hour of the night.

Three minutes later I was back at the door, with the mask zipped over my head and the neckflap tucked into my shirt. I knocked twice, then leaped into the room when Bundini opened the door, screaming some brainless slogan like "DEATH TO THE WEIRD!"

For a second or two there was no sound at all in the room—then the whole place exploded in wild laughter as I pranced around, smoking and drinking through the molded rubber mouth and raving about whatever came into my head.

The moment I saw the expression on Muhammad's face, I knew my mask would never get back to Woody Creek. His eyes lit up like he'd just seen the one toy he'd wanted all his life, and he almost came out of the bed after me. . . .

"Okay," I said, lifting it off my head and tossing it across the room to the bed. "It's yours, my man—but let me warn you that not *everybody* thinks this thing is real funny."

("Especially *black* people," Conrad told me later. "Jesus," he said, "I just about flipped when you jumped into the room with that goddamn mask on your head. That *was* really pushing your luck.")

Ali put the mask on immediately and was just starting to enjoy himself in the mirror when . . . ye Gods, we all went stiff as the sound of harsh knock, ing came through the door, along with the voice of Pat Patterson. "Open up," he was shouting. "What the hell is going on in there?"

I rushed for the bathroom, but Bundini was two steps ahead of me. . . . Ali, still wearing the hideous mask, ducked under the covers and Conrad went to open the door.

It all happened so fast that we all simply *froze* in position as Patterson came in like Dick Butkus on a blood scent . . . and that was when Muham, mad came out of the bed with a wild cry and a mushroom cloud of flying sheets, point one long brown arm and a finger like Satan's own cattle prod, straight into Pat Patterson's face.

And that, folks, was a moment that I'd just as soon not have to live through again. We were all lucky, I think, that Patterson didn't go for his gun and blow Muhammad away in that moment of madness before he recog, nized the body under the mask.

It was only a split second, but it could easily have been a hell of a lot longer for all of us if Ali hadn't dissolved in a fit of whooping laughter at the sight of Pat Patterson's face. . . . And although Pat recovered instantly, the smile he finally showed us was uncomfortably thin.

The problem, I think, was not so much the mask itself and the shock it had caused him—but *why* The Champ was wearing the goddamn thing at all; where had it come from? And why? These were serious times, but a scene like this could have ominous implications for the future—particularly with Ali so pleased with his new toy that he kept it on his head for the next ten or fifteen minutes, staring around the room and saying with no hint of a smile in his voice that he would definitely wear it for his appearance on the Dick Cavett show the next day. "This is the new *me*," he told us. "I'll wear it on TV tomorrow and tell Cavett that I promised Veronica that I won't take it off until I win my title back. I'm gonna wear this ugly thing everywhere I go—

even when I get into the ring with Spinks next time." He laughed wildly and jabbed at himself in the mirror. "Yes indeed!" he chuckled. "They thought I was crazy *before,* but they ain't seen *nothin'* yet."

I was feeling a little on the crazy side myself, at that point—and Patterson's accusing presence soon told us it was time to go.

I agreed, and went upstairs to my room for a bit of the good smoke.

THE ROVING TRIPOD, THE EXPERTS AT THE HILTON BAR. . . .

Muhammad Ali has interested a lot of different people for a lot of very different reasons since he became a media superstar and a high-energy national presence almost two decades ago. . . . And he has interested me, too, for reasons that ranged from a sort of amused camaraderie in the beginning, to wary admiration, then sympathy & a level of personal respect, followed by a dip into a different kind of wariness that was more exasperation than admiration . . . and finally into a mix of all these things that never really surfaced and came together until I heard that he'd signed to fight Leon Spinks as a "warmup" for his $16 million swan song against Ken Norton.

This was the point where my interest in Muhammad Ali moved almost subconsciously to a new and higher gear. I had seen all of Leon's fights in the 1976 Montreal Olympics, and I recall being impressed to the point of awe at the way he attacked and destroyed whatever they put in front of him. I had never seen a *young* fighter who could get away with planting *both* feet and leaning forward when he hooked with either hand.

Archie Moore was probably the last *big* fighter with that rare combination of power, reflexes, and high tactical instinct that a boxer *must* have to get away with risking moments of total commitment even occasionally. . . . But Leon did it *constantly,* and in most of his fights that was *all* he did.

It was a pure *kamikaze* style: The Roving Tripod, as it were—with Leon's legs forming two poles of the tripod, and the body of his opponent forming the third. Which is interesting for at least two reasons: (1) There *is no tripod* until a punch off that stance connects with the opponent's head or body, so the effect of a miss can range from fatal to unnerving, or at the very least it will cause raised eyebrows and even a faint smile or two among the ringside judges who are scoring the fight . . . and (2) If the punch connects solidly, then the tripod is formed and an almost preternatural blast of energy is delivered at the point of impact, especially if the hapless target is leaning as far back on the ropes as he can get with his head ducked in and forward in a coverup stance—like Ali's Rope-a-Dope.

A boxer who plants both feet and then leans forward to lash out with a hook has his whole weight *and also his whole balance* behind it; he cannot pull back at that point, and if he fails to connect he will not only lose points for dumb awkwardness, but he'll plunge his head out front, low and wide open for one of those close-in jackhammer combinations that usually end with a knockdown.

That was Leon's style in the Olympics, and it was a terrifying thing to see. All he had to do was catch his opponent with no place to run, then land one or two of those brain-rattling tripod shots in the first round—and once you get stunned and intimidated like that in the first round of a three-round (Olympic) bout, there is not enough time to recover . . .

. . . or even *want* to, for that matter, once you begin to think that this brute they pushed you into the ring with has no reverse gear and would just as soon attack a telephone pole as a human being.

Not many fighters can handle that style of all-out assault without having to back off and devise a new game plan. But there is not time for devising new plans in a three-round fight—and perhaps not in ten, twelve, or fifteen rounds, either, because Leon doesn't give you much time to think. He keeps coming, swarming, pounding; and he can land three or four shots from *both* directions once he gets braced and leans out to meet that third leg of the tripod.

On the other hand, those poor geeks that Leon beat silly in the Olympics were *amateurs* . . . and we are all a bit poorer for the fact that he was a *light-heavyweight* when he won that Gold Medal; because if he'd been a few pounds heavier he would have had to go against the elegant Cuban heavyweight champion Teofilo Stevenson, who would have beaten him like a gong for all three rounds.

But Stevenson, the Olympic heavyweight champ in both 1972 and '76, and the only modern heavyweight with the physical and mental equipment to compete with Muhammad Ali, has insisted for reasons of his own and Fidel Castro's on remaining the "*amateur* heavyweight champion of the world," instead of taking that one final leap for the great ring that a fight against Muhammad Ali could have been for him.

Whatever reasons might have led Castro to decide that an Ali/Stevenson match—sometime in 1973 or '74 after Muhammad had won the hearts and minds of the whole world with his win over George Foreman in Zaire—was not in the interest of either Cuba, Castro, or perhaps even Stevenson himself, will always be clouded in the dark fog of politics and the conviction of people like me that the same low/rent political priorities that heaped a legacy of failure and shame on every other main issue of this generation was also the real reason why the two great heavyweight artists of our time were never allowed in the ring with each other.

This is one of those private opinions of my own that even my friends in the "boxing industry" still dismiss as the flaky gibberish of a half/smart writer who was doing okay with things like drugs, violence, and presidential politics, but who couldn't quite cut the mustard in *their* world.

Boxing.

These were the same people who chuckled indulgently when I said, in Las Vegas, that I'd take every bet I could get on Leon Spinks against Muhammad Ali at ten to one, and with anybody who was seriously into numbers I was ready to haggle all the way down to five to one, or maybe even four . . . but even at eight to one it was somewhere between hard and impossible to get a bet down on Spinks with anybody in Vegas who was even a fifty/fifty bet to pay off in real money.

One of the few consistent traits shared by "experts" in any field is that they will almost never bet money or anything else that might turn up in public on whatever they call their convictions. That is why they are "experts." They have waltzed through that mine field of high/risk commitments that separates politicians from gamblers, and once you've reached that plateau where you can pass for an expert, the best way to stay there is to hedge all your bets, private and public, so artistically that nothing short of a thing so bizarre that it can pass for an "act of God" can damage your high/priced reputation . . .

I remember vividly, for instance, my frustration at Norman Mailer's refusal to bet money on his almost certain conviction that George Foreman was too powerful for Muhammad Ali to cope with in Zaire. . . . And I also recall being slapped on the chest by an Associated Press boxing writer in Las Vegas while we were talking about the fight one afternoon at the casino bar in the Hilton. "Leon Spinks is a *dumb midget*," he snarled in the teeth of all the other experts who'd gathered on that afternoon to get each other's fix on the fight.

"He has about as much chance of winning the heavyweight championship as *this guy*."

"*This guy*" was me, and the AP writer emphasized his total conviction by giving me a swift backhand to the sternum . . . and I thought: "Well you *dumb* loudmouth cocksucker, you're going to remember that stupid mistake as long as you live."

And he will. I have talked to him since, on this subject, and when I said I planned to quote him *absolutely verbatim* with regard to his prefight wisdom in Vegas, he seemed like a different man and said that if I was going to quote him on his outburst of public stupidity that I should at least be fair enough to explain that he had "been with Muhammad Ali for so long and through so many wild scenes that he *simply couldn't go against him on this one*."

Well . . . how's *that* for equal time? It's a hell of a lot more than you pompous big-time bullies ever even thought about giving me, and if you want to add anything else, there's always the Letters to the Editor page in [*Rolling Stone*]. . . . But the next time you whack some idle bystander in the chest with one of your deeply felt expert opinions, keep in mind that you might hit somebody who will want to insist on betting real money.

THE BROWN JAY GATSBY. . . . A DOOMED GENERATION

"No Vietcong Ever Called Me 'Nigger.'"

Muhammad Ali said that, back in 1967, and he almost went to prison for it—which says all that needs to be said right now about justice & gibberish in the White House.

Indeed. And that's all we need to say on this strange tangent, too. What began as a quick note on Muhammad Ali and the harsh techniques of boxing has gone totally amok, and I still haven't written the lead for this goddamn thing. . . . But the evil beeping of that filthy mojo wire is telling me, now, that maybe I should get back on the story: no more fun, no more of these high speedy runs and queer memories. . . . So let's get this rotten outburst over with and move on to something else.

Some people write their novels and others roll high enough to live them and some fools try to do both—but Ali can barely read, much less write, so he came to that fork in the road a long time ago and he had the rare instinct to find that one seam in the defense that let him opt for a third choice: He would get rid of words altogether and live his own movie.

A brown Jay Gatsby—not black and with a head that would never be white: He moved from the very beginning with the same instinct that drove Gatsby—an endless fascination with that green light at the end of the pier. He had shirts for Daisy, magic leverage for Wolfsheim, a delicate and danger-ously vulnerable Ali-Gatsby shuttle for Tom Buchanan, and no answers at all for Nick Carraway, the word junkie.

There are two kinds of counter punchers in this world—one learns early to live by his reactions and quick reflexes—and the other, the one with a taste for high rolling has the instinct to make an aggressor's art of what is essen-tially the defensive, survivor's style of the Counter Puncher.

Muhammad Ali decided one day a long time ago not long after his twenty-first birthday that he was not only going to be King of the World *on his own turf,* but Crown Prince on *everybody else's.* . . .

Which is very, very *High* Thinking—even if you can't pull it off. Most people can't handle the action on whatever they chose or have to call their own turf; and the few who can, usually have better sense than to push their luck any further.

That was always the difference between Muhammad Ali and the rest of us. He came, he saw, and if he didn't entirely conquer—he came as close as anybody we are likely to see in the lifetime of this doomed generation.

Res Ipsa Loquitor.

[May, 1978]

Please note that this piece has been edited for this volume and does not appear in its entirety.

THE FOURTH ALI

ISHMAEL REED

In the films *Mandingo* and *Drum* former WBA Heavyweight Champion Ken Norton plays a slave boxer, moving through scenes, his flesh handled by people who have such intense feelings for him they wish to stab him or boil him in a pot. The women want to ball him, and the men want to do battle with him; some people want to do both.

The Heavyweight Champion of the World is, most of all, a grand hunk of flesh, capable of devastating physical destruction when instructed by a brain, or a group of brains. I'm not saying he's stupid. He may be brilliant, but even his brilliance is used to praise his flesh.

The Heavyweight Championship of the World is a sex show, a fashion show, scene of intrigue between different religions, politics, class war, a gathering of stars, ex-stars, their hangers-on and hangers-on's assistants.

It's part Mardi Gras with New Orleans jazz providing the background for the main events while the embattled Be-boppers, led by former Sonny Rollins and Ornette Coleman sideman Earl Turbington, held forth in one of the restaurants facing the Hilton's French Garden bar.

Driving into town on Route 61 past the authentic Cajun music and food joints, motels with imitation French-styled balconies, car lots—heading on Canal Street toward Decatur, I heard Dick Gregory on the car radio. A saint of the prime flesh movement was naming "Carlos," a New Orleans man, as a conspirator in JFK's assassination. Gregory was one of Ali's advisers, though an insider told me that Ali didn't pay attention to Gregory's nutritions.

In the evening, Mayor Ernest N. Morial, New Orleans' "black" mayor, who'd be considered white in most parts of the world, gave a reception at the Fairmont Hotel honoring Muhammad Ali and Leon Spinks. I walked into the lobby toward a big room on the first floor. There was a commotion behind the door. The first man to exit was Ali. I was standing face-to-face with a $100 million industry which included everything from candy bars to a forthcoming automobile capable of traveling across the desert. He was huge and awesome looking, but not the "Abysmal Brute" Jack London had pined after. "Hi, Champ," I said. I shook hands with the black man they let beat up Superman.

He was followed by his wife, Veronica ("Veronica belongs to me," he said later). A procession followed the couple to the upstairs ballroom, the whole scene illuminated by photographers' flashbulbs. I fell in behind them. When Ali reached the top of the escalator I heard a loud exchange between Ali and a figure who was coming down. It was Joe Frazier. He would sing "The Star Spangled Banner" before the fight and perform at the Isaac Hayes victory show at the Hilton Friday night.

Ali has so much control over his body he can turn the juice on and off. In contrast to the somber and downcast-looking fighter I'd seen emerge from the downstairs room, with whom I was alone for about fifteen seconds, the upstairs Ali began to shuffle up and down the stage, jabbing at invisible opponents, dancing, all the while speaking rapidly. He doesn't have the brittle dry irony of Archie Moore or the eloquent Victorian style of the bookish Jack Johnson, but he is more effective because he speaks to Americans in American images, images mostly derived from comic books, television, and folklore. To be a good black poet in the sixties meant capturing the rhythms of Ali and Malcolm X on the page. His opponents were "Mummies" and "Vampires"; he was "The Man from Shock." In his bitter press conference he discussed "The Six Million Dollar Man." His prose is derived from the trickster world of Bugs Bunny and Mad Comics. The world of Creature Features. Thus, after victory, he was able to get a whole room of grown and worldly men and women to chant with him; "Mannnnnnnnn, Mannnnnnnnn. That's gone be the new thing," he said, "Mannnnnnnnn."

"I don't know what to say," he said. "Where's the champ? If he stays out of jail, I'll get his tail." Ali referred to [Leon] Spinks as a "nigger," then caught himself to explain that "niggers can say niggers, but white folks can't," which is as good an answer as any to the man running for office in Alabama who requested that he have the same right to say "nigger" as "the Jews" and "the niggers."

When the question-and-answer period came, I had my hand up and so he pointed to "the young man over there." I was on his side after that.

"Mr. Ali, do you plan to run for Congress as the *Nation* magazine has suggested?"

"No, I plan to run for vice president, that way the President won't get shot." He called himself the "Savior of Boxing," and predicted that he'd punch Spinks out of the ring. "Spinks," he said, "will become the first spook satellite." He flirted with the ladies and praised his body.

Dick Gregory followed Ali with some familiar jokes about Spinks's arrest for driving without a license and possessing $1.98 worth of cocaine (St. Louis cocaine). Gregory strongly believes that the coke was planted on Spinks. "Why did they alert the press before he was brought into the station?"

I asked Gregory to repeat what he'd said on the radio, that the killers of JFK resided in New Orleans. I figured that since the mayor and the police were on the stage the conspirators would be arrested, immediately. The laughter vanished. The mayor and Ali stood silently. Dick Gregory refused to discuss it.

During the broadcast he urged black-Italian cooperation. "If the Mafia is so big," he said, "why won't Henry Ford invite it to his next garden party?"

After Ali left, Gregory came over to the bar where I was standing. The black waiters, dressed in black bow ties and green satinish jackets, weren't serving beer or wine, so I asked for what Gregory was drinking. Vodka and orange juice. UMMMMMM.

Thursday, hundreds of people were pushing into the Grand Ballroom for the official weigh-in ceremonies. Bright, unnatural lights from the television cameras. Total confusion. People were standing on chairs, craning their necks to see celebrities. It was ten fifty-five when Angelo Dundee arrived. He looks like a mild-mannered math teacher at a boys' high school. Jimmy Ellis, who has a teenager's bright face, and Ali's brother, Rahaman—whom I mistakenly called Rudolph Valentino Clay—following. He could have been Valentino standing against the pillar in the French Garden bar, dressed in a white suit.

The platform was so full of the press that it began to reel. Arum threatened to cancel the press conference. I see Don King.

He is followed by Ali, toothpick in mouth, and Veronica Ali. A man next to me says, "Ali is the best-known person in the world." Ali weighs in at 221 pounds, Spinks 201. I'm tempted to bid.

After the weigh-in I asked former Light Heavyweight Champion of the World Jose Torres to assess Ali's chances. Torres was pessimistic. He'd seen Ali work out and he didn't like his color. "Too gray." He thought Ali's eyes

were "dead," and that he was bored. "Ali no longer enjoys fighting and de-
spises training," Torres said. "I want Ali to win for nostalgic reasons." He
liked Spinks. "The more criticism he gets the more I like him," Torres said.
Leroy Diggs, Spinks's bodyguard and sparring partner, standing behind
Torres, said that Spinks looked real good.

I saw Don King's famous crown poking above the crowds in the aisle,
moving and mashing their bodies against each other. He was blandly prais-
ing Ali but at the same time voiced hope that he would retire. He said that
Ali was the most identifiable man in the world. "Strong on the inside as well
as the outside." He praised Larry Holmes, "The other champion," in a short
speech dotted with words like "cognizant." The most frequent adjective people use in talking about King is "flamboyant."

I went up to the second floor to inquire about my credentials. A white-
haired Norman Mailer was standing in the middle of the room. I met him in
1962 at Stefan's and had gone to a couple of his parties. Gone were the pug
breaks and the frantic fast-talking. He seemed at peace. We exchanged greetings.

I asked Mailer who was going to win. He gave me one of those answers for
which he has a patent. "Ali. He's worked the death out." So had Mailer.

The packed press bus headed for the Superdome at four o'clock. I felt
sorry for the working press. I thought about the newspapers they worked for.
The cities they had to return to. I was standing next to Ed Cannon, a Muslim
reporter who was wearing a sweater which read "There Is No God Greater
Than Allah." That night he was hassled on the floor by a "famous movie
star." The Superdome resembled a giant concrete jaw jutting out at the end of
the street. Soon we were inside the jaw. There were a lot of police. After one
round a few rows of state troopers gave Ali a standing ovation. Spinks
looked like the kind of guy who'd say "motherfucker, kiss my ass," as they put
the handcuffs on him. The seats were of red and blue hues and extended to
the roof of the building. Strobe lights blinked on and off. Processions of flag
bearers headed up and down the aisle.

One blue flag carried the letters "Moron." Nobody would believe me. I
asked Nick Browne of the *Soho News,* who was sitting next to me, to examine
the flag through his binoculars and sure enough it said "Moron." After the
chaotic weigh-in there had been a threat to call out the National Guard. Fistfights broke out on the floor during the bouts.

All during the fights, even the championship fights, people were entering and exiting. "They don't care about this crowd," somebody said, "what they care about is television." Over two hundred million people watched the fight.

As the main event approached fistfights began to really break out, "over bets" I was told. About six rows of state troopers spilled over one another just to stop two guys. It was like a rowdy 1890s audience which used to hurl liquor bottles at the actors, or mercilessly heckle politicians on the stump.

Sylvester Stallone, Joe Frazier, and Larry Holmes had entered the ring, Holmes receiving a few boos, but much less than the governor of Louisiana received when he was introduced. Isaac Hayes did a disco version of "America the Beautiful," and Joe Frazier sang "The Star Spangled Banner," grimacing as if in pain. Somebody seated beneath me said, "I ain't gonna stand." When Ali entered he was mobbed. He was alternately lifted and buried by the crowd. His party seemed to sway from side to side and as they moved him down the aisle the crowds pressed in for a souvenir of The Greatest's flesh.

"My thing was to dance, come right out and start moving, win the first, win the second, win the third, get away from the ropes, dance, do everything I know how to do. Get my body in shape so that it could do what my brains tell me. The fight's almost over, if you lose eight rounds, you lose the whole fight—so after I won about ten rounds, naturally, the opponent gets frustrated. He can't win unless he knocks me out, and I get more confident," was the way Ali described his victorious strategy at a later press conference. He fought the way the pros said he had to fight in order to win. "He cut out that Rope-a-Dope bullshit," as one old-timer said to me.

His left jabs worried Spinks silly, and Spinks looked like a brawler, engaged in a St. Louis street fight, the most vicious east of the Mississippi. His trainer, George Benton, left his corner during the fight, in frustration at the amateurs Spinks had at ringside yelling to him "wiggle, Leon, wiggle." Arguments broke out among them over who should give Spinks advice. Spinks was twenty-five, lacked craftsmanship, was a sensational head-hunter. I remember a trainer at an exhibition fight pleading with Spinks to go for the opponent's body. Ali had followed the advice Archie Moore had given to an Old Man in the Ring. "You hone whatever skills you have left."

A reporter from the *Washington Evening Star* told me that it was Ali's most serious fight in three years. At the end of the fifteenth round there was no doubt in my mind that Ali had won, and so I headed for the dressing room without hearing the decision. Veronica Ali, Jayne Kennedy, members of the family, boxing people, and show business personalities were watching a small TV set as the decision was being announced. Stallone entered, and John Travolta was standing off to the side chatting with some people. I asked Liza Minnelli, who was standing in front of me, wearing a red dress, what she thought of the fight. She thought it was "sensational."

As soon as Ali left the ring, the crowd began swaying and moving like a papier-mâché dragon, moving through the interview room to the dressing room. When Ali finally entered it was impossible to gain entrance unless you were a celebrity or an important member of the Champ's entourage. "Make way for Wyatt Earp," they said when Hugh O'Brien walked by.

Congratulations were going all around as well-wishers entered the dressing-room area. Ali's brother was standing in the middle of the room chanting Muslim phrases. In English he kept repeating, "He said he's from the world of shock." Ali had told the inner circle that he would surprise everybody and he was from the world of shock. I decided that the silence among his aides that afternoon was not due to sullenness but to gloom. Ali had to cheer them up.

I caught up with Dick Gregory. Gregory said he was surprised that the fight went as long as it did. "It was a lesson for the world, a health and body lesson. If you take the physical body God has given you and purify it, there's nothing that the body won't do for you. Anything made by the universal force won't get old. That's what it was, with the right mineral balance and combination of nutrients you can make it." I overheard one of the trainers remark, "He did six thousand calisthenics. Six thousand. No athlete has ever done that."

But then there was something unique about Ali. Bob Arum had put his finger on it. He argued that "elements of deterioration" had set in during Ali's layoff, just as they had to Louis during his army stint, and Jack Johnson after his exile abroad. But then he spoke of Ali's regenerative capacities. He said he'd seen three Alis—the Supreme Court victory, the victory over Frazier, the defeat of George Foreman—and that Ali might win if he had a fourth Ali in him. That night in the Superdome we'd seen a fourth Ali.

He had his skills, he had his personality, and he had the will; what else did he have at ringside? Spinks's manager, George Benton, mentioned a "mysti-

cal force guiding Ali's life. . . ." After the Zaire fight, George Foreman's corner complained that Foreman didn't fight the fight that was planned. That he
seemed distracted. After Spinks lost he said that his "mind wasn't on the
fight." Was an incredible amount of "other" energy in Ali's corner? His de-
votion to Allah is well known.

It was a "mystical" night. The Superdome audience had watched a man
turn the clock back, a rare event. I noticed pigeons inside, circling the Superdome, flying above the heads of the crowd.

Spinks's six-door white Lincoln Continental was brought up by a bald
man, wearing dark glasses and an earring, named Mr. T. He was surrounded
by a few people including his brother Michael. Spinks waved at some people
who stood on a balcony. Nobody waved back. Somebody announced that
Ali was holding a press conference upstairs. He was seated, flanked by Veronica Ali and Jayne Kennedy, the actress, who resembled each other so they
could be sisters.

"Immona hold it six months. I'm going to go all over the world. Do you
know what I did? I was great in defeat, can you imagine how great I am now?
How many endorsements, how many movies, how many commercials I will
get? I was great when I lost fights. I got eight months I can hold my title . . . mannnnnn. See how big I am? Can you imagine what will happen if
I walk down the street in any city?

"Do you know I danced fifteen rounds with a twenty-five-year-old boy?
I'm thirty-six years old. Man, do you realize how great I am now? The doctor
checked my temperature and my blood, and took it to the hospital, and told
Dick Gregory what I needed. Do you know how my stamina was up? Do
you know what he told me to do?

"Take honey and ice cream thirty minutes before the fight. Half a pint of
ice cream and five or six spoonfuls of real honey. My doctor told me to eat ice
cream and honey. He gave me a big hunk of honey and melted ice cream. I
didn't get tired. Did you see me explode all during the fight? I said, go!

"I'm the three-time champion. I'm the only man to win it three times. The
greatest champion of all time. [Audience: "Of all time."] Of all time. Was
I pretty? [Man in audience: "You was pretty."] Was I moving? Was I fighting?
Was I sticking? Was I a Master?

The political, cultural, and entertainment establishments were rooting for
Ali. His victory would be seen as another sign of sixtomania now sweeping

the country because, even though some of his most heroic fights occurred in the seventies, he would still remind us of the turbulent decade, of Muslims, Malcolm X, Rap Brown, the Great Society, LBJ, Vietnam, General Hershey, dashikis, afros, Black Power, MLK, RFK. He represented the New Black of the 1960s, who was the successor to the New Negro of the 1920s, glamorous, sophisticated, intelligent, international, and militant.

The stars were for Ali, but the busboys were for Spinks. They said he lost because he was "too wild." His critics claimed that he drank in "New Orleans dives," where the stateside Palestinians hang out—the people the establishment has told to get lost. The people who've been shunted off to the cities' ruins where they live next to abandoned buildings.

They could identify with Spinks. If they put handcuffs on him for a traffic offense, then they do the same thing to them. If he was tricked into signing for a longer period in the armed forces than he thought, the same thing happens to them. For seven months, he was "The People's Champ."

Ali and his party left the stadium, with people lined up on each side to say farewell to the champion. The night before, the streets were empty, but now they were crowded, reminding one of the excitement among the night crowds in American cities during the 1930s and 1940s, or when the expositions were held in St. Louis and Washington. The black players' bars were filling up. The traffic was bumper to bumper. Hundreds were standing outside the Hilton, or standing body to body inside of the hotel. In the French Quarter, many more moved down Bourbon Street as the sounds of B. B. King and Louis Armstrong came from the restaurants and bars. Every thirty-six-year-old had a smile on his face.

[September, 1978]

Please note that this piece has been edited for this volume and does not appear in its entirety.

THE 1980S

"The difference between fighters of today and in my day is that they all look the same. There's nothing that sets them apart. . . . Even the talent stays at the same level."

—*Muhammad Ali quoted in Rebekah K. Brown,*
"The Press Box," in the Michigan Chronicle, *December 16, 1989*

"I'm a spiritual man. I believe in God. I believe in Islamic faith, Allah, so I believe that he controls destinies. If something as serious as a cut means the fight's gotta stop, I thank God, and accept the extemporary causes that have prevented me from getting it. My skin is not so brittle, I'm not so old. People crazy, 38 years old, that's not an old man. It's old if you drink liquor, I don't drink; it's old if you smoke nicotine, I don't smoke; it's old if you're carousing with women, which I don't; it's old if you eat pork flesh, the wrong foods, see, so my body's not a 35- or 38-year-old body. I'm a Superman."

—*Q and A: Muhammad Ali, "Heavyweight in a Larger Ring,"*
in Maclean's, *July 7, 1980*

"That's what I've been sitting here trying to figure out."

— *Muhammad Ali, on being asked what he planned to do*
in retirement after his loss to Larry Holmes from
"Muhammad Ali's Biggest Mistake,"
by A. S. Doc Young, in Sepia,
December 1980

SPORT INTERVIEW
MUHAMMAD ALI

JOSE TORRES

The first time I saw him was in 1960. He was Cassius Clay then and he was standing in a Toledo, Ohio, boxing ring.

"Hey," he yelled to the crowd, feigning amazement. "Do you know who that man is? That's Hosay Torres. I am surely the greatest and the prettiest of the heavyweights, but this man is the prettiest middleweight around." He went on that night to win the light heavyweight amateur championship, but he impressed no boxing man in the place.

History lurched ahead and Cassius Clay became Muhammad Ali who became the greatest heavyweight champion in history. His performance in and out of the ring transcended pugilism and conventional politics. He became the antithesis of the traditional American hero, but a hero all the same.

At thirty-nine, Ali is returning to the ring. Perhaps. He hopes to meet Trevor Berbick in the Bahamas this December for a reported $500,000 purse. It is at the same time surprising and predictable, like the man himself.

Recently, he called my house. My wife answered.

"Who is calling?" she asked.

"The greatest fighter in the history of the world."

Some things never change.

Sport: Why are you coming back to the ring? Do you need the money?

Ali: People ask me, "Champ, why you doing it? Why?" I say, why does man go to the moon? I say, because it's there. Why did those blind people climb that mountain? Because it was there. Why am I fighting for the title for a fourth time? Because it's there. No man but me has ever won it three times. No man has ever had a chance to do it four times. "Champ, you may get hurt. Champ, don't do it," they say. Most people can only see as far as their eyes can see. I can see farther than most humans.

Sport: How so?

Ali: The Vietnam War. Didn't I take the stand when it was unpopular? Wasn't I right? I changed my name to Muhammad Ali. Aren't black kids changing their names today? I was the first to talk in boxing. Now all boxers talk. They're writing poems, doing the shuffle, clowning in the ring, using my gimmicks, giving interviews. They never did that until someone who could see farther came along.

Sport: Is money playing any role in your comeback?

Ali: Yes, part of it. But the main thing in my idea of coming back is to go down in history. Regardless of how much money I get, nothing can buy history. To be four-time champion is greater than all the money in the world to me.

Sport: But you had that chance with Larry Holmes.

Ali: I had a bad night with Holmes. We all have them. Look at Roberto Duran. He quit. He threw up his hands and quit! Did they make him stop? Did they deny him the right to box? He came back. Look at Ken Norton. He got knocked down and came back. Frazier got knocked out—look at Joe Frazier, he's coming back and he's been knocked out a couple of times.

Sport: But people are also criticizing Joe Frazier for coming back. What people see is that you're almost forty years old.

Ali: I'll tell you about age. Age is a number. Being a Muslim, to me age is not important. I don't drink, smoke, move in fast circles. My body is equivalent to that of a thirty-two- or thirty-three-year-old.

Sport: What do you think of the idea of getting up early to do roadwork?

Ali: I can still do the same things I used to do, but I have to plan better. I just can't do things on the spur of the moment. We have to work, longer, not harder. Where it used to take four weeks to get into shape, now it takes twelve. Instead of running three miles a day, I might just run two miles, but for a longer time. Instead of boxing twelve rounds in a gym with the speed bag, heavy bag, ropes, and shadowboxing, now I might cut to eight rounds. And instead of working one month straight in the gym, going twelve rounds, I might work six weeks doing eight rounds. You have to take a little out, put a little in, change this, change that.

Sport: Looking back now, what would you have done differently to prepare for the Holmes fight?

Ali: I wouldn't have lost weight as quick as I did. I was on a crash diet, sometimes not eating. I was taking thyroid pills because I wasn't feeling too good and I was told my thyroid wasn't producing right. I would change that. I'd run more, do more roadwork, because I didn't run a lot. And I'd box more; I didn't box enough.

Sport: What will happen to your comeback if you don't beat Berbick?

Ali: It's a risk, it's a gamble, but it's according to how I go down. If I lose a close decision and I'm not hurt, it won't be that bad. Holmes beat me. But he didn't hurt me, he didn't knock me down, they didn't count me out. They didn't pull him off me. I was in the corner and we were debating whether to go one more round.

Sport: You once told me, "I don't want to quit like Sugar Ray Robinson, I don't want to quit like Joe Louis, I don't want to go out broke and beaten." You said you will know when to quit. Do you still think that way?

Ali: Naturally. That's why I'm coming back. I lost against Holmes. If I don't come back, that will be the last image, I'm just coming back to show that I was off that night. My main desire is to have a couple of fights that will lead to a championship fight.

Sport: If you never fought again, in what shape would you be financially?

Ali: The interest on the money I have and the things I have going would take care of me well, and my family, too.

Sport: Do you feel you still have the coordination to fight?

Ali: I don't have the same coordination I had when I fought Frazier in my twenties. But I was so super then, so fast, so unreal. I still have a little over the best man you got in there, just a little bit.

Sport: People talk about your speech. They say you used to speak more clearly. Are you aware of any deterioration there?

Ali: Only when I'm tired. When I got tired they caught me in a couple of instances where I was slurring my speech. I was lazy, didn't feel like talking. But right now, as I'm talking to you this moment, I'm sure you can tell that I'm talking as good and as proper as anybody that's been hit on the head.

Sport: Is your wife, Veronica, in favor of your return?

Ali: She would rather I didn't. But if I fight, if I want to, she's with me.

Sport: Would you encourage your son to be a fighter?

Ali: No.

Sport: Why not?

Ali: Too dangerous. Too savage. Too risky. I want him to be educated and be a doctor or lawyer. Or an interpreter, to speak the truth and learn many languages. Or a government official or a politician. Anything but sports, because that was my life's history.

Sport: In the ring you pull back from punches, which is wrong technically. You also carry your hands down and expose your jaw, as if you are daring your opponent. And your punches to the body are almost nonexistent. Nevertheless, you were probably the greatest of all heavyweights. Were you con-sciously defying the rules of boxing?

Ali: I consciously defied the so-called right rules of boxing—keeping your guard up. I had my hands down because that would suck a man in, make him come to me. I was faking, I was opened up, but I could pull back just enough—like radar. I would judge my distance and leave him about an inch out of his range. He would throw a punch and I'd move back another inch and he'd miss me by two inches and I'd look for the counter. I did it and I still do it deliberately. But not just anybody can do it.

Sport: Do you feel more comfortable with boxers or with sluggers?

Ali: I felt more comfortable fighting sluggers. Sluggers don't move and run. They walk into you. Gerry Cooney is a slugger. Joe Frazier was a slugger. George Chuvalo was a slugger. They are easier for me because they come to you; you don't have to run after them.

Sport: What was your greatest disappointment in the ring?

Ali: The first loss to Joe Frazier. I lost the championship after the layoff. I had never lost before.

Sport: Have you ever been afraid in the ring?

Ali: I've never been in fear of a fighter, but I've been afraid of all the things involved in the outcome of a fight. I knew that if I lost, I would lose a lot of money for future fights as well as prestige and influence, and that humiliation would be in store. I fear death. I didn't fear getting beat or getting hurt by the man. In the Holmes fight, for example, I feared the outcome of how I per-formed, not the man himself.

Sport: I think fear is part of boxing, it is what keeps you alert.

Ali: I don't call it fear, I call it being scared to death.

Sport: Do you feel anger when you are in the ring?

Ali: No, I never feel anger because it causes frustration, and when you are frustrated you can't think like you would if you were cool and calm. You can't get excited and panic or get angry, you have to stay cool and calm in order to think better.

Sport: You always said that you were "the greatest," but you never said that you were "the perfect one." What was the biggest mistake you ever made as a man?

Ali: The biggest mistake I ever made was when I made the statement that I had no quarrels with the Viet Cong. I made it too early. I was right, but I should have said it later.

Sport: If you wanted to reveal a flaw in your character, what would it be?

Ali: It's been too easy for people to put one over on me because of my working on feelings, not brains, being too weak with people, not checking things out.

Sport: Compare the qualities of Cassius Clay with those of Muhammad Ali.

Ali: The basic quality of Cassius Clay was believing in himself, having confidence, living a clean life, training like he should. Doing all the things a boxer should do, obeying all the rules of boxing. What really pushed Muhammad Ali was the change of his name, joining the Islamic faith, believing in his religion, praying to God sincerely.

Sport: There is a federal investigation into boxing and there are rumors that promoter Don King might be indicted and that boxing is going to be cleaned up. Are you in favor of this?

Ali: If they have facts, if something is wrong, if they have some kind of proof and can make a case, I think it should be brought to light. I can't imagine Don King or Robert Arum doing something wrong. With as much money as they make on top, they would have no reason to do something wrong under the table.

Sport: Harold Smith ran Muhammad Ali Professional Sports. How do you feel about his troubles with the law?

Ali: All I know is good about him. He's done so much good for kids and amateur boxing. I never noticed nothing crooked or shady, and it's hard for me to believe he's involved deliberately with robbing a bank of $21 million. I think that if he was guilty, by now he would have run and got out of the country. He's free, nobody's watching him. But it's something for the courts to decide.

Sport: If you were a federal boxing commissioner, what would you do about the current state of the sport?

Ali: If I was a man of power in boxing, I would make *one* organization. No WBA and WBC. I'd have one championship. And those like Don King and Bob Arum, as long as they were clean and honest, I'd welcome them to the game, to keep promoting, because they're helping boxing.

Sport: What will happen to Muhammad Ali once he makes the decision to retire from boxing?

Ali: My mind is made up to promote the Islamic religion and be an evangelist for Islam. That's all I want. Like Billy Graham is a Christian evangelist, I want to be an Islamic evangelist. I won't be making no movies. I don't want nothing to do with sports. I want nothing except to raise my eight children and be with my beautiful wife.

Sport: If you become champion again, will you quit right away?

Ali: I have about seven more years. I'm not finished yet. I plan to retire at forty-seven. They all think I'm through now, but I'm just getting started.

Sport: Why are you smiling when you say that?

Ali: Because I'm lying!

Sport: What do you have to prove?

Ali: I don't have to fight. It's not important to prove nothing, but I want to do it. I want them to believe. How do you know I'm serious? I'm not back yet. Who knows, I could be bluffing the whole world. I could just be getting all this publicity.

Sport: What do you say to critics who think you won't make it past Berbick?

Ali: All those who don't think I can make it, watch. Keep your eyes open, keep listening to your radio and your television. Watch me return! Don't tell me I can't do it. This is why we got problems in the world, mainly among American minority groups. Mothers and fathers tell their kids, "You'll never be nothing." Kids have a hard time in school, they drop out. People quit too easy. I'm not a quitter. I shall return!

[December, 1981]

Please note that this piece has been edited for this volume and does not appear in its entirety.

MUHAMMAD ALI IS THE MOST FAMOUS MAN IN THE WORLD

BOB GREENE

It was the voice that was shocking.

"How much you going to pay me?"

The voice was slurry, blurred, almost a whisper. Coming over the long-distance line, the words seemed to be filled with effort.

I said that as far as I knew, *Esquire* did not pay people who were written about in the magazine. In any event, this was a special sort of issue; fifty men and women from the past fifty years had been selected as the most influential of their time. He was one of them. The magazine wanted to include him in the issue.

"You're just using me to sell magazines," Muhammad Ali said. The voice was fading. "You just want to put me on the cover."

No, I said, Ali would not be on the cover. But he would be in very good company.

"I'm the most famous man in the world," the voice said.

I said that there would be other famous people in the issue; people, perhaps, as famous as he.

"Who?" Ali said.

I said that some of the others were John F. Kennedy, Franklin D. Roosevelt, Martin Luther King.

"They're all dead," Ali said.

I waited for American Airlines' Flight 184 from Los Angeles to arrive at Chicago's O'Hare International Airport. Ali's manager, Herbert Muhammad, had told me that Ali would be on board, and then would be switching to another flight to Washington, D.C. Ali would be addressing a rally of Muslims in Washington.

Herbert Muhammad had said he could not guarantee that Ali would speak with me; it would be up to him. He said that if I wanted to take a chance I should pack a bag, buy a ticket to Washington, and be at the gate when Ali's plane arrived.

So I sat on a chair directly next to where the jetway opened into the terminal. The plane was a few minutes early. About a dozen passengers disembarked, and then came Ali. He was wearing a gray suit; he wore no belt with the pants. The suit was expensive, but his brown shoes were worn and scuffed.

I walked up to him and introduced myself. He did not look at me, but he said: "Where's Herbert?" The voice was as soft and fuzzy as it had been on the phone.

I said I didn't know; I said the Washington flight would be leaving in forty-five minutes from a gate just down the corridor.

Ali removed his suit jacket. Even though it was a frigid winter day, he was wearing a short-sleeve blue shirt. He began to walk toward the next gate.

The scene in the airport was like one of those brokerage commercials in which everyone freezes in place. I have traveled with celebrities before; I had never seen anything like this. Everyone—everyone—stopped in their tracks when they caught sight of Ali. He was considerably heavier than in the days when he had been fighting; now, in 1983, he had just turned forty-one, and his hair was flecked with gray. But there was no question about his recognition factor; each pair of eyes stared at him, each mouth silently formed the word "Ali."

"Champ, you're the greatest there ever was," a man cried. Ali walked past him, not looking.

"Where's Herbert?" his voice said again.

I said again that I didn't know. A woman—she was middle-aged, well dressed, not eccentric-looking in the least—caught sight of Ali and dropped to her knees in front of him, as if praying. He stepped around her.

I led him to the proper gate. We took seats in the boarding area. He was carrying a briefcase; actually, it was bigger than that, more like a salesman's sample case. He opened it and took out a book called *The Spectre of Death, Including Glimpses of Life Beyond the Grave.*

He opened the book. He leaned over to me and began reading aloud from it, but so softly that I could barely make out the words:

"Life will soon come to an end, and we will part with the comforts. Whenever you see a dead man being led to the grave, remind yourself that one day you will also meet your end. . . .

I asked him what else he had in the salesman's case. He began to rummage through it; the contents looked like something in a bag lady's sack. Pamphlets, old photographs, receipts, scraps of paper—the case was chock-full. He pulled out a copy of the Bible and opened the cover. There was an autograph I could not quite make out.

"Oral Roberts," he whispered.

A woman was standing in front of us. Her young daughter—she said that the girl's name was Clarice, and that she was six—was with her. The woman shoved the girl gently in Ali's direction. The girl kissed Ali on the cheek.

"She's not real, real friendly," the mother said. Ali, saying nothing, stood up and kissed the mother on the cheek, too.

"See," the mother said to her daughter, "now you met somebody great."

A man named Joseph Loughry, manager of international banking programs for General Electric Information Services in Rockville, Maryland, stopped in front of Ali. "I have a little guy named James," Loughry said. Ali, not looking up, not saying anything, accepted a piece of paper from Loughry, and wrote on it: "To James from Muhammad Ali."

Loughry said some words of thanks to Ali, but Ali neither spoke to him nor looked at him. When he walked away, Ali said to me: "The least little thing we do, God marks it down. Each little atom, He sees. On the day of judgment, all the good and all the bad will be weighed. Every leaf that falls from a tree, God sees. Think of all the trees."

A man was sitting behind us, in a chair facing the other way. "Watch me do this," Ali said. He rubbed his thumb and first two fingers together in a way that resulted in a cricket sound. He turned around, placed his fingers next to the man's ear, rubbed the fingers together, and made the sound. By the time the man turned around, Ali was looking away, as if nothing had happened. But then he did it to the man again. The man jerked his head to the side. He rubbed his ear. When he had gone back to his newspaper, Ali reached back again, made the cricket sound with his fingers again.

The man stood up and looked around. But Ali was talking to me again, as if nothing had happened. I said something about him being treated as a "super figure."

"Super nigger?" Ali said.

"Figure," I said. "Super figure."

"I know," he said. "I heard you the first time. I was just joking. I don't know about 'super figures.' But I do know that I am the most famous person in the world."

"Are you sure?" I said.

"Who's more famous?" Ali said.

"What about Reagan?" I said.

"Be serious," Ali said. "If Reagan were to go to Morocco or Persia, he could walk down the street and no one would bother him. If I go there, they have to call out soldiers to guard me. I can't go outside."

"Why?" I said.

"What do you mean 'why'?" Ali said.

"Why you?" I said. "You were a great boxer, But all of this other stuff . . . why you?"

"I don't know," he said. "I'm not smart. I'm dumber than you are. I can't spell as good as you. I can't read as good as you. But people don't care. Because that shows I'm a common person, just like they are."

At that moment a woman named Pam Lontos interrupted us. She handed Ali a business card; the card indicated that she was the president of a sales motivation firm based in Dallas, and that she made motivational speeches.

"Have you ever done any motivational talks about how to believe in yourself?" she said to Ali.

He did not speak, did not look at her.

"I'd like to talk to you about making public speeches," she said. "Are you with any booking agency? I think you'd be amazed at how much money you can make for just forty-five minutes' work. You can make just a ton of money."

Ali still did not look up at her.

"The booking agency I'm with handles David Brinkley and Norman Vincent Peale," she said. " Wouldn't you like to make a lot of money just by getting up and talking?"

"I talk for free," Ali said. "For God."

Just then Herbert Muhammad arrived. Ali's manager was a rotund man wearing a fur cap. "Ali, where have you been?" he said. "I've been looking all over the terminal for you."

The gate agent announced that the flight was boarding; Pam Lontos walked away and we got in line to get on the plane. There was a businessman in front of us. Ali reached forward, put his fingers next to the man's ears, and make the cricket noise. When the man turned around, Ali was looking in another direction.

We sat in the first row of first class on the right side of the plane. Ali was by the window; I was on the aisle. Other passengers were filing on. Ali didn't seem to be paying any attention to them, but then he said to me, "I have to do something."

He climbed over me. He reached for a man who was heading back into the coach section. He tapped the man on the shoulder.

"Psst," Ali said.

The man turned around. His face frozen at the sight of Ali. Ali pointed to the floor of the plane, where a ticket envelope lay.

"You dropped something," Ali said.

"Why . . . why, thank you," the man said.

But Ali had already turned away. He walked up to the cockpit. He bent over slightly and ducked inside. He tapped the pilot on the shoulder.

The pilot and the first officer and the flight engineer looked up in wonder. Ali nodded at them. Then he turned and came back toward his seat by the window. Before he could get there, though, a flight attendant who was struggling to lift a carton onto the overhead rack said to him: "Would you like to put that up there? You have more muscles than me."

Silently Ali put the box away. He slid past me. Another flight attendant leaned over and said: "Would you like a cocktail or a soft drink after we take off?"

"Milk," Ali said, so softly that the woman could not hear.

"I beg your pardon?" she said.

"Milk," Ali said, looking straight forward.

We taxied out onto the runway. As we picked up speed and then lifted off, Ali said to me: "You never know when your time to die will come."

About five minutes into the flight, he turned to me and said, "I'm not going to say anything to you for a while. It's time for me to pray." He held up his wrist; he was wearing a fancy watch with a floating arrow inside.

"This is a Muslim prayer watch," Ali said. "We have to pray at different times during the day. An alarm goes off every time I have to pray. The arrow is always pointing toward Mecca."

"Where'd you get it?" I asked.

"The king of Saudi Arabia gave it to me," he said. "He was wearing it on his arm and he took it off and gave it to me. I was wearing a Timex before." He closed his eyes, as if in prayer.

When he opened his eyes, he said to me: "My desire, my main goal now, is to prepare myself for the hereafter. That should be all men's goal."

"But what about life right now?" I said.

"This life is not real," Ali said. "I conquered the world, and it didn't give me satisfaction. The boxing, the fame, the publicity, the attention—it didn't satisfy my soul.

"Who could be more popular? Who could achieve greater heights? It's all nothing unless you go to heaven. You can have pleasure, but it means nothing unless you please God."

A man who had been sitting across the aisle unbuckled his seat belt and came over to us. He was William Doré, the president of Global Divers & Contractors, Inc., in Lafayette, Louisiana.

"Ali," he said, "I want to shake your hand. I made twelve dollars on you when you fought against Sonny Liston."

"Is that all?" Ali said.

"I only bet three," Doré said.

Ali was looking away by now.

"It's been a pleasure to watch you over the years," Doré said. "You've done a lot for the game."

When Doré had returned to his seat, Ali said to me: "Boxing was nothing. It wasn't important at all. Boxing was just meant as a way to introduce me to the world."

But he was interrupted in midthought. Pam Lontos, the motivational speaker, had come up from the coach section; she was kneeling in the aisle, and she was pushing a brochure at Ali. The brochure began: "The basics of broadcast selling help you find your true potential, to turn that potential into profit . . ."

A flight attendant put both hands on Lontos's shoulders. "Ma'am," the flight attendant said, "if you want an autograph, we'll be happy to bring you one back."

"But I don't want an autograph," Lontos said as she was led back into coach.

Ali was sniffling. He seemed to be getting the beginnings of a cold. He took the small pillow from behind my head, tore a piece from its paper casing, and blew his nose. In a moment he was sleeping.

We were approaching Washington. Ali tapped me on the shoulder. He pointed out the window. The lights of the monuments and government buildings were below.

"What do you think of that?" he said.

"It's pretty," I said.

"Look at all those lights on all those houses," he said. "Those are all my fans. Do you know I could walk up to any one of those houses, and knock on the door, and they would know me?

"It's a funny feeling to look down on the world and know that every person knows me. Sometimes I think about hitchhiking around the world, with no money, and just knocking on a different door every time I needed a meal or a place to sleep. I could do it."

We walked into Washington's National Airport. A group of Muslims were waiting in the concourse for Ali; they were sponsoring the rally he had come to address.

We walked toward the baggage claim area. There was an immediate difference in Ali. On the airplane, even though his voice had still been slurred and vague, his mind and his attention had appeared to be fairly sharp. In here, though—with every person calling to him and stopping to gaze at him—he seemed to put himself back into the same sort of trance he had apparently been under back at O'Hare. His eyes glazed over; he looked at no one; his face took on a blank, numb expression. As the voices spoke his name, this grew more marked.

All I could think of was: He's not punch-drunk in the traditional sense.

He's not woozy from being hit too many times. Rather, he is suffering from a different kind of continual beating. For twenty years and more, he has been assaulted with constant attention, constant badgering, constant touching, every time he has ventured out in public. That is what he has had too much of—not the fists, but the nonstop contact from strangers. Clearly it had done something to him; and what it had done was most noticeable when he was in the midst of more onslaughts.

He moved through the crowds. His eyes stayed unfocused. Only once did he speak. A man stepped right in front of him. The man talked not to Ali, but me. He said: "Hey, ask Ali if he can still fly like a butterfly and sting like a bee."

"Float," Ali whispered, not looking at the man. "Float like a butterfly."

There was screaming and shouting as Ali was led to a car waiting outside. We were driven by one of the Muslims to a Holiday Inn downtown. It was not one of Washington's fancier hotels. Ali's suite was on the far end of the seventh floor.

The manager of the hotel, Thomas Buckley, was waiting for Ali in the living room of the suite. "Is there anything I can do for you?" Buckley said.

Ali's cold seemed to be getting worse. "How do you make it hotter in here?" Ali said.

Buckley went to the thermostat and adjusted its lever. "I'm in the service business," Buckley said.

Ali's eyes still seemed to be somewhere else. His voice was barely decipherable.

"Service to others is the rent you pay for your room in heaven," he said.

In the morning, Ali sat in the hotel's coffee shop with Herbert Muhammad and several of the Washington-based Muslims. He wore the same suit he had been wearing the day before. His address at the Muslim rally was not for another day; today he had been scheduled to appear at several inner-city schools.

"Herbert," Ali said, his voice as soft as it had been the day before, "what does Allah give you credit for?"

"What do you mean?" Herbert Muhammad said.

"Well," Ali said, "if you help an old lady across the street, does Allah give you credit for that?"

"I'm sure He does," Herbert said. Ali nodded; Herbert turned to me and said, "Ali has a good heart."

Ali had ordered some wheat toast; it was slow in arriving. He reached across the table and took a piece of toast from one of the Muslims' plates. When Ali's toast came, he took the top piece and handed it back to the Muslim.

The woman at the coffee shop's cash register picked up the ringing telephone. She listened for a second, and then came over. "Mr. Ali," she said, "it's for you."

"Who is it?" Ali said, looking at his wheat toast.

"The person said he was Eddie Cantor," the woman said.

Ali stood up and walked to the phone.

"Ali," Herbert called to him before he got there, "who are you going to talk to?"

"Eddie Cantor," Ali said in an emotionless tone.

"Ali," said Herbert, laughing, "Eddie Cantor's dead. If he's calling you I want to hear about it."

Ali picked up the telephone and started talking. As he did, he used his fingers to make the cricket sound next to the ear of the cashier. She looked around, then rubbed her ear furiously. Ali did it again. She rubbed her ear again.

He came back to the table. I asked him who had been on the phone.

"Eddie Kendricks," he said. "He used to sing with the Temptations."

"How did he know to find you here?" I said.

Ali shrugged. He looked at his Muslim prayer watch, then gave me a signal to be silent. As the others in the coffee shop worked on their breakfasts, he closed his eyes and prayed.

We drove through the streets. At the Sister Clara Muhammad Elementary School, up a flight of stairs in a run-down section of town, Ali stood in front of a class of seventy-five students. He crossed his arms while the children sang to him. Once in a while he motioned back and forth with a finger, as if conducting an orchestra.

"I'm so happy to see all you children," he whispered to them. They were very young; it was obvious that they knew he was an important man, but unclear if they knew precisely who he was.

At Shaw Junior High School, in a modern, low-slung building, faculty members and students ran toward him and pawed at him as he was led to the school auditorium. Lipstick smeared his cheeks from where the female teachers had kissed him.

We were shoved back and forth in a sea of bodies as we tried to get to the stage. The school band was playing; the auditorium was alive with shrieks and shouts.

"This is the whole world," he said to me. "This is what my whole life is like."

He made it to the stage. While the band played the theme from *Rocky* he took a blue comb from his pocket and ran it through his hair.

"Boys and girls," the principal said into the microphone, "being here on this stage with this man is probably the greatest moment of my life. And it should be the greatest moment of your life."

Ali, whose cold had seemed worse all morning, took out a handkerchief. A cook from the school's kitchen yelled, "Muhammad Ali, I love you." Ali blew his nose.

The principal called Ali to the lectern. He said that he wanted the students to ask questions of Ali, but that he wanted to ask the first one himself.

"Muhammad," he said, "would you say your toughest fight was with Frazier?"

"My toughest fight was with my first wife," Ali said.

He talked with the students for about fifteen minutes. On the way out he stopped in front of a couple of boys. Ali began to shadowbox with them, moving his feet back and forth in the famous "Ali Shuffle." The boys held up their hands and backed off. A woman teacher who had not been at the assembly caught sight of him and began to tremble. "Oh, Lord," she said, her eyes wide.

At Cardozo High School, in one of Washington's toughest neighborhoods, police officers stood guard at the front door. The students were gathered in an assembly, but had not been told that Ali was scheduled to come.

So they were listening to another speaker when, unannounced, Ali walked in a back door of the auditorium. First a few of them caught sight of him, then a few more. A buzz moved through the room as he walked, sniffling, down the aisle toward the stage.

By the time he was halfway there the chants had begun: "Ali! Ali! Ali! Ali!"

When he started to speak, though, his voice was so soft and slurred that no one could hear him. They began to call out for him to speak louder; but he didn't seem to notice, he just kept calling them "boys and girls" in that whispered tone.

He asked if there were any questions. A pretty young woman in the front row, who had been visibly puzzled by his slow, quiet, faltering speech pattern, raised her hand, and he pointed at her.

"Are you really Muhammad Ali?" she said.

Ali stared at her. "I'll see you after school," he said. "And tell your boyfriend that if he don't like it, I'll see him after school, too."

A fellow who apparently was her boyfriend stood up. "Fool," Ali said, "I'll see you after school." But beyond the first five or six rows, no one could hear him.

Ali turned to the principal and, with his fists raised, again went into the boxing routine and the Ali Shuffle. The principal shook his head and backed away.

Ali was coughing badly as we arrived at Dunbar High School. He followed wherever the local Muslims led him; in this case, into an administration office.

Ali stood there coughing and wiping his nose, waiting to be instructed where to go next. A female administrator looked up at him and said, "This man is sick. Has anyone called a doctor for him?"

But he was already being taken to a classroom. In the hallway a young mother who was visiting the school ran up to him and handed her baby to him. Ali reached out for the child, but Herbert Muhammad said, "Ali, you have too bad a cold to be handling that baby." Ali handed the infant back.

We moved through the corridors. Children moved to the doors of their classrooms. Ali leaned close to me and said, "They're all mine. This is what Allah has given me. This is heaven in the world." We moved past an elderly man who for some reason was at the school. Ali made the cricket sound with his fingers next to the old man's ear, but the man, apparently hard of hearing, did not react.

We went into the school library. Everyone in the room stopped what they were doing. One boy, though, had his back to us: He was reading at a table, and was immersed in his book.

Ali approached him. He put his hand on the boy's shoulder. The boy looked up and his mouth fell open. He started to say something, but Ali held a finger up to his own mouth, as if to silence the boy.

On the way out of the room, Ali passed by a tall, muscular young man. Ali stopped.

They looked at each other. Then Ali held up his fists. He went into the Ali Shuffle and began to leap about in front of the young man.

The young man did not back off. He held up his own fists. He did not attempt to strike Ali, but neither did he give an inch. He moved with Ali, making it clear that he was not afraid. Ali began to perspire. The young man moved closer. The young man had a confident smile on his face. He started to push Ali, establishing command of the situation.

No one in the room stirred. Ali coughed. The young man brought his punches closer and closer to Ali's face. Their arms began to make contact. The sound of their forearms slapping against each other echoed off the walls, and suddenly there was a clattering sound, and everything stopped.

There, on the yellow carpeting, was Ali's Muslim prayer watch. Ali slowly leaned over. He picked up the watch and fastened it back onto his wrist.

"Come on, Ali," Herbert Muhammad said. "We're running late." They moved toward the door of the school library. Ali's eyes met the eyes of the tall young man for just a moment. Then they clouded over, and once again he seemed to be somewhere else.

[December, 1983]

MUHAMMAD ALI
AT THE RINGSIDE, 1985

WOLE SOYINKA

The arena is darkened. A feast of blood
Will follow duly; the spotlights have been borrowed
For a while. These ringside prances
Merely serve to whet the appetite. Gladiators,
Clad tonight in formal mufti, customised,
Milk recognition, savour the night-off, show-off
Rites. Ill-fitted in this voyeur company,
The desperate arm-wrap of the tiring heart
Gives place to social hugs, the slow-count
One to ten to a snappy "Give-me-five!"
Toothpaste grins replace the death-mask
Rubber gumshield grimaces. Promiscuous
Peck-a-cheek supplants the Maestro's peek-a-boo.
The roped arena waits; an umpire tests the floor,
Tests whiplash boundaries of the rope.
The gallants' exhibition rounds possess
These foreplay moments. Gloves in silk-white sheen
Rout lint and leather. Paco Rabane rules the air.
A tight-arsed soubriette checks her placard smile
To sign the rounds for blood and gore.
Eased from the navel of Bitch-Mother Fame
A microphone, neck-ruffed silver-filigree,
As one who would usurp the victor's garland—stabs the air
for instant prophesies. In cosy insulation, bathed
In tele-glow, the distant homes have built
Their own vicarious rings—the forecast claimed
Four million viewers on the cable deal alone;
Much "bread" was loaded on the scales

At weighing hour—till scores are settled. One
Will leave the fickle womb tonight
Smeared in combat fluids, a broken foetus.
The other, toned in fire, a dogged phoenix
Oblivious of the slow countdown of inner hurts
Will thrust his leaden fists in air
Night prince of the world of dreams.
One sits still. His silence is a dying count.
At last the lens acknowledges the tested
Hulk that dominates, even in repose
The giddy rounds of furs and diamond pins.
A brief salute—the camera is kind,
Discreetly pans, and masks the double‑talk
Of medicine‑men—"Has the syndrome
But not the consequence." Promoters, handlers
It's time to throw in the towel—Parkinson's
Polysyllables have failed to tease a rhyme
From the once nimble Louisville lips.

The camera flees, distressed. But not before
The fire of battle flashes in those eyes
Re‑kindled by the moment's urge to centre‑stage.
He rules the night‑space even now, bestrides
The treacherous domain with thighs of bronze,
A dancing mural of delights. Oh Ali! Ale‑e‑e. . . .
What music hurts the massive head tonight, Ali!
The drums, the tin‑cans, the guitars and mbira of Zaire?
Aa‑lee! Aa‑lee! Aa‑lee Bomaye! Ali Bomaye!
The Rumble in the Jungle? Beauty and the Beast?
Roll‑call of Bum‑a‑Month. The rope‑a‑dope?
The Thrilla in Manila?—Ah‑lee! Ah‑lee!
"The closest thing to death" you said. Was that
The greatest, saddest prophesy of all? Oh, Ali!
Black Tarantula whose antics hypnotise the foe!
Butterfly side‑slipping death from rocket probes
Bee whose sting, unsheathed, picks the teeth

Of the raging hippopotamus, then fans
The jaws' convergence with its flighty wings.
Needle that threads the snapping fangs
Of crocodiles, knots the tusks of elephants
On rampage. Cricket that claps and chirrups
Round the flailing horn of the rhinoceros,
Then shuffles, does a bugalloo, tap-dances on its tip.
Esu with faces turned to all four compass points,
Astride a weather-vane; they sought to trap him,
Slapped the wind each time. He brings a message—
All know the messenger, the neighborhood is roused—
Yet no one sees his face, he waits for no reply,
Only that combination three-four calling-card,
The wasp-tail legend: I've been there and gone.
Mortar that goads the pestle: Do you call that
Pounding? The yam is not yet smooth—
Pound, dope, pound! When I have eaten the yam,
I'll chew the fibre that once called itself
A pestle! Warrior who said, I will not fight,
Yet proved a prophet's call-to-arms against a war.

[1985]

MY DINNER WITH ALI

DAVIS MILLER

I'd been waiting for years. When it finally happened, it wasn't what I expected. But he's been fooling many of us for most of our lives.

Several people had been trying to connect me with him at his farm in Michigan for the previous six months. Yet when I finally got to see him, it wasn't in Michigan and I didn't have an appointment. I simply drove past his mother's house in Louisville. It was midafternoon on Good Friday, April 1, two days before Resurrection Day. A block-long white Winnebago with Virginia plates was parked out front. Though he hadn't often been in town lately, I knew it was his vehicle.

I was certain it was him because I know his patterns and his style. Since 1962, when he has traveled unhurried in this country, he has driven either buses or RVs. And he owns another farm in Virginia. The connections were obvious. Some people study faults in the earth's crust or the habits of storms or of galaxies, hoping to make sense of the world and of their own lives. Others meditate on the life and work of only one social movement or one man. Since I was ten years old, I have been a Muhammad Ali scholar.

I parked my car behind the Winnebago and grabbed a few old magazines and a special stack of papers I'd been storing under the front seat, waiting for the meeting with Ali that I'd been sure would come. Like everyone else, I wondered in what shape I would find The Champ. I'd heard all about his condition and had watched him stumble through the ropes when introduced at recent big fights. But when I thought of Ali, I remembered him as I'd seen him several times years before, when he was luminous. I was in my early twenties, trying to make a living as a kickboxer, and, on one occasion, was fortunate enough to spar with him. I later wrote a couple of stories about the experience and had copies of those with me today, hoping he would sign them.

Yes, in those days he had shone. There was an aura of light and confidence around him. He had told the world of his importance: "I am the center of the universe," he had said, and we almost believed him. But recent reports had Ali sounding like a turtle spilled onto his back.

It was his brother Rahaman who opened the door. He saw the stack of papers and magazines under my arm, smiled an understanding smile, and said, "He's out in the Winnebago. Just knock on the door. He'll be happy to sign those for you." Rahaman looked pretty much the way I remembered him, a little like a black, aging Errol Flynn. There was no indication in his voice or on his face that I would find his brother less than healthy.

I recrossed the yard, climbed the couple of steps on the side of the Winnebago, and prepared to knock. Ali opened the door before I got the chance. He is, of course, a huge man. His presence filled the doorway. He had to lean under the frame to see me.

I felt no nervousness. Ali's face, in many ways, is as familiar to me as my father's. His skin remains unmarked, his countenance has a nearly perfect symmetry. Yet something is different: Ali is no longer the world's prettiest man. This has little relationship to his sickness; it is largely because he is heavier than he needs to be. He remains handsome, but in the way of a youngish granddad who likes to tell stories about how he could have been a movie star, if he'd wanted.

"Come on in," he said and waved me past him. His voice had a gurgle to it, like he needed to clear his throat. He offered his massive hand. His grip was not a grip at all—his touch was gentle, almost feminine. His palm was cool and uncalloused, his fingers were the long, tapered digits of a hypnotist, his knuckles large and slightly swollen. They looked like he had recently been punching the heavy bag.

He was dressed in white: new leather tennis shoes, cotton socks, custom-tailored linen slacks, and short-sleeved safari-style shirt crisp with starch. I told him I thought white was a better color for him than the black he often wears.

He motioned for me to sit, but didn't speak. His mouth was a little tense at the corners; it looked like a kid's who has been forced by a parent or teacher to keep it closed. He slowly lowered himself into a chair beside the window. I took a seat across from him and laid my magazines on the table between us. He immediately picked them up, produced a pen, and began signing them. He asked, "What's your name?" without looking up and when I told him, he continued writing. His eyes were not glazed, as I'd heard, but they looked tired. A wet cough rattled in his throat. His left hand tremored continuously. In the silence around us, I felt a need to tell him some of the things I'd been wanting to say for years.

"Champ, you changed my life," I said. It was true. "When I was a kid, I was messed up, couldn't even talk to people."

He raised his eyes from an old healthy image of himself on a magazine cover.

"You made me believe I could do anything," I said. "Now I'm a writer. I've sold several stories about you. And I've just finished a first novel that you're in."

He was watching me while I talked, not judging, just watching. I picked up a magazine from the stack in front of him. "This is a story I wrote about the ways you've influenced my life."

"What's your name?" he asked again, this time looking right at me. I told him. He nodded. "I'll finish signing these for your in a little while," he said. He put his pen on the table. "Read me your story."

"You have a good face," he said when I was through. "I like your face."

He'd listened seriously as I'd read, laughing at the funny lines and when I'd tried to imitate his voice. He had not been bored. It was a lot more than I could have expected—Muhammad Ali doesn't like to read, but he had listened to, and seemed to enjoy, my story.

"You ever seen any magic?" he asked. "You like magic?"

"Not in years," I said.

He stood and walked to the back of his RV. He moved mechanically. It was my great-grandfather's walk. He motioned for me to follow. There was a sad, yet lovely, noble, and intimate quality to his movements.

He did about ten tricks. The one that interested me the most required no props. It was a very simple deception. "Watch my feet," he said. He was standing about eight feet in front of me, with his back to me and his arms perpendicular to his sides. Then, though he has real trouble walking and talking, he seemed to levitate about four inches off of the floor. He turned to me and in his thick, slow voice said, "I'm *baadd*," and gave me the old easy Ali smile.

I laughed and asked him to do it again; it was a good one. I thought I might like to try it myself, just as twenty years earlier I had stood in front of the mirror in my dad's hallway for hours, pushing my worm of a left arm out at the reflection, trying feebly to imitate Ali's cobra jab. And I had found an old laundry bag, filled it with rags, and hung it from a ceiling beam in the basement. I pushed my left hand into that twenty-pound marshmallow two hundred, three hundred, five hundred times a day, concentrating on speed: dazzling, cracking speed, in pursuit of godly speed—*zing, ting, ding* went the punches on the bag, and I strove to make the three sounds as one (like Ali's), strove to make my fists move quicker than thought, and then I would try to spring up on my toes, as I had watched Ali do: I would try to fly like Ali, bouncing away from the bag and to my left.

After the levitation trick, Ali grabbed an empty plastic milk jug from beside a sink. He asked me to examine it. "What if I make this jug rise up from the sink about this high and sit there? Will you believe?"

"I'm not much of a believer these days, Champ," I said. I wasn't exactly sure what he was selling.

"Watch," he said, pointed at the plastic container, and took three or four steps back. I was trying to see both the milk jug and Ali. He waved his hands a couple of times in front of his body, said, "Arise, ghost, arise," in a foggy-sounding voice. The plastic container did not move from the counter.

"April Fools," Ali said. We both chuckled and he walked over and slipped his arm around my shoulders.

He autographed the stories and wrote a special note on a page of my book-length manuscript I'd asked him to take a look at. "To Davis Miller, The Greatest Fan of All Times," he wrote, "From Muhammad Ali, King of Boxing." I felt my stories were finally complete, now that he had confirmed their existence. He handed me the magazines and asked me into his mother's house. We left the Winnebago. I unlocked my car and leaned across the front seat, carefully placing the magazines and manuscript on the passenger's side, not wanting to take a chance on damaging them or leaving them behind. Suddenly there was a chirping, insectlike noise in my ear. I jumped back, swatted the air, turned around. It had been Ali's hand. He was standing right behind me, still the practical joker.

"How'd you do that?" I wanted to know. It was a question I'd find myself asking several times that day.

He didn't answer, but raised both fists to shoulder height and motioned me out into the yard. We walked about five paces, I put up my hands, and he tossed a slow jab at me. I blocked and countered with my own. Fighters and ex-fighters are always throwing punches at each other or at the air or at whatever happens to be around. It's the way we play. I'd bet Ali must still toss over a hundred lefts a day. He and I had both thrown our punches a full half-foot away from the other, but my adrenal gland was pumping at high gear from being around Ali and my jab had come out fast—it had made the air sing. He slid back a half-step and took a serious look at me. A couple of kids were riding past on bikes; they recognized Ali and stopped.

"He doesn't understand I'm the greatest boxer of all times," he yelled to the kids. He pulled his watch from his arm, stuck it in his pants pocket; he'd get down to business now. He danced to his left a little, loosening up his legs. Just a couple of minutes before, climbing down the steps of his RV, he'd moved so awkwardly that he'd almost lost his balance. I'd wanted to give him a hand, but knew not to. I'd remembered seeing old Joe Louis "escorted" in that fashion by lesser mortals, and I couldn't do that to Muhammad Ali. But now that Ali was on his toes and boxing, he was moving fluidly.

He flung another jab in my direction, a second, a third. He wasn't one-fifth as fast as he had been in 1975, when I'd first sparred with him, but his eyes were alert, shining like black electric marbles, and he saw everything and was real relaxed. That's precisely why old fighters keep making comebacks: We are more alive when boxing than at any other time. The grass around us was green and was already getting high; it would soon need its first cutting. A jay squawked from an oak tree to the left. There were five or six robins around us in the yard. I instinctively blocked all three of his blows, or slid to the side of them, then immediately felt guilty about it, like being fourteen years old and knowing for the first time that you can beat your dad at Ping-Pong. I wished I could stop myself from slipping Ali's jabs, but I couldn't. Reflexive training runs faster and deeper than thought. I zipped a jab to his nose, one to his body, a straight right to the chin, and was dead certain all three would have scored. A couple of cars stopped in front of the house. His mom's is on a corner lot. Two or three more were parked on the side.

"Check out the left," I heard a young-sounding voice say from some-where. I knew the owner of the voice was talking about mine, not Ali's.

"He's in with the triple greatest of all times," Ali was shouting. "Gonna let him tire himself out. He'll get tired soon."

I didn't, but pretended to, anyway. "You're right, Champ," I told him and dropped my hands. "I'm thirty-five. I can't go like I used to."

I held my right hand to my chest, acting out of breath. I looked at Ali; his hand was in exactly the same position. We were both smiling, but he was sizing me up a little.

"He got scared," he shouted. All of the onlookers laughed from their bicycles or through their car windows. Some of them blew their horns and yelled "Hey, Champ!"

"Come on in the house," he said softly in my ear. We walked toward the door, Ali in the lead, moving woodenly through the new grass, while all around us people rolled up their car windows and started their engines.

Ali's family easily accepted me. They were not surprised to have a visitor and handled me with ritualistic grace and charm. It was obvious that many people still come to see Ali when he is in Louisville. Rahaman told me to make myself at home, offered a root beer, and went to get it. I took a seat on the sofa beside Ali's mother, Mrs. Odessa Clay. Mrs. Clay must be in her early seventies, yet her face has few wrinkles. Short, her hair nearly as orange as a hazy Louisville sunset, she is freckled, fragile-looking, and pretty. Ali's face is shaped much like his mother's. When he was fighting she was quite heavy, but she has lost what looks to be about seventy-five pounds over the last ten years.

Mrs. Clay was watching Oprah Winfrey on TV. Ali had disappeared from the room and I was wondering where he had gone. Rahaman brought the drink and a paper napkin and a coaster. Mrs. Clay patted me on the hand. "Don't worry," she said. "Ali hasn't left you here. I'm sure he's just gone upstairs to say his prayers." I hadn't realized my anxiety had shown. But Ali's mother has watched him bring home puppies many times during his sixteen years. "He's always been a restless man. Can't ever sit still." She spoke carefully, with a mother's sweet sadness about her. The dignified clip to her voice must have once been affected, but after cometing all over the globe with Ali, it now sounds genuinely British and Virginian in its inflections.

"Have you met Lonnie, Ali's new wife?" she asked. "He's known her since she was a baby. I'm so happy for him. She's my best friend's daughter, we used to all travel to his fights together. She's a smart girl, has a master's degree in business. She's so good to him, doesn't use him. He told me, 'Mom, Lonnie's better to me than all the other three put together.' She treats him so good. He needs somebody to take care of him."

Just then, Ali came back into the room, carrying himself high and with statesmanly dignity, though his footing was ever-so-slightly unsteady. He fell deep into a chair on the other side of the room.

"You tired, baby?" Mrs. Clay asked.

"Tired, I'm always tired," he said, then rubbed his face a couple of times and closed his eyes.

He must have felt me watching him or was simply conscious of someone other than family being in the room. His eyes weren't closed ten seconds before he shook himself awake, balled his hands into fists again, and started making typical Ali faces and noises at me—grimacing, growling, other playful cartoon kid stuff. After a few seconds he asked, "Y-y-you okay?" He was so difficult to understand that I didn't so much hear him as I conjectured what he must have been saying. "Y-y-you need anything? They taking care of you?" I assured him I was fine.

He made a loud clicking noise by pressing his tongue against the roof of his mouth. Rahaman came quickly from the kitchen. Ali motioned him close and whispered a brief message in his ear. Rahaman went back to the kitchen. Ali turned to me. "Come sit beside me," he said, patting a bar stool just to his right. He waited for me to take my place, then said, "You had any dinner? Sit and eat with me."

"Can I use the phone? I need to call home and let my wife know."

"You got kids?" he asked. I told him I had two. He asked how old. I told him the ages.

"They know me?" he asked.

"Even the two-year-old. He throws punches at the TV whenever I play your old fights."

He nodded, satisfied. "Bring 'em over Sunday," he said, matter-of-factly. "I'll do my magic for 'em. Here's Mom's number. Be sure to phone first."

I called Lynn and told her where I was and what I was doing. She didn't seem surprised. She asked me to pick up a gallon of milk on the way home. I knew she was excited for me but she wouldn't show it in her voice on the phone. In September 1977, when Lynn and I were in college, we skipped class, took most of the money from our bank accounts, drove to New York, and attended the Ali–Earnie Shavers fight at Madison Square Garden. For the rest of the year, we had to live off what little money I was making teaching karate at the university two nights a week. But it was worth it to both of us to have seen Ali in what we knew would be one of his last fights.

Rahaman brought two large bowls of chili and two enormous slices of bread from the kitchen. Ali and I sat at our chairs and ate. He put his face down close to the bowl and the food was gone. Three minutes tops.

The entire time I continued to eat, the telephone was ringing. It was always for Ali. He spent only a few seconds with each caller; he no longer likes to talk to most people on the phone, having to frequently repeat himself to be understood. He handles calls, other than from his immediate family, the same way he deals with being expected to speak in public—he says what he has to say in as few words as possible. His situation is similar to that of a person with a stuttering problem in that he performs much better when he doesn't feel pressured to perform. Between calls, he spoke easily to me.

"Do you know how many people in the world would like to have the opportunity you're getting, how many people would like to come into my house and spend the day with me?" he said. "Haven't fought in seven years and I still get over four hundred letters a week."

I asked how people got this address.

"I don't know," he answered. "Sometimes they come addressed 'Muhammad Ali, Los Angeles, California, USA.' I don't have a house in LA anymore, but the letters still get to me.

"I want to get me a place, a coffee shop, where I can give away free coffee and doughnuts and people can just sit around and talk, people of all races, and I can go and talk to people. Have some of my old robes and trunks and gloves around, show old fight films, call it 'Ali's Place.'"

"I'd call it 'Ali's,'" I said, not believing there would or ever could be such a place, but enjoying sharing his dream with him. "Just 'Ali's,' that's enough. People would know what it was."

"'Ali's'?" he repeated, and his eyes focused inward, visualizing the dream.

"Do you have copies of your old fights?" I asked. He shook his head no. "Well, look," I said, "why don't I go to a video place and see if I can rent some and we can watch them tonight. Would you like that? You want to ride with me?"

"I'll drive," Ali said.

There was a rubber monster mask in the Winnebago and I wore it on my hand on the way to the video store. I pressed the mask against the window at stoplights. A couple of times people in the cars would see the mask, then recognize Ali. Ali wears glasses when he reads and when he drives. When he saw someone looking at him, he'd carefully remove his glasses, place them in his lap, make his hands into fists and put them up beside his head. People would lay on their horns and wave and cheer and shriek and lean out of their car windows.

We rented a tape of his fights and interviews called *Ali: Skill, Brains and Guts* that was directed by Jimmy Jacobs, the great handball champ and fight historian and Mike Tyson's co-manager. Jacobs had died of a deteriorative illness. Ali hadn't known of Jacob's death until I told him. "He was a good man," Ali said. His voice had that same quality that an older person's takes on who daily reads obituaries.

I stopped by my car again on the way back into Mrs. Clay's house. There was one more picture I hoped Ali would sign, but earlier I'd felt I might be imposing on him. It was a facial shot in a biography by Wilfrid Sheed that features hundreds of wonderfully reproduced color plates. I grabbed the book from the car and followed Ali into the house.

When we were seated, I handed him the book and he signed the picture on the title page. I was about to ask if he'd mind autographing the photo I especially wanted, but he turned to page two, signed that picture, then the next page and the next. He continued to sign photographs for about fifteen minutes, writing notes about opponents, wives, parents, Elijah Muhammad, Malcolm X, Howard Cosell, then passing the book to his mother and brother to sign a family portrait. Ali autographed nearly every photo in the book, pointing out special comments as he signed.

I carefully placed the book on a table and excused myself to the bathroom. I locked the door behind me. A pair of Ali's huge black shoes were beside the toilet. The toe of one had been crushed, the other was lying on its side. When I unlocked the door to leave, it wouldn't budge. I couldn't even turn the handle. I knocked. There was laughter from the other room. I yanked fairly hard on the door a couple of times. Nothing.

Finally it easily opened. I caught just a glimpse of Ali bounding into a side room to the right, laughing and high-stepping like some oversized, out-of-shape Nubian leprechaun. I peeked around the corner into the room. He was standing with his back flat against the wall. He saw me, jumped from the room, and began tickling me. Next thing I knew, he had me on the floor, balled-up in a fetal position, with tears flowing down both sides of my face, laughing. Then he stopped tickling me and helped me to my feet.

Everybody kept laughing. Mrs. Clay's face was round and wide with laughter. She looked like the mom of a leprechaun. "What'd you think happened to the door?" Rahaman asked. I told him I figured it was Ali. "Then why are you turning red?" he wanted to know.

"It's not every day," I said, "that I go to Muhammad Ali's, he locks me in the bathroom, then tickles me into submission." Everyone laughed again.

Suddenly I realized the obvious, that all day I'd been acting like a teenage admirer again. And that Muhammad Ali has not yet lost perhaps his highest talent—the ability to transport people past thoughts and words to a world of play. Being around Ali, or watching him perform on TV, has always made me feel genuinely childlike.

We finally slipped the Ali tape into the VCR. Rahaman brought everyone another root beer and we settled back to watch, Rahaman to my left, Ali beside me on the right and Mrs. Clay beside Ali. The family's reactions to the tape were not dissimilar to those you or I would have looking at old home movies or high school annuals. Everyone sighed and their mouths arced at tender angles. "Oh, look at Bundini," Mrs. Clay would say or, "Hey, there's Otis," Rahaman would offer. Whenever there was a film clip of Ali reciting verse, we'd all recite with him. "Those were the days," Rahaman said several times, to which Mrs. Clay would respond, "Yes, yes they were," in a high, lamentative lilt. After a half-hour or so, she left the room. Rahaman continued to watch the tape with us for a while, but then said he needed to be going.

It was just Ali and me. On the TV, it was 1963 and he was framed on the left by Jim Jacobs and on the right by Drew "Bundini" Brown. "They're both dead now," he said, an acute awareness of his own mortality in his tone.

For a time he continued to smile at the old Ali on the screen, but eventually he lost interest in peering at the distant mountains of his youth. "Did my mom go upstairs? Do you know?" he asked.

"Yeah, I think she's probably asleep."

He nodded, stood, and left the room to check on her. When he came back he was moving heavily. His shoulder hit the side of the doorway to the kitchen. He went in and brought out two fistfuls of cookies. Crumbs were all over his mouth. He sat beside me on the sofa. Our knees were touching. Usually when a man gets this close I pull away. He offered me a couple of cookies. When he was through eating, he yawned a giant's yawn, closed his eyes, and seemed to go dead asleep.

"Champ, you want me to leave?" I said. "Am I keeping you up?"

He slowly opened his eyes and was back to our side of The Great Mystery.

The pores on his face suddenly looked huge, his features elongated, dis-torted, like someone's in an El Greco. He rubbed his face the way I rub mine when I haven't shaved in a week.

"No, stay," he said. His voice was very gentle.

"You'd let me know if I was staying too late?"

"I go to bed at eleven," he said.

With the volume turned this low on the TV, you could hear the video-tape's steady whir. "Can I ask you a serious question?" I said. He nodded okay.

"You're still a great man, Champ, I see that, but a lot of people think your mind is fried. Does that bother you?"

He didn't hesitate before he answered. "No, there are ignorant people everywhere," he said. "Even educated people can be ignorant."

"Does it bother you that you're a great man who's not being allowed to be great?"

"Wh-wh-what do you mean, 'not allowed to be great'?" he said.

"I mean . . . let me think about what I mean . . . I mean the things you seem to care most about, the things you really enjoy doing, the things the rest of us think of as *being* Muhammad Ali, those are exactly the things that have been taken from you. It just doesn't seem fair."

"You don't question God," he said.

"Okay, I respect that, but . . . Aw, man, I don't have any business talking to you about this."

"No, no, go on," he said.

"It just bothers me," I told him. I was thinking about the obvious ironies, thinking about Ali continuing to invent, and be invented by, his own late twentieth century mythology. About how he used to talk more easily, maybe better, than anybody in the world; how he often still *thinks* with speed and dazzle, but it takes serious effort for him to communicate even with the people closest to him. About how he may have been the world's best athlete—when just walking he used to have the grace of a cat turning corners; now, at night, he stumbles around the house. About how it's his left hand, the most visible source of his boxing greatness, the hand that won more that 150 fights, it's *his left hand,* not his right, that shakes almost continuously. And I was thinking how his major source of pride, his "prettiness," remains more or less intact. If Ali lost thirty pounds, he would still look classically Greek. Despite not expecting to encounter the miraculous any more than any other agnostic, I'm sort of spooked by the seeming precision with which things have been excised from Ali's life.

"I know why this has happened," Ali said. "God is showing me, and showing *you*"—he pointed his shaking index finger at me and widened his eyes—"that I'm just a man, just like everybody else."

We sat a long quiet time then, and watched Ali's flickering image on the television screen. It was now 1971 and there was footage of him in training for the first Joe Frazier fight. Our Most Public Figure was then The World's Most Beautiful Man and The Greatest Athlete of All Time, his tight, copper-colored skin glowing under the fluorescents, secret rhythms springing in loose firmness from his fingertips.

"Champ, I think it's time for me to go," I said and made an effort to stand.

"No, stay. You my man," he says and pats my leg. It seems almost tragic that he needs company this badly, but it has nothing to do with his illness; he's always been this way, and I take his accolade as the greatest compliment of my life.

"I'll tell you a secret," he says and leans close. "I'm gonna make a comback."

"What?" I think he's joking, hope he is, but something in the way he's speaking makes me uncertain. "You're not serious."

And suddenly there is musk in his voice. "I'm gonna make a comeback," he repeats louder, more firmly.

"Are you serious?"

"The timing is perfect. They'd think it was a miracle, wouldn't they?" He's speaking in a distinct, familiar voice; he is very easy to understand. It is almost the voice I remember from when I first met him in 1975, the one that seemed to come rolling up from deep in his abdomen. In short, Ali sounds like Ali.

"Wouldn't they?" he asks again.

"It *would* be a miracle," I say.

"Nobody'll take me serious at first. But then I'll get my weight down to 215 and have an exhibition at Yankee Stadium or someplace. Then they'll believe. I'll fight for the title. It'll be bigger than the Resurrection." He stands and walks out to the center of the room.

"It'd be good for you to get your weight down," I say.

"Watch this," he says and begins dancing to his left. He is watching himself in the mirror above the TV. His clean white shoes bounce around the room; I marvel at how easily he moves. His white clothing accentuates his movements in the dark room. The white appears to make him glow. Then he starts throwing punches, not the kind he'd tossed at me earlier, but now really letting them zing. I'd honestly thought what he'd thrown in the yard was indicative of what he had left. But what he'd done was allow me to play; he'd wanted me to enjoy myself.

"Look at the TV. That's 1971 and I'm just as fast now." It's true, the old man can still do it. He can still make the fire appear in the air. One second, two seconds, sixteen punches flash in the night. Actually, he looks faster standing in front of me than does the ghostlike Ali images still running on the screen. God, I wish I had a video camera to tape this. Nobody would believe me.

"And I'll be even faster when I get my weight down," he tells me.

"You know more now, too," I find myself admitting. Jesus, what am I saying? This is a sick man.

"Do you believe?" he asks.

"Well . . ." I say. Is this Parkinson's syndrome affecting his sanity? Look at the gray shining in his hair. And Ali throws another three dozen punches at the gods of mortality—he springs a *triple* hook off of a jab, drops straight right leads in multiples, explodes into a blur of uppercuts, and the air pops, and his fists and feet whir. This was his best work. His highest art. When Ali was fighting, he typically held back a little; this is the stuff he seldom chose to use against opponents.

"Do you believe?" he asks, breathing no harder than I would if I'd thrown the punches he's just thrown.

They wouldn't let you, even if you could do it, I'm thinking. There's too much concern everywhere for your health. Everybody thinks they see old Mr. Thanatos waiting for you.

"Do you *believe?*" he asks again.

"I believe," I hear myself say.

He stops dancing and points a magician's finger at me. Then I get the look, the smile, that has closed ten thousand interviews. "April Fools," he says and sits down beside me yet again. He looks confident, relaxed, satisfied, alive. We sit in silence for several minutes. I look at my watch. It's eleven-eighteen. I hadn't realized it was that late. I'd told Lynn I'd be in by eight.

"Champ, I better go home. I have a wife and kids waiting."

"Okay," he says almost inaudibly and yawns the kind of long uncovered yawn people usually do only among family and friends.

He's bone-tired, I'm tired, too, but I want to leave him by saying something that will mean something to him, something that will set me apart from the two billion other people he's met, that will imprint me indelibly in his memory and will make the kind of impact on his life he has made on mine. I want to say the words that will cure his Parkinson's.

Instead I say, "We'll see you Easter, Champ."

He coughs and gives me his hand. "Be cool and look out for the ladies." His words are so volumeless and full of fluid that I don't realize what he's said until I'm halfway out the door.

I don't recall picking up the book he signed, but I must have; it's sitting beside my typewriter now. I can't remember walking across his mom's yard and don't remember starting the car.

I didn't forget Lynn's gallon of milk. The doors to the grocery store whooshed closed behind me. For this time of night, there were quite a few customers in the store. They seemed to move more as floating shadows than as people. An old feeling came across me that I immediately recognized. The sensation was much like going out into the day-to-day world soon after making love for the first time. It was the same sense of having landed in a lesser reality. And of having a secret that the rest of the world can't see. I'd have to wake Lynn and share the memory of this feeling with her.

I reached to grab a milk jug and caught a reflection of myself in the chrome at the dairy counter. There was a half-smile on my face and I hadn't realized it.

[May, 1989]

GREAT MEN DIE TWICE

MARK KRAM

There is the feel of a cold offshore mist to the hospital room, a life-is-a-bitch feel, made sharp by the hostile ganglia of medical technology, plasma bags dripping, vile tubing snaking in and out of the body, blinking monitors leveling illusion, muffling existence down to a sort of digital bingo. The Champ, Muhammad Ali, lies there now, propped up slightly, a skim of sweat on his lips and forehead, eyes closed, an almost imperceptible tremor to his arms and head. For all his claims to the contrary, his surface romance with immortality, Ali had a spooky bead on his future; he never saw it sweeping grandly toward him but bellying quietly along the jungle floor. "We just flies in a room," he liked to say, moving quickly across the ruins of daily life, plane crashes, train wrecks, matricide, infanticide; then after swatting half of humanity, he'd lower his voice and whisper, as if imparting a secret, "We just flies, that's all. Got nowhere to fly, do we?"

Images and echoes fill the room, diffuse and speeding, shot through with ineluctable light and the mythopoeic for so long, the glass darkened to a degree no one thought possible; his immense talent, his ring wisdom, his antipathy for chemicals, argued against destructibility; all he would ever do is grow old. For twenty years, while he turned the porno shop of sports into international theater, attention was paid in a way it never was before or has been since. The crowds were a wonder to behold. Kids scaled the wings of jets to get a glimpse of him; thousands, young and old, tailed him in masses during his roadwork. World leaders marveled at the spell he cast over the crowds. "If you were a Filipino," joked Ferdinand Marcos, "I'd have to shoot you." The pope asked for his autograph; Sure, he said, pointing to a picture, but why ain't Jesus black? A young Libyan student in London sat on his bed, kept him up half the night with dithyrambic visions of Muslim revolution. "Watch, one day you will see," said Muammar Qaddafi. Half asleep, Ali said: "Sheeeet, you crazy." Leonid Brezhnev once dispatched a note to an official at *Izvestia:* "I would like to see more on Muhammad Ali. Who is this man?"

The Ali Watch: how absurd that it would one day drop down here on a little hospital on Hilton Head Island, South Carolina. The nurse dabs his face dry. What is he thinking? Never has his favorite phrase sounded so dis-mally precise: *My, my, ain't the world strange.* If he could root back through the maze of moment and incident, would he find premonitory signs sticking out like dire figurations of chicken entrails? Does he remember King Levinsky, one of the many heavy bags for Joe Louis, in the corridor after the Miami Beach weigh-in? Boldly colored ties draped Levinsky's neck (he sold them on the street), his synapses now like two eggs over-light, in permanent sizzle, as he tried to move into stride with a young Cassius Clay. Over and over, like a one-man Greek chorus, Levinsky croaked, eyes spinning, spittle bubbling from his lips: *"He's gonna take you, kid. Liston's gonna take you, make you a guy sellin' ties. . . . Partners with me kid, ya kin be partners with me."* Does he remember a shadowed evening in his hotel room a day or so after the third Joe Frazier fight, moving to the window, his body still on fire from the assault? He stood there watching the bloodred sun drop into Manila Bay, then took a visitor's hand and guided it over his forehead, each bump sending a vague dread through the fingers. "Why I do this?" he said softly. Does he remember the Bahamian cowbell tinkling the end of his final, pathetic fight, a derisive good-bye sound stark with omen? What is he thinking?

Ali poses a question, his eyes closed, his lips parting as if he were sliding open manhole covers. "You die here . . . they take you home?" he asks. The nurses roll their eyes and smile, struck by his innocence; it has nothing to do, they know, with morbidity. He is not joking, either. The practical aftermath of death seems to stimulate his curiosity these days; nothing urgent, mind you, just something that begins to get in your mind when you're watching blood move in and out of your body for half the day. Though he is very much a mystic, there is a part of Ali that has always found security and a skewed understanding of life in the quantifiable: amounts, calibrated outcomes, the creaking, reassuring machinery of living. The night before in the hotel lounge, with his wife, Lonnie, beside him, bemusedly aghast, he grilled a pleasant waitress until he knew how many tips she got each week, how many children she had, the frequency of men hitting on her, and the general con-tour of her reality. "She have a sad life," he said later. The nurse now cracks with a deadpan expression: "You die, we take you home, Muhammad."

Still, a certain chiaroscuro grimness attaches to their surreal exchange and cries out for some brainless, comic intervention. He himself had long been a specialist in such relief when he would instantly brighten faces during his favorite tours of prisons, orphanages, and nursing homes. When down himself (very seldom), he could count on a pratfall from his hysterical shaman, Drew "Bundini" Brown, on the latest bizarre news from his scheming court, maybe a straight line from some reporter that he would turn into a ricocheting soliloquy on, say, the disgusting aesthetics of dining on pig. No laughs today, though.

"Don't make him laugh," a nurse insisted when leading a writer and a photographer into the room. "Laughing shakes the tubing loose." The photographer is Howard Bingham, Ali's closest friend; he's been with the Champ from the start, in the face of much abuse from the Black Muslims. Ali calls him "the enemy" or "the nonbeliever." His natural instinct is to make Ali laugh; today he has to settle for biting his lower lip and gazing warily back and forth between Ali and his nurses. He doesn't know what to do with his hands. Ali had requested that he leave his cameras outside; just one shot of this scene, of Ali on his back, the forbidding purge in progress, of fame and mystique splayed raw, would bring Bingham a minor fortune. "He doesn't want the world to see him like this," says Howard. "I wouldn't take the picture for a million dollars."

The process is called plasmapheresis. It lasts five hours and is being conducted by Dr. Rajko Medenica. The procedure, popular in Europe, is a cleansing of the blood. Ali is hooked up to an electrocardiograph and a blood-pressure monitor; there is always some risk when blood is not making its customary passage. But the procedure is not dangerous and he is in no pain, we are told. Two things, though, that he surely can't abide about the treatment: the injection of those big needles and the ceaseless tedium. When he was a young fighter, a doctor had to chase him around a desk to give him a shot, and chaotic mobility to him is at least as important as breathing. Bingham can't take his eyes off Ali; the still life of his friend, tethered so completely, seems as incomprehensible to him as it would to others who followed the radiated glow of Ali's invulnerability. The nurses cast an eye at his blood pressure and look at each other. His pressure once jumped twelve points while he watched a TV report on Mike Tyson's street fight with Mitch Green in Harlem. It's rising a bit now, and the nurses think he has to urinate. He can't bear relieving himself in the presence of women; he resists, and his anxiety climbs.

"Ali," one of them calls. His eyes remain closed, his breathing is hardly audible. The nurse calls to him again; no response. "Come on now, Ali," she complains, knowing that he likes to feign death. "Now, stop it, Ali." He doesn't move, then suddenly his head gives a small jerk forward and his eyes buck wide open, the way they used to when he'd made some incoherent claim to lineage to the gods. The nurses flinch, or are they in on the joke, too? Eyes still wide, with a growing smile, he says to the writer, weakly: "You thought I dead, tell the truth. You the only one ever here to see this and I die for ya. You git some scoop, big news 'round the whole world, won't it be?" He leans his head back on the pillow, saying: "Got no funny people 'round me anymore. Have to make myself laugh." The nurse wants to know if he has to urinate. "No," he says with a trace of irritation. "Yes, you do," the nurse says. "Your pressure..." Ali looks over at Lonnie with mischievous eyes. "I just thinkin' 'bout a pretty woman." The nurse asks him what he'd like for lunch. "Give him some pork," cracks Bingham. Ali censures the heretic with a playful stare. Ali requests chicken and some cherry pie with "two scoops of ice cream." He turns to the writer again: "Abraham Lincoln went on a three-day drunk, and you know what he say when he wake up?" He waits for a beat, then says: "I freed whooooooo?" His body starts to shake with laughter. The nurse yells: "Stop it, Muhammad! You'll drive the needles through your veins." He calms down, rasps, "I'll never grow up, will I? I'll be fifty in three years. Old age just make you ugly, that's all."

Not all, exactly; getting old is the last display for the bread-and-circuses culture. Legends must suffer for all the gifts and luck and privilege given to them. Great men, it's been noted, die twice—once as great and once as men. With grace, preferably, which adds an uplifting, stirring Homeric touch. If the fall is too messy, the national psyche will rush toward it, then re-coil; there is no suspense, no example in the mundane. The captivating, as-piring sociopath Sonny Liston had a primitive hold on the equation of greatness. "Clay [he never called him Ali] beeeg now," Sonny once said while gnawing on some ribs. "He flyin' high now. Like an eagle. So high. Where he gonna land, how he gonna land? He gonna have any wings? I wanna see." Sonny, of course, never made it for the final show. Soon after, he checked out in Vegas, the suspicion of murder hovering over the coroner's report.

Who wanted to ask the question back then, or even be allowed to examine in depth its many possibilities? It was too serious for the carnival, immediately at odds with the cartoon bombast that swirled around Ali, the unassailable appeal of the phenomenon, the breathtaking climb of the arc. Before him, the ring, if not moribund, had been a dark, somber corner of sports, best described by the passing sight of then-middleweight-king Dick Tiger, leaving his beat-up hotel wearing a roomy black homburg and a long pawnshop overcoat, a black satchel in his hand, heading for the subway and a title fight at the Garden. But the heavyweight champions—as they always will—illuminated the image sent out to the public. There was the stoic, mute Joe Louis, with his cruising menace; the street fighter Rocky Marciano, with his trade-unionist obedience; the arresting and dogged Floyd Patterson, who would bare his soul to a telephone pole at the sight of a pencil; all unfrivolous men who left no doubt as to the nature of their work.

With the emergence of Muhammad Ali, no one would ever see the ring the same way again, not even the fighters themselves; a TV go, a purse, and a sheared lip would never be enough; and a title was just a belt unless you did something with it. A fighter had to *be;* a product, an event, transcendental. Ali and the new age met stern, early resistance. He was the demon loose at a holy rite. With his preening narcissism, braggart mouth, and stylistic quirks, he was viewed as a vandal of ring tenets and etiquette. Besides, they said, he couldn't punch, did not like to get hit, and seemed to lack a sufficient amount of killer adrenaline. True, on the latter two counts. "I git no pleasure from hurtin' another human bein'," he used to say. "I do what I gotta do, nothin' more, nothin' less." As far as eating punches, he said, "Only a fool wanna be hit. Boxin' just today, my face is forever." Others saw much more. The ballet master Balanchine, for one, showed up at a workout and gazed in wonder. "My God," he said, "he fights with his legs, he actually fights with his legs. What an astonishing creature." Ali's jab (more like a straight left of jolting electricity) came in triplets, each a thousandth of a second in execution. He'd double up cruelly with a left hook (rarely seen) and a razor in a right—and then he'd be gone. Even so, it took many years for Ali to ascend to a preeminent light in the national consciousness. In the sixties, as a converted Black Muslim, he vilified white people as blond, blue-eyed devils. His position on Vietnam—"I ain't got no quarrel with those Vietcong, anyway. They never called me nigger"—was innocent at first, but then taken up as if he were the provocateur of a national crisis. The politicians, promoters, and sweeping sentiment converged to conspire against his constitutional right to work: States barred him from fighting. He resisted the draft and drifted into exile. Three years later he returned, heavier, slower, but with a new kind of fire in his belly. Though he had defeated heavyweight champion Sonny Liston and defended his title nine times, Ali had never had a dramatic constituency before. Now a huge one awaited him, liberals looking for expression, eager literati to put it in scripture, worn-out hippies, anyone who wanted to see right done for once. The rest is history: the two symphonic conflicts with Joe Frazier; the tingling walk with him into the darkness of George Foreman. Then, the Hegelian "bad infinite" of repeating diminishing cycles: retiring, unretiring, the torture of losing weight, the oiling of mushy reflexes. The margins of dominance compressed perilously, and the head shots (negligible before exile) mounted.

Greatness trickled from the corpus of his image, his career now like a gut-shot that was going to take its time before killing. His signing to fight Larry Holmes, after retiring a second time, provoked worried comment. After watching some of Ali's films, a London neurologist said that he was convinced Ali had brain damage. Diagnosis by long distance, the promoters scoffed. Yet among those in his camp, the few who cared, there was an edginess. They approached Holmes, saying, "Don't hurt him, Larry." Moved, Holmes replied: "No way. I love Ali." With compassion he then took Ali apart with the studied carefulness of a diamond cutter; still, not enough to mask the winces at ringside. Ali failed to go the route for the first time in his career. Incredibly, fourteen months later, in 1981, his ego goaded him to the Bahamas and another fight, the fat jellied on his middle, his hand-speed sighing and wheezing like a busted old fan; tropic rot on the trade winds. Trevor Berbick, an earnest plug, outpointed him easily. Afterward, Angelo Dundee, who had trained Ali from the start and had to be talked into showing up for this one, watched him slumped in the dressing room, then turned away and rubbed his eyes as certain people tried to convince Ali that he had been robbed and that a fourth title was still possible.

The public prefers, indeed seems to insist on, the precedent set by Rocky Marciano, who quit undefeated, kept self-delusion at bay. Ali knew the importance of a clean farewell, not only as a health measure but as good commercial sense. His ring classicism had always argued so persuasively against excessive physical harm, his pride was beyond anything but a regal exit. But his prolonged decline had been nasty, unseemly. Who or what pressured him to continue on? Some blamed his manager, Herbert Muhammad, who had made millions with Ali. Herbert said that his influence wasn't that strong.

Two years after the last fight, Ali seemed as mystified as everyone else as to why he hadn't ended his career earlier. He was living with his third wife, the ice goddess Veronica, in an L.A. mansion, surrounded by the gifts of a life-time—a six-foot hand-carved tiger given to him by Teng Hsiao-ping, a robe given to him by Elvis Presley. Fatigued, his hands tremoring badly, he sat in front of the fire and could only say: "Everybody git lost in life. I just git lost, that's all."

Now, five years later, the question *why* still lingers, along with the warn-ing of the old aphorism that "we live beyond what we enact." The re-suscitation of Ali's image has been a sporadic exercise for a long time now, some of it coming from friends who have experienced heartfelt pain over his illness. Others seem to be trying to assuage a guilt known only to themselves, and a few are out to keep Ali a player, a lure to those who might want to use his name in business; though the marketplace turns away from billboards in decline. Not long ago, a piece in the *New York Times Magazine* pronounced him the Ali of old, just about terminally perky. Then, Ali surfaced in a front-page telephone interview in the *Washington Post.* He appeared to have a hard grasp on politics, current states' rights issues, and federal judgeships be-ing contested—a scenario that had seemed as likely as the fusillade of laser fire Ali said Muslim spaceships would one day loose on the white devils.

Noses began to twitch. What and who was behind the new Ali, the wily Washington lobbyist who had the ear of everyone from Strom Thurmond to Orrin Hatch? The wife of Senator Arlen Specter even baked Ali a double-chocolate-mousse pie. For a good while, most of these senators, and others, knew only the voice of Ali on the phone. Dave Kindred, a columnist for the *Atlanta Journal-Constitution* who has known Ali since his Louisville days, concluded that it was most likely Ali's attorney, Richard Hirschfeld, widely regarded as a brilliant impersonator of Ali, who had made the calls. (Hirschfeld has refused to comment on whether or not he did so.) Hirschfeld and Ali had cut up a lot of money over the years on numerous enterprises (funded by other people), from hotels to cars, most of them failing. Ali's lobbying seemed to center on a federal judgeship for a Hirschfeld friend, and a federal lawsuit in which Ali sought $50 million in damages from his "wrongful conviction in the 1967 draft evasion case." He lost the suit but succeeded in getting Senator Hatch and others to explore a loophole that might remedy the verdict. Ali eventually had to materialize (with Hirschfeld hard by his side), and many on Capitol Hill were unable to match the man with the voice. One of Sam Nunn's aides, noting Ali's listlessness and Hirschfeld's aggressive quizzing, wondered: "Is Ali being carted around like a puppet?" Certainly a serpentine tale; but had Ali been a collaborator all along?

At his farm in Berrien Springs, Michigan, Ali sits at the end of a table in the living room. The 247 pounds of weight have made him a bit short of breath. He's battled his appetite (two, three desserts, meals back to back) and sedentary lapses for years. Several months before, he had been almost sleek, thanks to fourteen-mile walks and his wife's efforts to police him at the table. But what is disturbing is the general profile of his condition.

For a long time now, he has appeared indifferent to the ravages of his problem. But he dispels that notion when asked how seriously he considered a dangerous brain operation in Mexico before his family talked him out of it. "Scale of ten," he says, "a six." The answer reflects the terrible frustration that must exist within him, the daily, fierce struggle with a body and mind that will not capitulate to his bidding. He sits there, his hands shaking, his movements robotic, the look on his face similar to what the Marines call a thousand-yard stare.

Why is it, do you think, that after all these years, the dominant sound around Ali is silence? Look at the cataract of noise caught by TV sound men, look at the verbosity that snared some novelists into thinking he was a primitive intelligence capable of Ciceronian insight. Part of the fever of the times; if the Black Panther Huey Newton, posing with rifle and spear, could be written up as a theoretical genius and his partner, Bobby Seale, interpreted as a tactical wizard, then how much a symbol was Ali, the first to tap and manifest glinting black pride, to dispute with vigor erosive self-laceration.

The fact was that he was not cerebral; he was a reflex of confusing emotions and instant passions. He did have street cunning, most of it aimed at keeping himself a mystery. "People like mystery," he used to say. "Who is he?

What's he all about? Who's he gonna be tomorrow?" To that end, he tossed the media rabble dripping hunks of redundant, rote monologue; his loudness provided a great show and diverted probing questions. By nature, he was a gentle, sensitive man, and even in the throes of angry threats against whites it was hard to hide a smile, for he loved what the blacks call "selling wolf tick, ets," tricking people into fear. The Black Panthers used that gambit well, and the TV crews followed their presence. Thinking of all this, how could some, one so alien to ideas and thought, who communicated privately, in scraps and remote silences, be capable of fooling Washington politicians? Absurd, of course, but then the question emerges: Did he allow himself to be used?

"How about all those phone calls?" he is asked.

"What calls?" he responds, vacantly.

"To politicians this past summer."

"You can't believe that," he says. "Man wrote that, he's a cracker from way back in Louisville. Always hated blacks."

"But the piece had the goods."

"I'm signin' my autographs now," he says. "This the only important thing in my life. Keepin' in touch with the people."

"Were you used?"

"Spend a hundred dollars on stamps every week. Give 'em all my auto, graph that write me."

"Were you used?"

"For what?"

"To influence your lawsuit."

"I ain't worried about money," he says.

"Maybe you just want to be big again. Remember what you told Elvis. 'Elvis, you have to keep singin' or die to stay big. I'm gonna be big forever.'"

He smiles thinly: "I say anything shock the world."

"You like politics now?"

"Politics put me to sleep."

"You were at the Republican National Convention."

"You borin' me, putting me to sleep."

"Reagan, Hatch, Quayle, they would've clapped you in jail in the old days."

His eyes widen slightly: "That right?" He adds: "I'm tired. You better than a sleepin' pill."

But don't let the exchange mislead. Ali is not up to repartee these days, never was, really, unless he was in the mood, and then he'd fade you with one of his standard lines ("You not as dumb as you look"). He speaks very, very slowly, and you have to lean in to hear him. It takes nearly an hour to negotiate the course of a conversation. Typically, he hadn't been enlightening on the Capitol Hill scam. Over the years, he has been easily led, told by any number of rogues what his best interests were. If the advisers were friends who appealed to his instinct to help them move up a rung, he was even more of a setup. Later, Bingham says: "Ali was pissed about that impersonation stuff. He had no idea." Why didn't he just say that he didn't make the calls? "You know him," he says. "He'll never betray who he thinks has tried to help him. The idea that people will think less of him now bothers him a lot."

If there was ever any doubt about the staying power of Ali, it is swept aside when you travel with him. His favorite place in the world—next to his worktable at his farm—is an airport. So he should be in high spirits now; he'll be in three airports before the day's over. But he's a bit petulant with Lonnie, who aims to see that he keeps his date at Hilton Head Island. He can't stand hospitals. They get in the way of life. He found it hard even to visit his old sidekick Bundini when he was dying. Paralyzed from the neck down, Bundini could only move his eyes. Ali bent down close to his ear and whispered: "You in pain?" The eyes signaled yes. Ali turned his head away, then came back to those eyes, saying: "We had some good times, didn't we?" Bundini's eyes went up and down. Ali talks about this in the Chicago airport. He's calmed down now, sits off by himself, ramrodstraight and waiting. He wears a pinstripe suit, red tie, and next to him is his black magician's bag; he never lets it out of his sight. The bag is filled with religious tracts already autographed; which is the first thing he does every day at six A.M. when he gets up. All he has to do is fill in the person's name.

His autograph ritual and travel are his consuming interests. He'll go anywhere at the ring of a phone, and he spends much time on the road. Perhaps the travel buoys him; he certainly gets an energy charge from people. Soon they begin to drop like birds to his side. "You see," he says, "all I gotta do is sit here. Somethin', ain't it? Why they like me?" He is not trying to be humble, he is genuinely perplexed by the chemistry that exists between himself and other people. "Maybe they just like celebrities," he says. Maybe, he's told, he's much more than a celebrity. He ponders that for a moment, and says: "That right?" By now, a hundred people have lined up in front of him, and a security guard begins to keep them in line. Ali asks them their name, writes, then gives them his autographed tracts. Some ask him to pose for pictures, others kid him about unretiring. He raises his fist: "Kong [Mike Tyson], I'm comin' after you." Near the end, he does a magic trick for a lady, using a fake thumb. "Where you going, Muhammad?" she asks. He thinks, and then leans over to the writer and asks: "Where we going?" The lady's eyes fill, she hugs him, and says: "We love you so much." What is it that so movingly draws so many people—his innocent, childlike way, the stony visual he projects, set off against his highly visible symptoms?

That night over dinner, Ali's eyes open and close between courses. He fades in and out of the conversation, has a hint of trouble lifting the fork to his mouth. His every day includes periods like this, he's in and out like a faraway signal. Sometimes he's full of play. He likes to swing his long arm near a person's ear, then create a friction with thumb and forefinger to produce a cricket effect in the ear. Then the play is gone, and so is he. "One day," Lonnie is saying, "I want someone to catch his soul, to show what a fine human being he is." Ali says, head down: "Nobody know me. I fool 'em all." Lonnie is Ali's fourth wife. She was a little girl who lived across from Ali's old Louisville home when he was at the top. She is a woman of wit and intelligence, with a master's degree in business administration. She plans his trips, is the tough cop with him and his medicine, and generally seems to brighten his life. Ice cream dribbles down Ali's chin. "Now, Muhammad," she says, wiping it away. "You're a big baby." He orders another dessert, then says: "Where are we?" A blade of silence cuts across the table.

Bingham says: "Hilton Head Island."

Ali says: "Ya ever wake up and don't know where you are?" Sure, he is told, steady travel can make a person feel like that for an instant; yet it is obvious that short-term memory for him is like a labyrinth.

Ali's day at the hospital is nearly over. He will soon be counting down the minutes. Right now he's in high spirits. A nurse has secretly slipped him some strips of paper. He has a complete piece of paper in his hands. He crumples the paper, pretends to put it in his mouth, then billows his cheeks until he regurgitates tiny pieces all over his chest. "Ain't magic a happy thing," he says, trying to contain his giggling. When Dr. Medenica comes,

Ali jokes with him. The doctor goes about examining the day's results. He looks at the bags of plasma: fifteen thousand cc's have been moved through Ali. Floyd Patterson has expressed dismay over the current treatment. "No brain damage?" Floyd had said. "Next you'll be hearing he was bit by a cock-roach. He's gonna kill Clay. . . . He'll drop dead in a year." Medenica bridles at the comment. "He's rather ignorant. I'm going to have to call that man." Ali wants to know what Patterson said. Nobody wants to tell him. "Tell me," says Ali. Everyone looks at each other, and someone finally says: "Floyd says you'll drop dead in a year." Ali shrugs it off: "Floyd mean well."

It is Medenica's contention that Ali suffers from pesticide poisoning. Though his work has met with some skepticism in the medical community, Medenica is respected in South Carolina. His desk is rimmed with pictures of prominent people—a senator, a Saudi prince, an ambassador—patients for whom he has retarded death by cancer. He is supposed to have done won-ders for Marshal Tito of Yugoslavia. Tito was so grateful, he arranged fund-ing for Medenica's clinic in Switzerland. When he died, the funds were cut off and Medenica was left with bills and criminal indictment by the Yugosla-vians and the Swiss. "Don't ask how Ali got the pesticides," Medenica says.

Plasmapheresis is a solid treatment for pesticide poisoning, which occurs more than ever these days. The blood cleaning removes the immune com-plex, which in turn removes toxins. But how can Medenica be so sure that Ali's problem is not brain damage? Dr. Dennis Cope, of UCLA, has said that Ali is a victim of "Parkinson's syndrome secondary to pugilistic brain syndrome." In short, he took too many head shots. Medenica, though, is a confident man.

He predicts Ali will be completely recovered. "I find absolutely no brain damage. The magnetic resonator tests show no damage. Before I took him as a patient, I watched many of his fight films. He did not take many head blows."

Is he kidding?

"No, I do not see many head blows. When he came this summer, he was in bad shape. Poor gait. Difficult speech. Vocal-cord syndrome, extended and inflamed. He is much better. His problem is he misses taking his medi-cine, and he travels too much. He should be here once a month."

Finally, Ali is helped out of his medical harness. He dresses slowly. Then, ready to go out, he puts that famous upper-teeth clamp on his bottom lip to show determination and circles the doctor with a cocked right fist. His next stop is for an interferon shot. It is used to stimulate the white blood cells. Afterward, he is weak, and there is a certain sadness in his eyes. On the way to the car, he is asked if the treatment helps. He says: "Sheeeet, nothin' help."

The Lincoln Town Car moves through the night. Bingham, who is driving, fumbles with the tape player. Earlier in the day he had searched anxiously for a tape of Whitney Houston doing "The Greatest Love of All," a song written especially for Ali years ago. He had sensed that Ali would be quite low when the day was over, and he wanted something to pick him up. The words, beautiful and haunting, fill the car.

"You hear that," Bingham says, his voice cracking. "Everything's gonna be just fine, Ali."

The dark trees spin by. There is no answer. What is he thinking?

[June, 1989]

THE 1990S

"It's dyin'. I always said it would die when I left. Just look at it—there's Holyfield, there used to be Tyson. But he's no Muhammad Ali, no kind of real hero."

—Muhammad Ali on boxing, quoted in Davis Miller,
"'I'm More Human Now,'" the Detroit News, *January 17, 1997*

"I've seen the whole world. I learn somethin' from people everywhere. There's truth in Hinduism, Christianity, Islam, all religions. And in just plain talkin'. The only religion that matters is the real religion—love."

—Muhammad Ali quoted in Davis Miller,
"'I'm More Human Now,'" the Detroit News, *January 17, 1997*

"Can you believe it? Dancin' at 50! . . . Oooohhh. . . . Dancin' at 50. Maaannn. It'll be bigger than the moon shot! I'm dedicatin' the fight to the baby boomers, the people who were six years old when I beat Sonny Liston. Now they're thirty-four. I'll do the Ali shuffle!"

—Muhammad Ali, on being asked about fighting
either Evander Holyfield or Mike Tyson, in
"Young Cassius" by William Nock,
Sports Illustrated, *January 13, 1992*

THE CRUELEST SPORT

JOYCE CAROL OATES

Muhammad Ali, born Cassius Marcellus Clay in Louisville, Kentucky, on January 17, 1942, grandson of a slave, began boxing at the age of twelve, and, by eighteen, had fought 108 amateur bouts. How is it possible that the young man who, in his twenties, would astonish the world not just with the brilliance of his boxing but the sharpness of his wit seems to have been a dull-average student in high school who graduated 376th out of a class of 391? In 1966, his score on a mental aptitude test was an Army IQ of 78, well below military qualification. In 1975, Ali confessed to a reporter that he "can't read too good" and had not read ten pages of all the material written about him. I remember the television interview in which, asked what else he might have done with his life, Ali paused, for several seconds, clearly not knowing how to reply. All he'd ever known, he said finally, was boxing.

Mental aptitude tests cannot measure genius except in certain narrow ranges, and the genius of the body, the play of lightning-swift reflexes coupled with unwavering precision and confidence, eludes comprehension. All great boxers possess this genius, which scrupulous training hones, but can never create. "Styles make fights," as Ali's great trainer Angelo Dundee says, and "style" was young Ali's trademark. Yet even after early wins over such veterans as Archie Moore and Henry Cooper, the idiosyncrasies of Ali's style aroused skepticism in boxing experts. After winning the Olympic gold medal in 1960, Ali was described by A. J. Leibling as "skittering . . . like a pebble over water." Everyone could see that this brash young boxer held his hands too low; he leaned away from punches instead of properly slipping them; his jab was light and flicking; he seemed to be perpetually on the brink of disaster. As a seven-to-one underdog in his first title fight with Sonny Liston, the twenty-two-year-old challenger astounded the experts with his performance, which was like none other they had ever seen in the heavyweight division; he so outboxed and demoralized Liston that Liston "quit on his stool" after the sixth round. A new era in boxing had begun, like a new music.

"Ali rode the crest of a new wave of athletes—competitors who were both big and fast. . . . Ali had a combination of size and speed that had never been seen in a fighter before, along with incredible will and courage. He also brought a new style to boxing. Jack Dempsey changed fisticuffs from a kind of constipated science where fighters fought in a tense defensive style to a wild sensual assault. Ali revo-lutionized boxing the way black basketball players have changed basketball today. He changed what happened in the ring, and elevated it to a level that was pre-viously unknown."

—*Larry Merchant, quoted in* Muhammad Ali

In the context of contemporary boxing—the sport is in one of its periodic slumps—there is nothing more instructive and rejuvenating than to see again these old, early fights of Ali's, when, as his happy boast had it, he floated like a butterfly and stung like a bee and threw punches faster than op-ponents could see—like the "mystery" right to the temple of Liston that felled him, in the first minute of the first round of their rematch. These early fights, the most brilliant being against Cleveland Williams, in 1966, predate by a decade the long, grueling, punishing fights of Ali's later career, whose accumulative effects hurt Ali irrevocably, resulting in what doctors call, care-fully, his "Parkinsonianism"—to distinguish it from Parkinson's disease. There is a true visceral shock in observing a heavyweight with the grace, agil-ity, swiftness of hands and feet, defensive skills, and ring cunning of a mid-dleweight Ray Robinson, or a lightweight Willie Pep—like all great athletes, Ali has to be seen to be believed.

In a secular, yet pseudo-religious and sentimental nation like the United States, it is quite natural that sports stars emerge as "heroes"—"legends"—"icons." Who else? George Santayana described religion as "another world to live in" and no world is so set off from the disorganization and disenchant-ment of the quotidian than the world, or worlds, of sports. Immediately fol-lowing his first victory over Liston, the young Cassius Clay declared himself a convert to the Nation of Islam (more popularly known as the Black Mus-lims) and "no longer a Christian." He repudiated his "slave name" of Cas-sius Marcellus Clay to become Muhammad Ali (a name which, incidentally, the *New York Times,* among other censorious white publications, would not honor through the 1960s). Ali became, virtually overnight, a spokesman for black America as no other athlete, certainly not the purposefully reticent Joe

Louis, had ever done—"I don't have to be what you want me to be," he told white America. "I'm free to be me." Two years later, refusing to be inducted into the army to fight in Vietnam, Ali, beleaguered by reporters, uttered one of the memorable incendiary remarks of that era: "Man, I ain't got no quarrel with them Vietcong."

How ingloriously white America responded to Ali: The government retaliated by overruling a judge who had granted Ali the status of conscientious objector, fined Ali $10,000, and sentenced him to five years in prison; he was stripped of his heavyweight title and deprived of his license to box. Eventually, the U.S. Supreme Court would overturn the conviction, and, as the tide of opinion shifted in the country, in the early 1970s as the Vietnam War wound down Ali returned triumphantly to boxing again, and regained the heavyweight title not once but twice. Years of exile during which he'd endured the angry self-righteousness of the conservative white press seemed, wonderfully not to have embittered him. He had become a hero. He had entered myth.

Yet the elegiac title of Angelo Dundee's chapter in Dave Anderson's *In The Corner*—"We Never Saw Muhammad Ali at His best"—defines the nature of Ali's sacrifice for his principles, and the loss to boxing. When, after the three-and-a-half-year layoff, Ali returned to the ring, he was of course no longer the seemingly invincible boxer he'd been; he'd lost his legs, thus his primary line of defense. Like the maturing writer who learns to replace the incandescent head-on energies of youth with what is called technique, Ali would have to descend into his physical being and experience for the first time the punishment ("the nearest thing to death") that is the lot of the great boxer willing to put himself to the test. As Ali's personal physician at that time, Ferdie Pacheco, said,

> [Ali] discovered something which was both very good and
> very bad. Very bad in that it led to the physical damage he
> suffered later in his career; very good in that it eventually got
> him back the championship. He discovered that he could take
> a punch.

The secret of Ali's mature success, and the secret of his tragedy: *He could take a punch.*

For the remainder of his twenty-year career, Muhammad Ali took punches, many of the kind that, delivered to a nonboxer, would kill him or her outright—from Joe Frazier in their three exhausting marathon bouts, from George Foreman, from Ken Norton, Leon Spinks, Larry Holmes. Where in his feckless youth Ali was a dazzling figure combining, say, the brashness of Hotspur and the insouciance of Lear's Fool, he became in these dark, brooding, increasingly willed fights the closest analogue boxing contains to Lear himself; or, rather, since there is no great fight without two great boxers, the title matches Ali-Frazier I (which Frazier won by a decision) and Ali-Frazier III (which Ali won, just barely, when Frazier virtually collapsed after the fourteenth round) are boxing's analogues to *King Lear*—ordeals of unfathomable human courage and resilience raised to the level of classic tragedy. These somber and terrifying boxing matches make us weep for their very futility; we seem to be in the presence of human experience too profound to be named—beyond the strategies and diminishments of language. The mystic's dark night of the soul, transmogrified as a brutal meditation of the body.

And Ali-Foreman, Zaire, 1974: the occasion of the infamous "Rope-a-Dope" defense, by which the thirty-two-year-old Ali exhausted his twenty-six-year-old opponent by the inspired method of simply, and horribly, allowing him to punch himself out on Ali's body and arms. This is a fight of such a magical quality that even to watch it closely is not to see how it was done, its fairy-tale reversal in the eighth round executed. (One of Norman Mailer's most impassioned books, *The Fight,* is about this fight; watching a tape of Ali on the ropes enticing, and infuriating, and frustrating, and finally exhausting his opponent by an offense in the guise of a defense, I pondered what sly lessons of masochism Mailer absorbed from being at ringside that day, what deep-imprinted resolve to outwear all adversaries.)

These hard-won victories began irreversible loss: progressive deterioration of Ali's kidneys, hands, reflexes, stamina. By the time of that most depressing of modern-day matches, Ali-Holmes, 1980, when Ali was thirty-eight years old, Ferdie Pacheco had long departed the Ali camp, dismissed for having advised Ali to retire; those who supported Ali's decision to fight, like the bout's promoter, Don King, had questionable motives. It is a wonder that Ali survived this fight at all: The fight was, in Sylvester Stallone's words, "like watching an autopsy on a man who's still alive." Incredibly, Ali was allowed to fight once more, with Trevor Berbick, in December 1981, before retiring permanently.

The brash rap-style egoism of young Cassius Clay underwent a consider-able transformation during Ali's long public career, yet strikes us, perhaps, as altered only in tone. Mystically involved in the Nation of Islam, Ali sincerely believes himself an international emissary for peace, love, and understanding (he who once wreaked such violence upon his opponents!); and who is to presume to feel sorry for one who will not feel sorry for himself?

[1994]

Please note that this piece has been edited for this volume and does not appear in its entirety.

BOXING FIDEL

GAY TALESE

It is a warm, breezy, palm-flapping winter evening in Havana, and the leading restaurants are crowded with tourists from Europe, Asia, and South America being serenaded by guitarists relentlessly singing *"Guan-tan-a-mera . . . guajira . . . Guan-tan-a-mera"*; and at the Café Cantante there are clamorous salsa dancers, mambo kings, grunting, bare-chested male performers lifting tables with their teeth, and turbaned women swathed in hip-hugging skirts, blowing whistles while gyrating their glistening bodies into an erotic frenzy. In the café's audience as well as in the restaurants, hotels, and other public places throughout the island, cigarettes and cigars are smoked without restraint or restriction. Two prostitutes are smoking and talking privately on the corner of a dimly lit street bordering the manicured lawns of Havana's five-star Hotel Nacional. They are copper-colored women in their early twenties wearing faded miniskirts and halters, and as they chat, they are watching attentively while two men—one white, the other black—huddle over the raised trunk of a parked red Toyota, arguing about the prices of the boxes of black-market Havana cigars that are stacked within.

The white man is a square-jawed Hungarian in his mid-thirties, wearing a beige tropical suit and a wide yellow tie, and he is one of Havana's leading entrepreneurs in the thriving illegal business of selling top-quality hand-rolled Cuban cigars below the local and international market price. The black man behind the car is a well-built, baldish, gray-bearded individual in his mid-fifties from Los Angeles named Howard Bingham; and no matter what price the Hungarian quotes, Bingham shakes his head and says, "No, no—that's too much!"

"You're crazy!" cries the Hungarian in slightly accented English, taking one of the boxes from the trunk and waving it in Howard Bingham's face. "These are Cohiba Esplendidos! The best in the world! You will pay $1,000 for a box like this in the States."

"Not me," says Bingham, who wears a Hawaiian shirt with a camera strapped around his neck. He is a professional photographer, and he is stay-

266

ing at the Hotel Nacional with his friend Muhammad Ali. "I wouldn't give you more than fifty dollars."

"You really are crazy," says the Hungarian, slicing through the box's paper seal with his fingernail, opening the lid to reveal a gleaming row of labeled Esplendidos.

"Fifty dollars," says Bingham.

"A hundred dollars," insists the Hungarian. "And hurry! The police could be driving around." The Hungarian straightens up and stares over the car toward the palm-lined lawn and stanchioned lights that glow in the distance along the road leading to the hotel's ornate portico, which is now jammed with people and vehicles; then he turns and flings a glance back toward the nearby public street, where he notices that the prostitutes are now blowing smoke in his direction. He frowns.

"Quick, quick," he says to Bingham, handing him the box. "One hundred dollars."

Howard Bingham does not smoke. He and Muhammad Ali and their traveling companions are leaving Havana tomorrow, after participating in a five-day American humanitarian-aid mission that brought a planeload of medical supplies to hospitals and clinics depleted by the United States' embargo, and Bingham would like to return home with some fine contraband cigars for his friends. But, on the other hand, one hundred is still too much.

"Fifty dollars," says Bingham determinedly, looking at his watch. He begins to walk away.

"Okay, okay," the Hungarian says petulantly. "Fifty."

Bingham reaches into his pocket for the money, and the Hungarian grabs it and gives him the Esplendidos before driving off in the Toyota. One of the prostitutes takes a few steps toward Bingham, but the photographer hurries on to the hotel. Fidel Castro is having a reception tonight for Muhammad Ali and Bingham has only a half hour to change and be at the portico to catch the chartered bus that will take them to the government's headquarters. He will be bringing one of his photographs to the Cuban leader—an enlarged, framed portrait showing Muhammad Ali and Malcolm X walking together along a Harlem sidewalk in 1963. Malcolm X was thirty-seven at the time, two years away from an assassin's bullet; the twenty-one-year-old Ali was about to win the heavyweight title in a remarkable upset over Sonny Liston in Miami. Bingham's photograph is inscribed, TO PRESIDENT FIDEL

CASTRO, FROM MUHAMMAD ALI. Under his signature, the former cham/
pion has sketched a little heart.

Although Muhammad Ali is now fifty/four and has been retired from
boxing for more than fifteen years, he is still one of the most famous men
in the world, being identifiable throughout five continents; and as he walks
through the lobby of the Hotel Nacional toward the bus, wearing a gray
sharkskin suit and a white cotton shirt buttoned at the neck without a tie, sev/
eral guests approach him and request his autograph. It takes him about thirty
seconds to write "Muhammad Ali," so shaky are his hands from the effects of
Parkinson's syndrome; and though he walks without support, his movements
are quite slow, and Howard Bingham and Ali's fourth wife, Yolanda, are fol/
lowing nearby.

Bingham met Ali thirty/five years ago in Los Angeles, shortly after the
fighter had turned professional and before he discarded his "slave name"
(Cassius Marcellus Clay) and joined the Black Muslims. Bingham subse/
quently became his closest male friend and has photographed every aspect of
Ali's life: his rise and fall three times as the heavyweight champion; his three/
year expulsion from boxing, beginning in 1967, for refusing to serve in the
American military during the Vietnam War ("I ain't got no quarrel with
them Vietcong"); his four marriages; his fatherhood of nine children (one
adopted, two out of wedlock); his endless public appearances in all parts of
the world—Germany, England, Egypt (sailing on the Nile with a son of Eli/
jah Muhammad's), Sweden, Libya, Pakistan (hugging refugees from Af/
ghanistan), Japan, Indonesia, Ghana (wearing a dashiki and posing with
President Kwame Nkrumah), Zaire (beating George Foreman), Manila
(beating Joe Frazier) . . . and now, on the final night of his 1996 visit to
Cuba, he is en route to a social encounter with an aging contender he has
long admired—one who has survived at the top for nearly forty years despite
the ill will of nine American presidents, the CIA, the Mafia, and various
militant Cuban Americans.

Bingham waits for Ali near the open door of the charter bus that is block/
ing the hotel's entrance; but Ali lingers within the crowd in the lobby, and
Yolanda steps aside to let some people get closer to her husband.

She is a large and pretty woman of thirty/eight, with a radiant smile and a
freckled, fair complexion that reflects her interracial ancestry. A scarf is

loosely draped over her head and shoulders, her arms are covered by long sleeves, and her well-designed dress in vivid hues hangs below her knees. She converted to Islam from Catholicism when she married Ali, a man sixteen years her senior but one with whom she shared a familial bond dating back to her girlhood in their native Louisville, where her mother and Ali's mother were sisterly soul mates who traveled together to attend his fights. Yolanda had occasionally joined Ali's entourage, becoming acquainted with not only the boxing element but with Ali's female contemporaries who were his lovers, his wives, the mothers of his children; and she remained in touch with Ali through the 1970s, while she majored in psychology at Vanderbilt and later earned her master's degree in business at UCLA. Then—with the end of Ali's boxing career, his third marriage, and his vibrant health—Yolanda intimately entered his life as casually and naturally as she now stands waiting to reclaim her place at his side.

She knows that he is enjoying himself. There is a slight twinkle in his eyes, not much expression on his face, and no words forthcoming from this once most talkative of champions. But the mind behind his Parkinson's mask is functioning normally, and he is characteristically committed to what he is doing: He is spelling out his full name on whatever cards or scraps of paper his admirers are handing him. "Muhammad Ali." He does not settle for a time-saving "Ali" or his mere initials. He has never shortchanged his audience.

And in his audience tonight are people from Latin America, Canada, Africa, Russia, China, Germany, France. There are two hundred French travel agents staying at the hotel in conjunction with the Cuban government's campaign to increase its growing tourist trade (which last year saw about 745,000 visitors spending an estimated $1 billion on the island). There is also on hand an Italian movie producer and his lady friend from Rome and a one-time Japanese wrestler, Antonio Inoki, who inured Ali's legs during a 1976 exhibition in Tokyo (but who warmly embraced him two nights ago in the hotel's lounge as they sat listening to Cuban pianist Chucho Valdes playing jazz on a Russian-made Moskva baby grand); and there is also in the crowd, standing taller than the rest, the forty-three-year-old, six-foot five-inch Cuban heavyweight hero Teófilo Stevenson, who was a three-time Olympic gold medalist, in 1972, 1976, and 1980, and who, on this island at least, is every bit as renowned as Ali or Castro.

Though part of Stevenson's reputation derives from his erstwhile power and skill in the ring (although he never fought Ali), it is also attributable to his not having succumbed to the offers of professional boxing promoters, stubbornly resisting the Yankee dollar—although Stevenson hardly seems deprived. He dwells among his countrymen like a towering Cuban peacock, occupying high positions within the government's athletic programs and gaining sufficient attention from the island's women to have garnered four wives so far, who are testimony to his eclectic taste.

His first wife was a dance instructor. His second was an industrial engineer. His third was a medical doctor. His fourth and present wife is a criminal attorney. Her name is Fraymari, and she is a girlishly petite olive-skinned woman of twenty-three who, standing next to her husband in the lobby, rises barely higher than the midsection of his embroidered guayabera—a tightly tailored, short-sleeved shirt that accentuates his tapered torso, his broad shoulders, and the length of his dark, muscular arms, which once prevented his opponents from doing any injustice to his winning Latin looks.

Stevenson always fought from an upright position, and he maintains that posture today. When people talk to him, his eyes look downward, but his head remains high. The firm jaw of his oval-shaped head seems to be locked at a right angle to his straight-spined back. He is a proud man who exhibits all of his height. But he does listen, especially when the words being directed up at him are coming from the perky little attorney who is his wife. Fraymari is now reminding him that it is getting late—everyone should be on the bus; Fidel may be waiting.

Stevenson lowers his eyes toward her and winks. He has gotten the message. He has been Ali's principal escort throughout this visit. He was also Ali's guest in the United States during the fall of 1995; and though he knows only a few words of English, and Ali no Spanish, they are brotherly in their body language.

Stevenson edges himself into the crowd and gently places his right arm around the shoulders of his fellow champion. And then, slowly but firmly, he guides Ali toward the bus.

The road to Fidel Castro's Palace of the Revolution leads through a memory lane of old American automobiles chugging along at about twenty-five miles an hour—springless, preembargo Ford coupes and Plymouth sedans, DeSotos and LaSalles, Nashes and Studebakers, and various vehicular collages created out of Cadillac grilles and Oldsmobile axles and Buick fenders patched with pieces of oil-drum metal and powered by engines interlinked with kitchen utensils and pre-Batista lawn mowers and other gadgets that have elevated the craft of tinkering in Cuba to the status of high art.

The relatively newer forms of transportation seen on the road are, of course, non-American products—Polish Fiats, Russian Ladas, German motor scooters, Chinese bicycles, and the glistening, newly imported, air-conditioned Japanese bus from which Muhammad Ali is now gazing through a closed window out toward the street. At times, he raises a hand in response to one of the waving pedestrians or cyclists or motorists who recognize the bus, which has been shown repeatedly on the local TV news conveying Ali and his companions to the medical centers and tourist sites that have been part of the busy itinerary.

On the bus, as always, Ali is sitting alone, spread out across the two front seats in the left aisle directly behind the Cuban driver. Yolanda sits a few feet ahead of him to the right; she is adjacent to the driver and within inches of the windshield. The seats behind her are occupied by Teófilo Stevenson, Fraymari, and the photographer Bingham. Seated behind Ali, and also occupying two seats, is an American screenwriter named Greg Howard who weighs more than three hundred pounds. Although he has traveled with Ali for only a few months while researching a film on the fighter's life, Greg Howard has firmly established himself as an intimate sidekick and as such is among the very few on this trip who have heard Ali's voice. Ali speaks so softly that it is impossible to hear him in a crowd, and as a result whatever public comments or sentiments he is expected to, or chooses to, express are verbalized by Yolanda, or Bingham, or Teófilo Stevenson, or even at times by this stout young screenwriter.

"Ali is in his Zen period," Greg Howard has said more than once in reference to Ali's quiescence. Like Ali, he admires what he has seen so far in Cuba—"There's no racism here"—and as a black man he has long identified with many of Ali's frustrations and confrontations. His student thesis at Princeton analyzed the Newark race riots of 1967, and the Hollywood script he most recently completed focuses on the Negro baseball leagues of the pre–World War II years. He envisions his new work on Ali in the genre of *Gandhi.*

The two dozen bus seats behind those tacitly reserved to Ali's inner circle are occupied by the secretary-general of the Cuban Red Cross and the American humanitarian personnel who have entrusted him with $500,000 worth of donated medical supplies; and there are also the two Cuban interpreters and a dozen members of the American media, including the CBS-TV commentator Ed Bradley and his producers and camera crew from *60 Minutes*.

Ed Bradley is a gracious but reserved individualist who has appeared on television for a decade with his left earlobe pierced by a small circular ring—which, after some unfavorable comment initially expressed by his colleagues Mike Wallace and Andy Rooney, prompted Bradley's explanation: "It's *my* ear." Bradley also indulges in his identity as a cigar smoker; and as he sits in the midsection of the bus next to his Haitian lady friend, he is taking full advantage of the Communist regime's laissez-faire attitude toward tobacco, puffing away on a Cohiba Robusto, for which he paid full price at the Nacional's tobacco shop—and which now exudes a costly cloud of fragrance that appeals to his friend (who occasionally also smokes cigars) but is not appreciated by the two California women who are seated two rows back and are affiliated with a humanitarian-aid agency.

Indeed, the women have been commenting about the smoking habits of countless people they have encountered in Havana, being especially disappointed to discover earlier this very day that the pediatric hospital they visited (and to which they committed donations) is under the supervision of three tobacco-loving family physicians. When one of the American women, a blond from Santa Barbara, reproached one of the cigarette-smoking doctors indirectly for setting such a poor example, she was told in effect that the island's health statistics regarding longevity, infant mortality, and general fitness compared favorably with those in the United States and were probably better than those of Americans residing in the capital city of Washington. On the other hand, the doctor made it clear that he did not believe that smoking was good for one's health—after all, Fidel himself had given it up; but unfortunately, the doctor added, in a classic understatement, "some people have not followed him."

Nothing the doctor said appeased the woman from Santa Barbara. She did not, however, wish to appear confrontational at the hospital's news conference which was covered by the press; nor during her many bus rides with

Ed Bradley did she ever request that he discard his cigar. "Mr. Bradley intim-
idates me," she confided to her California co-worker. But he was of course
living within the law on this island that the doctor had called "the cradle of
the best tobacco in the world." In Cuba, the most available American peri-
odical on the newsstands is *Cigar Aficionado*.

The bus passes through the plaza de la Revolución and comes to a halt at
a security checkpoint near the large glass doors that open onto the mar-
ble-floored foyer of a 1950s modern building that is the center of Communism's only stronghold in the Western Hemisphere.

As the bus door swings open, Greg Howard moves forward in his seat
and grabs the 235-pound Muhammad Ali by the arms and shoulders and
helps him to his feet; and after Ali has made his way down to the metal step
he turns and stretches back into the bus to take hold of the extended hands
and forearms of the 300-pound screenwriter and pulls him to a standing position. This routine, repeated at each and every bus stop throughout the week,
is never accompanied by either man's acknowledging that he has received any
assistance, although Ali is aware that some passengers find the pas de deux
quite amusing, and he is not reluctant to use his friend to further comic effect.
After the bus had made an earlier stop in front of the sixteenth century Morro
Castle—where Ali had followed Teófilo Stevenson up a 117-step spiral
staircase for a rooftop view of Havana Harbor—he spotted the solitary figure
of Greg Howard standing below in the courtyard. Knowing that there was
no way the narrow staircase could accommodate Howard's wide body, Ali
suddenly began to wave his arms, summoning Howard to come up and join
him.

Castro's security guards, who know in advance the names of all the bus
passengers, guide Ali and the others through the glass doors and then
into a pair of waiting elevators for a brief ride that is followed by a short walk
through a corridor and finally into a large white-walled reception room,
where it is announced that Fidel Castro will soon join them. The room has
high ceilings and potted palms in every corner and is sparsely furnished with
modern tan leather furniture. Next to a sofa is a table with two telephones,
one gray and the other red. Overlooking the sofa is an oil painting of the
Viñales valley, which lies west of Havana; and among the primitive art dis-

played on a circular table in front of the sofa is a grotesque tribal figure similar to the one Ali had examined earlier in the week at a trinket stand while touring with the group in Havana's Old Square. Ali had then whispered into the ear of Howard Bingham, and Bingham had repeated aloud what Ali had said: "Joe Frazier."

Ali now stands in the middle of the room, next to Bingham, who carries under his arm the framed photograph he plans to give Castro. Teófilo Stevenson and Fraymari stand facing them. The diminutive and delicate-boned Fraymari has painted her lips scarlet and has pulled back her black hair in a matronly manner, hoping no doubt to appear more mature than her twenty-three years suggest, but standing next to the three much older and heavier and taller men transforms her image closer to that of an anorexic teenager. Ali's wife and Greg Howard are wandering about within the group that is exchanging comments in muted tones, either in English or Spanish, sometimes assisted by the interpreters. Ali's hands are shaking uncontrollably at his sides; but since his companions have witnessed this all week, the only people who are now paying attention are the security guards posted near the door.

Also waiting near the door for Castro is the four-man CBS camera team, and chatting with them and his two producers is Ed Bradley, without his cigar. There are no ashtrays in this room! This is a most uncommon sight in Cuba. Its implications might be political. Perhaps the sensibilities of the blond woman from Santa Barbara were taken into account by the doctors at the hospital and communicated to Castro's underlings, who are now making a conciliatory gesture toward their American benefactress.

Since the security guards have not invited the guests to be seated, everybody remains standing—for ten minutes, for twenty minutes, and then for a full half hour. Teófilo Stevenson shifts his weight from foot to foot and gazes over the heads of the crowd toward the upper level of the portal through which Castro is expected to enter—if he shows up. Stevenson knows from experience that Castro's schedule is unpredictable. There is always a crisis of some sort in Cuba, and it has long been rumored on the island that Castro constantly changes the location of where he sleeps. The identity of his bed partners is, of course, a state secret. Two nights ago, Stevenson and Ali and the rest were kept waiting until midnight for an expected meeting with Castro at the Hotel Biocaribe (to which Bingham had brought his gift photograph). But Castro never appeared. And no explanation was offered.

Now in this reception room, it is already nine P.M. Ali continues to shake. No one has had dinner. The small talk is getting smaller. A few people would like to smoke. The regime is not assuaging anyone in this crowd with a bartender. It is a cocktail party without cocktails. There are not even canapés or soft drinks. Everyone is becoming increasingly restless—and then suddenly there is a collective sigh. The very familiar man with the beard strides into the room, dressed for guerrilla combat; and in a cheerful, high-pitched voice that soars beyond his whiskers, he announces, *"Buenas noches!"*

In an even higher tone, he repeats, *"Buenas noches,"* this time with a few waves to the group while hastening toward the guest of honor; and then, with his arms extended, the seventy-year-old Fidel Castro immediately obscures the lower half of Ali's expressionless face with a gentle embrace and his flowing gray beard.

"I am glad to see you," Castro says to Ali, via the interpreter who followed him into the room, a comely, fair-skinned woman with a refined English accent. "I am very, very glad to see you," Castro continues, backing up to look into Ali's eyes while holding on to his trembling arms, "and I am thankful for your visit." Castro then releases his grip and awaits a possible reply. Ali says nothing. His expression remains characteristically fixed and benign, and his eyes to not blink despite the flashbulbs of several surrounding photographers. As the silence persists, Castro turns toward his old friend Teófilo Stevenson, feigning a jab. The Cuban boxing champion lowers his eyes and, with widened lips and cheeks, registers a smile. Castro then notices the tiny brunette standing beside Stevenson.

"Stevenson, who is this young woman?" Castro asks aloud in a tone of obvious approval. But before Stevenson can reply, Fraymari steps forward with a hint of lawyerly indication: "You mean you don't remember me?"

Castro seems stunned. He smiles feebly, trying to conceal his confusion. He turns inquiringly toward his boxing hero, but Stevenson's eyes only roll upward. Stevenson knows that Castro has met Fraymari socially on earlier occasions, but unfortunately the Cuban leader has forgotten, and it is equally unfortunate that Fraymari is now behaving like a prosecutor.

"You held my son in your arms before he was one year old!" she reminds him while Castro continues to ponder. The crowd is attentive; the television cameras are rolling.

"At a volleyball game?" Castro asks tentatively.

"No, no," Stevenson interrupts, before Fraymari can say anything more, "that was my former wife. The doctor."

Castro slowly shakes his head in mock disapproval. Then he abruptly turns away from the couple, but not before reminding Stevenson, "You should get name tags."

Castro redirects his attention to Muhammad Ali. He studies Ali's face.

"Where is your wife?" he asks softly. Ali says nothing. There is more silence and turning of heads in the group until Howard Bingham spots Yolanda standing near the back and waves her to Castro's side.

Before she arrives, Bingham steps forward and presents Castro with the photograph of Ali and Malcolm X in Harlem in 1963. Castro holds it up level with his eyes and studies it silently for several seconds. When this picture was taken, Castro had been in control of Cuba for nearly four years. He was then thirty-seven. In 1959, he defeated the USA-backed dictator Fulgencio Batista, overcoming odds greater than Ali's subsequent victory over the supposedly unbeatable Sonny Liston. Batista had actually announced Castro's death back in 1956. Castro, then hiding in a secret outpost, thirty years old and beardless, was a disgruntled Jesuit-trained lawyer who was born into a landowning family and who craved Batista's job. At thirty-two, he had it. Batista was force to flee to the Dominican Republic.

During this period, Muhammad Ali was only an amateur. His greatest achievement would come in 1960, when he received a gold medal in Rome as the member of the United States Olympic boxing team. But later in the sixties, he and Castro would share the world stage as figures moving against the American establishment—and now, in the twilight of their lives, on this winter's night in Havana, they meet for the first time: Ali silent and Castro isolated on his island.

"*Que bien!*" Castro says to Howard Bingham before showing the photograph to his interpreter. Then Castro is introduced by Bingham to Ali's wife. After they exchange greetings through the interpreter, he asks her, as if surprised, "You don't speak Spanish?"

"No," she says softly. She begins to caress her husband's left wrist, on which he wears a $250 silver Swiss Army watch she bought him. It is the only jewelry Ali wears.

"But I thought I saw you speaking Spanish on the TV news this week,"

Castro continues wonderingly before acknowledging that her voice had obviously been dubbed.

"Do you live in New York?"

"No, we live in Michigan."

"Cold," says Castro.

"Very cold," she repeats.

"In Michigan, don't you find many people that speak Spanish?"

"No, not many," she says. "Mostly in California, New York . . ." and, after a pause, "Florida."

Castro nods. It takes him a few seconds to think up another question.
Small talk has never been the forte of this man who specializes in nonstop ha-
ranguing monologues that can last for hours; and yet there he is, in a room
crowded with camera crews and news photographers—a talk-show host
with a guest of honor who is speechless. But Fidel Castro plods on, asking
Ali's wife if she has a favorite sport.

"I play a little tennis," Yolanda says, and then asks him, "Do you play
tennis?"

"Ping-Pong," he replies, quickly adding that during his youth he had
been active in the ring. "I spent hours boxing. . . ." he begins to reminisce,
but before he finishes his sentence, he sees the slowly rising right fist of Muhammad Ali moving toward his chin! Exuberant cheering and handclapping resound through the room, and Castro jumps sideways toward
Stevenson, shouting, *"Asesorame!"*—"Help me!"

Stevenson's long arms land upon Ali's shoulders from behind, squeezing
him gently; and then, after he releases him, the two ex-champions face each
other and begin to act out in slow motion the postures of competing
prizefighters—bobbing, weaving, swinging, ducking—all of it done without touching and all of it accompanied by three minutes of ongoing applause
and the clicking of cameras, and also some feelings of relief from Ali's
friends because, in his own way, he has decided to join them. Ali still says
nothing, his face still inscrutable, but he is less remote, less alone, and he does
not pull away from Stevenson's embrace as the latter eagerly tells Castro about
a boxing exhibition that he and Ali had staged earlier in the week at the Bal-
ado gym, in front of hundreds of fans and some of the island's up-and-com-
ing contenders.

Stevenson did not actually explain that it had been merely another photo opportunity, one in which they sparred openhanded in the ring, wearing their street clothes and barely touching each other's bodies and faces; but then Stevenson had climbed out of the ring, leaving Ali to the more taxing test of withstanding two abbreviated rounds against one and then another young bully of grade school age who clearly had not come to participate in a kiddie show. They had come to floor the champ. Their bellicose little bodies and hot-gloved hands and helmeted hell-bent heads were consumed with fury and ambition; and as they charged ahead, swinging wildly and swaggering to the roars of their teenage friends and relatives at ringside, one could imagine their future boastings to their grandchildren: On one fine day back in the winter of '96, I whacked Muhammad Ali! Except, in truth, on this particular day, Ali was still too fast for them. He backpedaled and shifted and swayed, stood on the toes of his black woven-leather pointed shoes, and showed that his body was made for motion—his Parkinson's problems were lost in his shuffle, in the thrusts of his butterfly sting that whistled two feet above the heads of his aspiring assailants, in the dazzling dips of his Rope-a-Dope that had confounded George Foreman in Zaire, in his ever-memorable style, which in this Cuban gym moistened the eyes of his ever-observant photographer friend and provoked the overweight screenwriter to cry out in a voice that few in this noisy Spanish crowd could understand, "Ali's on a high! Ali's on a high!"

Teófilo Stevenson raises Ali's right arm above the head of Castro, and the news photographers spend several minutes posing the three of them together in flashing light. Castro then sees Fraymari watching alone at some distance. She is not smiling. Castro nods toward her. He summons a photographer to take a picture of Fraymari and himself. But she relaxes only after her husband comes over to join her in the conversation, which Castro immediately directs to the health and growth of their son, who is not yet two years old.

"Will he be as tall as his father?" Castro asks.

"I assume so," Fraymari says, glancing up toward her husband. She also has to look up when talking to Fidel Castro, for the Cuban leader is taller than six feet and his posture is nearly as erect as her husband's. Only the six-foot three-inch Muhammad Ali, who is standing with Bingham on the far side of her husband—and whose skin coloring, oval-shaped head, and burr-style haircut are very similar to her husband's—betrays his height with the slope-shouldered forward slouch he has developed since his illness.

"How much does your son weigh?" Castro continues.

"When he was one year old, he was already twenty-six pounds," Fraymari says. "This is three above normal. He was walking at nine months."

"She still breast-feeds him," Teófilo Stevenson says, seeming pleased.

"Oh, that's very nourishing," agrees Castro.

"Sometimes the kid becomes confused and thinks my chest is his mother's breast," Stevenson says, and he could have added that his son is also confused by Ali's sunglasses. The little boy engraved teeth marks all over the plastic frames while chewing on them during the days he accompanied his parents on Ali's bus tour.

As a CBS boom pole swoops down closer to catch the conversation, Castro reaches out to touch Stevenson's belly and asks, "How much to you weigh?"

"Two hundred thirty-eight pounds, more or less."

"That's thirty-eight more than me," Castro says, but he complains, "I eat very little. Very little. The diet advice I get is never accurate. I eat around fifteen hundred calories—less than thirty grams of protein, less than that."

Castro slaps a hand against his own midsection, which is relatively flat. If he does have a potbelly, it is concealed within his well-tailored uniform. Indeed, for a man of seventy, he seems in fine health. His facial skin is florid and unsagging, his dark eyes dart around the room with ever-alert intensity, and he has a full head of lustrous gray hair not thinning at the crown. The attention he pays to himself might be measured from his manicured fingernails down to his square-toed boots, which are unscuffed and smoothly buffed without the burnish of a lackey's spit shine. But his beard seems to belong to another man and another time. It is excessively long and scraggly. Wispy white hairs mix with the faded black and dangle down the front of his uniform like an old shroud, weatherworn and drying out. It is the beard from the hills. Castro strokes it constantly, as if trying to revive the vitality of its fiber.

Castro now looks at Ali.

"How's your appetite?" he asks, forgetting that Ali is not speaking.

"Where's your wife?" he then asks aloud, and Howard Bingham calls out to her. Yolanda has once more drifted back into the group.

When she arrives, Castro hesitates before speaking to her. It is as if he is not absolutely sure who she is. He has met so many people since arriving, and with the group rotating constantly due to the jostling of the photographers, Castro cannot be certain whether the woman at his side is Muhammad Ali's wife or Ed Bradley's friend or some other woman he has met moments ago who has left him with an unlasting impression. Having already committed a faux pas regarding one of the wives of the two multimarried ex-champions standing nearby, Castro waits for some hint from his interpreter. None is offered. Fortunately, he does not have to worry in this country about the women's vote—or any vote, for that matter—but he does sigh in mild relief when Yolanda reintroduces herself as Ali's wife and does so by name.

"Ah, Yolanda," Castro repeats, "what a beautiful name. That's the name of a queen somewhere."

"In our household," she says.

"And how is your husband's appetite?"

"Good, but he likes sweets."

"We can send you some of our ice cream to Michigan," Castro says. Without waiting for her to comment, he asks, "Michigan is very cold?"

"Oh, yes," she replies, not indicating that they had already discussed Michigan's winter weather.

"How much snow?"

"We didn't get hit with the blizzard," Yolanda says, referring to a storm in January, "but it can get three, four feet—"

Teófilo Stevenson interrupts to say that he had been in Michigan during the previous October.

"Oh," Castro says, raising an eyebrow. He mentions that during the same month he had also been in the United States (attending the United Nations' fiftieth-anniversary tribute). He asks Stevenson the length of his American visit.

"I was there for nineteen days," says Stevenson.

"Nineteen days!" Castro repeats. "Longer than I was."

Castro complains that he was limited to five days and prohibited from traveling beyond New York.

"Well, *comandante*," Stevenson responds offhandedly, in a slightly superior tone, "if you like, I will sometime show you my video."

Stevenson appears to be very comfortable in the presence of the Cuban

leader, and perhaps the latter has habitually encouraged this; but at this moment, Castro may well be finding his boxing hero a bit condescending and
worthy of a retaliatory jab. He knows how to deliver it.

"When you visited the United States," Castro asks pointedly, "did you
bring your wife, the lawyer?"

Stevenson stiffens. He directs his eyes toward his wife. She turns away.

"No," Stevenson answers quietly. "I went alone."

Castro abruptly shifts his attention to the other side of the room, where the
CBS camera crew is positioned, and he asks Ed Bradley, "What do you do?"

"We're making a documentary on Ali," Bradley explains, "and we followed him to Cuba to see what he was doing in Cuba and . . ."

Bradley's voice is suddenly overwhelmed by the sounds of laughter and
handclapping. Bradley and Castro turn to discover that Muhammad Ali is
now reclaiming everyone's attention. He is holding his shaking left fist in the
air; but instead of assuming a boxer's pose, as he had done earlier, he is beginning to pull out from the top of his upraised fist, slowly and with dramatic
delicacy, the tip of a red silk handkerchief that is pinched between his right
index finger and thumb.

After he has pulled out the entire handkerchief, he dangles it in the air for
a few seconds, waving it closer and closer to the forehead of the wide-eyed Fidel Castro. Ali seems bewitched. He continues to stare stagnantly at Castro
and the others, surrounded by applause that he gives no indication he hears.
Then he proceeds to place the handkerchief back into the top of his cupped
left hand—pecking with the pinched fingers of his right—and then quickly
opens his palms toward his audience and reveals that the handkerchief has
disappeared.

"Where is it?" cries Castro, who seems to be genuinely surprised and
delighted. He approaches Ali and examines his hands, repeating,
"Where is it? Where have you put it?"

Everyone who has traveled on Ali's bus during the week knows where he
has hidden it. They have seen him perform the trick repeatedly in front of
some of the patients and doctors at the hospitals and clinics as well as before
countless tourists who have recognized him in his hotel lobby or during his
strolls through the town square. They have also seen him follow up each performance with a demonstration that exposes his method. He keeps hidden in

his fist a flesh-colored rubber thumb that contains the handkerchief that he will eventually pull out with the fingers of his other hand; and when he is re-inserting the handkerchief, he is actually shoving the material back into the concealed rubber thumb, into which he then inserts his own right thumb. When he opens his hands, the uninformed among his onlookers are seeing his empty palms and missing the fact that the handkerchief is tucked within the rubber thumb that is covering his outstretched right thumb. Sharing with his audience the mystery of his magic always earns him additional applause.

After Ali has performed and explained the trick to Castro, he gives Cas-tro the rubber thumb to examine—and, with more zest than he has shown all evening, Castro says, "Oh, let me try it, I want to try—it's the first time I have seen such a wonderful thing!" And after a few minutes of coaching from Howard Bingham, who long ago learned how to do it from Ali, the Cuban leader performs with sufficient dexterity and panache to satisfy his magical ambitions and to arouse another round of applause from the guests.

Meanwhile, more than ten minutes have passed since Ali began his comic routine. It is already about nine-thirty P.M., and the commentator Ed Brad-ley, whose conversation with Castro had been interrupted, is concerned that the Cuban leader might leave the room without responding to the questions Bradley has prepared for his show. Bradley edges close to Castro's interpreter, saying in a voice that is sure to be heard, "Would you ask him if he fol-lowed . . . was able to follow Ali when he was boxing professionally?"

The question is relayed and repeated until Castro, facing the CBS cam-eras, replies, "Yes, I recall the days when they were discussing the possibilities of a match between the two of them"—he nods toward Stevenson and Ali—"and I remember when he went to Africa."

"In Zaire," Bradley clarifies, referring to Ali's victory in 1974 over George Foreman. And he follows up: "What kind of impact did he have in this country, because he was a revolutionary as well as . . . ?"

"It was great," Castro says. "He was very much admired as a sportsman, as a boxer, as a person. There was always a high opinion of him. But I never guessed one day we would meet here, with this kind gesture of bringing med-icine, seeing our children, visiting our polyclinics. I am very glad, I am thrilled, to have the opportunity to meet him personally, to appreciate his kindness. I see he is strong. I see he has a very kind face."

Castro is speaking as if Ali were not in the room, standing a few feet away. Ali maintains his fixed facade even as Stevenson whispers into his ear, asking in English, "Muhammad, Muhammad, why you no speak?" Stevenson then turns to tell the journalist who stands behind him, "Muhammad does speak. He speaks to me." Stevenson says nothing more because Castro is now looking at him while continuing to tell Bradley, "I am very glad that he and Stevenson have met." After a pause, Castro adds, "And I am glad that they never fought."

"He's not so sure," Bradley interjects, smiling in the direction of Stevenson.

"I find in that friendship something beautiful," Castro insists softly.

"There is a tie between the two of them," Bradley says.

"Yes," says Castro. "It is true." He again looks at Ali, then at Stevenson, as if searching for something more profound to say.

"And how's the documentary?" he finally asks Bradley.

"It'll be on *60 Minutes.*"

"When?"

"Maybe one months," Bradley says, reminding Castro's interpreter, "This is the program on which the *comandante* has been interviewed by Dan Rather a number of times in the past, when Dan Rather was on *60 Minutes.*"

"And who's there now?" Castro wants to know.

"I am," Bradley answers.

"You," Castro repeats, with a quick glance at Bradley's earring. "So you are there—the boss now?"

Bradley responds as a media star without illusions: "I'm a worker."

Trays containing coffee, tea, and orange juice finally arrive, but only in amounts sufficient for Ali and Yolanda, Howard Bingham, Greg Howard, the Stevensons, and Castro—although Castro tells the waiters he wants nothing.

Castro motions for Ali and the others to join him across the room, around the circular table. The camera crews and the rest of the guests follow, standing as near to the principals as they can. But throughout the group, there is a discernible restlessness. They have been standing for more than an hour and a half. It is now approaching ten P.M. There has been no food. And for the vast majority, it is clear that there will also be nothing to drink. Even among the special guests, seated and sipping from chilled glasses or hot cups, there is a waning level of fascination with the evening. Indeed, Muhammad Ali's eyes are closed. He is sleeping.

Yolanda sits next to him on the sofa, pretending not to notice. Castro also ignores it, although he sits directly across the table, with the interpreter and the Stevensons.

"How large is Michigan?" Castro begins a new round of questioning with Yolanda, returning for the third time to a subject they had explored beyond the interest of anyone in the room except Castro himself.

"I don't know how big the state is as far as demographics," Yolanda says. "We live in a very small village [Berrien Springs] with about two thousand people."

"Are you going back to Michigan tomorrow?"

"Yes."

"What time?"

"Two-thirty."

"Via Miami?" Castro asks.

"Yes."

"From Miami, where do you fly?"

"We're flying to Michigan."

"How many hours' flight?"

"We have to change at Cincinnati—about two and a half hours."

"Flying time?" asks Castro.

Muhammad Ali opens his eyes, then closes them.

"Flying time," Yolanda repeats.

"From Miami to Michigan? Castro continues.

"No," she again explains, but still with patience, "we have to go to Cincinnati. There are no direct flights."

"So you have to take two planes?" Castro asks.

"Yes," she says, adding for clarification, "Miami to Cincinnati—and then Cincinnati to South Bend, Indiana."

"From Cincinnati . . . ?"

"To South Bend," she says. "That's the closest airport."

"So," Fidel goes on, "it is on the outskirts of the city?"

"Yes."

"You have a farm?"

"No," Yolanda says, "just land. We let someone else do the growing."

She mentions that Teófilo Stevenson has traveled through this part of the Midwest. The mention of his name gains Stevenson's attention.

"I was in Chicago," Stevenson tells Castro.

"You were at their home?" Castro asks.

"No," Yolanda corrects Stevenson, "you were in Michigan."

"I was in the countryside," Stevenson says. Unable to resist, he adds, "I have a video of that visit. I'll show it to you sometime."

Castro seems not to hear him. He directs his attention back to Yolanda, asking her were she was born, where she was educated, when she became married, and how many years separate her age from that of her husband, Muhammad Ali.

After Yolanda acknowledges being sixteen years younger that Ali, Castro turns toward Fraymari and with affected sympathy says that she married a man who is twenty years her senior.

"*Comandante!*" Stevenson intercedes, "I am in shape. Sports keep you healthy. Sports add years to your life and life to your years!"

"Oh, what conflict she has," Castro goes on, ignoring Stevenson and catering to Fraymari—and to the CBS cameraman who steps forward for a closer view of Castro's face. "She is a lawyer, and she does not put this husband in jail." Castro is enjoying much more than Fraymari the attention this topic is now getting from the group. Castro had lost his audience and now has it back and seemingly wants to retain it, no matter at what cost to Stevenson's harmony with Fraymari. Yes, Castro continues, Fraymari had the misfortune to select a husband "who can never settle down. . . . Jail would be an appropriate place for him."

"*Comandante,*" Stevenson interrupts in a jocular manner that seems intended to placate both the lawyer who is his spouse and the lawyer who rules the country, "I might as well be locked up!" He implies that should he deviate from marital fidelity, his lawyer wife "will surely put me in a place where she is the only woman who can visit me!"

Everyone around the table and within the circling group laughs. Ali is now awake. The banter between Castro and Stevenson resumes until Yolanda, all but rising in her chair, tells Castro, "We have to pack."

"You're going to have dinner now?" he asks.

"Yes, sir," she says. Ali stands, along with Howard Bingham. Yolanda thanks Castro's interpreter directly, saying, "Be sure to tell him, 'You're al-

ways welcome in our home.'" The interpreter quotes Castro as again complaining that when he visits America, he is usually restricted to New York,
but he adds, "Things change."

The group watches as Yolanda and Ali pass through, and Castro follows
them into the hallway. The elevator arrives, and its door is held open by a security guard. Castro extends his final farewell with handshakes—and only
then does he discover that he holds Ali's rubber thumb in his hand. Apologizing, he tries to hand it back to Ali, but Bingham politely protests. "No,
no," Bingham says, "Ali wants you to have it."

Castro's interpreter at first fails to understand what Bingham is saying.

"He wants you to keep it," Bingham repeats.

Bingham enters the elevator with Ali and Yolanda. Before the door closes,
Castro smiles, waves good-bye, and stares with curiosity at the rubber thumb.
Then he puts it in his pocket.

[September, 1996]

ALI'S AMAZING GRACE: STILL PREACHING, TEACHING, NOW HE CONTEMPLATES HIS 'HOUSE IN HEAVEN'

DAVID MARANISS

No words at first. The greeting comes from his eyes, then a handshake, light as a butterfly, followed by a gesture that says, "Follow me." He has just popped out the back door of his farm house wearing green pants and a light brown wool pullover with sunglasses tucked coolly into the mock tur/tleneck collar. He is carrying an old black briefcase. His hair is longer than usual and a bit uncombed. He starts walking toward his office, a converted barn on the lower end of the circular driveway.

He moves slowly, lurching slightly forward as he goes, never a stumble but sometimes seeming on the verge of one, as though his world slopes downhill. He opens the door and stands aside, following, not leading, on the way up/stairs to his second floor office. Halfway up, it becomes clear why. He sticks out a hand and catches his visitor's foot from behind. The old trip/up/the/stairs trick. Muhammad Ali loves tricks.

At the top of the stairs is the headquarters of GOAT. Another trick. It is the playfully ironic acronym for Greatest of All Time, Incorporated. Ali wants the world to know that he is just another goat, one living thing in this vast and miraculous universe. But also the greatest there ever was. He is fifty/five, his mouth and body slowed by Parkinson's disease, yet still arguably the best known and most beloved figure in the world. Who else? The Pope? Nel/son Mandela? Michael Jordan? Ali might win in a split decision.

Even the most dramatic lives move in cycles of loss and recovery. Last summer in Atlanta, when Ali stood alone in the spotlight, the world watch/

287

ing, his hands trembling, and lit the Olympic flame, he began another cycle, perhaps his ultimate comeback, as emotional as any he had staged in the ring against Joe Frazier or George Foreman. For sixteen years he had been retired from boxing. During that time he had gone through periods of boredom and uncertainty. Not that he was passe, but the world tends to forget its old kings when new ones come around.

He kept going as best he could, his health deteriorating, spreading good will with his smiling eyes, trying to keep his name alive. Then, finally, his moment arrived again, first at the Olympics, then at the Academy Awards, where he bore silent witness to *When We Were Kings,* the Oscar-winning documentary about his dramatic heavyweight championship fight in October 1974 against Foreman in what was then Zaire.

The shimmering house of movie stars seemed diminished, their egos preposterous, when Ali rose and stood before them. Yet some saw in that appearance a hint of the maudlin: poor Ali, enfeebled and paunchy, dragged out as another melodramatic Hollywood gimmick. Was he real or was he memory? What was left of him if he could no longer float and sting?

Quite a bit, it turns out. No sorrow and pity from the champ. He says he cherished his performances at the Olympics and Academy Awards more than anyone could know. Publicity is his lifeblood, more important to him than any medicine he is supposed to take. "Press keeps me alive, man," he says, with an honesty that softens the edge of his ego. "Press keeps me alive. Press and TV. The Olympics. Academy Awards. *When We Were Kings.* Keeps me alive."

When the producers sent him a videotape of "When We Were Kings," he stuck it into his VCR at home and watched it day after day. At a recent autograph extravaganza in Las Vegas, he conducted his own poll by comparing his line to those for Jim Brown, Paul Hornung, Bobby Hull and Ernie Banks. Twice as long as any of them. Staying alive. And the biggest life-saver of all: that night in Atlanta last July, thirty-six years after he had first danced onto the world scene as the brash young Olympic champion Cassius Marcellus Clay.

Long after the torch scene was over, Ali would not let go. He went back to his suite with his wife, Lonnie, and a few close friends. They were tired, emotionally drained from the surprise, anxiety, and thrill of the occasion, but Ali would not go to sleep. He was still holding the long white and gold torch, which he had kept as a prized memento. He cradled it in his arms, turning it over and over, just looking at it, not saying much, sitting in a big chair, smiling, hour after hour.

"I think the man was just awed. Just completely awed by the whole experience," Lonnie Ali recalled. "He was so excited. It took forever for him to go to bed. He was on such a high. He found it very hard to come back down to earth. There was just such a fabulous response. No one expected that. None of us did."

By the time he and Lonnie returned to their farm house here in southern Michigan, the mail was already backing up, flooding in at tenfold the previous pace. Letters from everywhere. The return of a trembling Ali had unloosed powerful feelings in people. They said they cried at his beauty and perseverance. They said he reminded them of what it means to stand up for something you believe in. Disabled people. Old sixties activists. Republicans. Black. White. Christian. Jewish. Muslim. A little boy from Germany, a boxing fan from England, a radiologist from Sudan, a secretary from Saudi Arabia—the multitudes thanked him for giving them hope.

When Ali reaches his office, he takes his customary chair against the side wall. There is work to be done, the room is overcrowded with mementos to be signed for charity, and his assistant, Kim Forburger, is waiting for him with a big blue felt pen. But Ali has something else in mind right now.

"Mmmmmm. Watch this, man," he says. His voice sounds like the soft, slurred grumble-whisper of someone trying to clear his throat on the way out of a deep sleep. Conversing with him for the first time, one unavoidably has to say, "I'm sorry, what?" now and then, or simply pretend to understand him, but soon enough one adjusts, and it becomes obvious that Parkinson's has not slowed his brain, only his motor skills.

Ali walks toward the doorway and looks back with a smile.

"Oh, have you see Muhammad levitate yet?" Forburger asks. She suddenly becomes the female assistant in a Vegas act. With a sweep of her hand, she says, "Come over here. Stand right behind him. Now watch his feet. Watch his feet."

Ali goes still and silent, meditating. His hands stop shaking. He seems to radiate something. A mystical aura? Ever so slowly, his feet rise from the floor, one inch, three inches, six inches. His hands are not touching anything.

"Ehhhh. Pretty heavy, mmmm," he says. His visitor, familiar with the lore of Ali's levitations, yet easily duped, watches slack-jawed as the champ floats in the air for several seconds.

Come over here, Ali motions. To the side. "Look," he says. He is not really levitating, of course. He has managed to balance himself perfectly, Parkinson's notwithstanding, all two hundred and fifty pounds of him, on the tiptoes of his right foot, creating an optical illusion from behind that both of his feet have lifted off the ground.

The tricks have only just begun. He hauls out a huge gray plastic toolbox, opens it and peers inside. His hands now move with the delicacy of a surgeon selecting the correct instrument from his bag. For the next quarter-hour, he performs the simple, delightful tricks of an apprentice magician. Balls and coins appear and disappear, ropes change lengths, sticks turn colors. "Maaann! Maaann! Heavy!" he says.

Then he turns to slapstick. Close your eyes and open your hand. The champ places something soft and fuzzy in it. "Mmmm. Okay. Open."

A fuzzy toy mouse.

Ali beams at the startled reaction. His voice becomes louder, higher, more animated. "Ehhh!" he shrieks. 'Kids go 'Ahhhh! Ahhhh!'"

Try it again. This time it's a cockroach.

And again. This time fake dog doo.

Ali closes his gray toolbox and puts it away, satisfied.

What is going on here? In part it is just Ali amusing himself with magic tricks that he has been doing over and over for many years for anyone who comes to see him. But he is also, as always, making a more profound point. He has transferred his old boxing skills and his poetry and his homespun philosophy to another realm, from words to magic. The world sees him now, lurching a bit, slurring some, getting old, trembling, and recalls that unspeakably great and gorgeous and garrulous young man that he once was. He understands that contrast. But, he is saying, nothing is as it appears. Life is always a matter of perception and deception.

Poets and philosophers contemplate this, and boxers know it intuitively. (Ali ghost boxing before the Foreman fight: "Come get me, sucker. I'm dancin'! I'm dancin'! No, I'm not here, I'm there! You're out, sucker!") Back when he was Cassius Clay, he pretended that he was demented before fighting Sonny Liston because he had heard that the only cons who scared big bad Sonny in prison were the madmen. By acting crazy, he not only injected a dose of fear into Liston, he took some out of himself. Life is a trick.

The Islamic religion, to which Ali has adhered for more than 30 years, disapproves of magic tricks, but he has found his way around that problem, as always.

"When . . . I . . . do . . . a . . . trick," he says now. He seems more easily understandable. Is he speaking more clearly or has the ear adjusted to him?

"I . . . always . . . show . . . people . . . how . . . to . . . do . . . it."

He smiles.

"Show . . . people . . . how . . . easy . . . it . . . is . . . to . . . be . . . tricked."

Perception and deception. He has returned to his chair in the office, with his black briefcase on his lap. Slowly and carefully he opens it up . . . click . . . click . . . and looks inside as though he is examining its contents for the first time.

Tucked in the upper compartment is his passport. Parkinson's has not slowed his travels. He's at home no more than 90 days a year. Washington, Los Angeles, Louisville, Las Vegas in a week, doing good deeds. He visits schools, campaigns against child abuse, for more Parkinson's funding, for peace and tolerance. Everyone wants to see the champ. Germany is clamoring for him. Its national television network just ran an hour-long documentary on him.

Next to the passport is a laminated trading card. He lifts it out and studies it. There's Ali next to Sugar Ray Robinson and Joe Louis.

"Two of the greatest fighters in the world," he says. He pauses. "Mmmmm. Both dead."

Ali thinks a lot about death. Aging and death and life after death. His philosophy is at once selfish and selfless. Publicity keeps him alive. He wants to stay alive so that he can make people happy and do good deeds. And "good deeds are the rent we pay for our house in heaven."

He is teaching and preaching now. A new poetry, slower, no rhymes, stream of consciousness, deeper meaning.

> "Twice a month they call us to sign autographs
> Make two hundred thousand a day.
> Signing. Hundred dollars a picture

Long lines. Bring in millions of dollars.
I'm not fighting no more
I'll sign for nothin.' Give it to charity.
Get the money, give it to the homeless
Give it to soup lines
If I see someone who needs some
Here's a hundred. Here's fifty.
Soup vendor. Wino. Old woman with varicose veins.
Good deeds. Judgment.
I'm well pleased with you my son. Come into heaven.
That's eternal life. Maann! Maann!
Look at all the buildings in downtown New York.
People built them. They're dead.
Buildings still standing.
You don't own nothin'. Just a trustee.
Think about it. You die.
This life's a test. A test.
Trying to pass the test. I'm tryin.
Warm bodies. Shake hands. Gone.
All dead now. President Kennedy.
Whatever color you are
No matter how much money you have
Politics. Sports. You're gonna die.
Sleep is the brother of death."

Ali closes his eyes. He starts snoring. Reopens his eyes.
"Turn over now. It's morning."
Back to the black briefcase.

Stacked in rows along the bottom are a collection of little leather books, five of them, in red and pink and green. It turns out they are Bibles. Why he needs five in a briefcase is not clear. What he does with them is part of the mystery of Muhammad Ali.

During the past several months, he and Lonnie and Thomas Hauser, author of his authorized biography, have made appearances around the country promoting the cause of universal understanding and tolerance.

(They are scheduled to come to the Smithsonian Institution on June 23.) Ali and Hauser, Muslim and Jew, put together a little book entitled *Healing* which they distribute at every stop. It contains quotations on tolerance from Cicero, Voltaire, Thoreau, and Ali. The book was inspired by Ali's habit of combing through the Koran and other books and writing down phrases that he found moving. Hauser chose the title one day when he studied a series of words and noticed A-L-I in the middle of H-E-A-L-I-N-G.

This crusade seems natural for Ali now. In the sixties, when he shed the name Cassius Clay, which he dismissed as his slave name, and refused to be inducted into the military to fight in Vietnam, temporarily giving up his freedom and wealth and title in the process, he stood as what Hauser called "a symbol of divided America." Now his popularity transcends politics, race, country, and religion. He is universally accepted as a man who stood up for what he believed in and paid the price and prevailed. He has endured enough intolerance to give the message deeper meaning. His shining eyes are the prize of peace.

Ali takes the little leather Bibles out of his briefcase and places them on a table beside him. He peers inside again and comes out with a stack of paper. Each page has a typed message. He hands over the first page. Could these be the quotations of tolerance and understanding he writes down each day?

Read it, Ali indicates, wordlessly, nodding his head.

"If God is all perfect his revelation must be perfect and accurate. Free from contradiction. . . . Since holy scripture is from God, it should be impossible to find mistakes and conflicting verses. If it doesn't, you can't trust it one hundred percent. There are many conflicting verses in the Bible."

Ali smiles, gestures to take that piece of paper back, and hands over one page after another of contradictions he has found in the Bible. Some contradictions in numbers, some about what Jesus was purported to have said. "All in the Bible," Ali says, as he finally puts the stack of paper back in his briefcase. "Heavy." He points to a filing cabinet behind the desk, which is overflowing with similar papers. It turns out that this is one of his favorite intellectual pastimes, searching his little leather Bibles for thousands of contradictions of fact or interpretation that have been cited by Islamic scholars. There seems to be no malice in his hobby, though it is hardly what one might expect from a missionary of universal healing.

What is going on here? The question is later put to Lonnie Ali. She is his fourth wife, wholly devoted to his well-being, a smart, funny, and gracious woman, a graduate of Vanderbilt University, who started cooking for him when he was getting sick, married him twelve years ago, and is serving more and more as his public voice. She knows that he is not perfect, but she also appreciates his larger meaning to the world. Muhammad, she says, is greater than his individual parts. He means so many things to so many people, and she is determined to preserve that, sometimes in spite of him. She has known him since she was six years old and growing up in Louisville in the house across the street from his mother, Odessa Clay.

Why is Ali doing this? She shrugs at the question. That, she says, "is part of the dichotomy that is Muhammad.

"Even when Muhammad was in the Nation of Islam where they considered whites devils he was putting little white kids on his lap and kissing them and loving them. Muhammad could really care less if a person is of another religion. But Muhammad found out that there are contradictions in the Bible and he's hooked on that. If he can get you to say, 'Oh, look, I never knew that,' then it's like he has accomplished a victory. Muhammad is a warrior. And he finds these little things to battle over."

There certainly seem to be more important battles now for Muhammad Ali. Perception and deception. How sick is he?

Ali began showing signs of trouble as far back as 1980, when he lost the heavyweight title in his sixtieth and next to last fight, against Larry Holmes. He visited several medical experts over the next few years and finally Parkinsonism, a syndrome related to Parkinson's disease, was diagnosed. Parkinson's is a slowly progressive disease, suffered by an estimated 1.5 million Americans, that causes cells in the middle part of the brain to degenerate, reducing the production of the chemical dopamine and leading to tremors, slowness of movement, memory loss, and other neurological symptoms. Its cause is unknown.

People who suffer from Parkinsonism have many of the same symptoms but in a milder and usually undegenerative form. Until recently, most of his doctors believed Ali had the syndrome, not the disease. Over the past eighteen months that diagnosis has been changing and the belief now is that he might have the disease.

Some doctors who have examined Ali remain convinced that his ailment was brought on by the pounding he took in the ring, especially the brutal fights late in his career against Frazier, Foreman, and Holmes. Mahlon De-Long, his Parkinson's physician at Emory University in Atlanta, and other experts argue, however, that Ali must have had a predisposition to the disease. They note that most "punch drunk" old fighters do not show signs of Parkinson's, but more often suffer from something known as Martland syndrome, with intellectual deficits that Ali does not show.

His disorder, in any case, is not as debilitating as one might suspect from catching a brief glimpse of him. He is agile enough to dress himself each morning. He knots his ties perfectly. He lifts his legs to put on his socks. Laces his shoes. Slips on his Swiss Army watch. Feeds himself. Opens doors. Performs magic tricks. Reads his Bibles and Korans. Writes legibly. Talks on the telephone. Understands everything said to him and around him. Flips the remote on his television to watch CNN and Biography and the Discovery Channel.

"He doesn't need any help from me," Lonnie Ali says, meaning in the physical sense. "The only thing I may assist Muhammad with, because he is nearsighted and doesn't wear glasses, is shaving. He misses some spots." His main problem, she said, is that he shows little interest in keeping up with medical treatments.

"I can offer him all the care in the world. His doctors can give him all the care in the world. It is up to him. Muhammad tends to ignore it."

Ali is on the move now, heading down the steps and out onto the grounds of his eighty-eight-acre farm. It is an unexpected paradise at the end of the road in the middle of Middle America, between South Bend Indiana and Benton Harbor Michigan. Once belonged to Al Capone, a mobster's hideaway. "Found . . . machine . . . guns," Ali says. There is a gentle pond, a gazebo where he prays to Allah, a playground for the youngest of his nine children, six-year-old Asaad, whom he and Lonnie adopted at birth; acres of sweet-blooming perennials, woods at the edge of the field, the St. Joe river rolling by, white picket fences, and white and green barns.

On his way down the looping driveway, Ali cannot resist some playful sparring. His hands stop shaking as he bobs and weaves and dances backwards. His condition seems irrelevant, or at least that is the point he wants to make. Could knock you out in ten seconds. His middle looks soft until it is felt: like steel.

At the turn in the driveway he reaches the far garage and his beige on brown Corniche sedan. He slowly eases himself into the driver's seat, then struggles out and onto his feet again, and starts fishing in his pants for the keys. He pulls out a set, examines them, picks a key, settles back into the car tries to insert it into the ignition. Doesn't fit. He starts over again, pulling more sets of keys out of his deep pocket. Two sets. Three sets. Four sets. Which is it? None fit.

He gets out again and walks to the rear of the car and points to the license: Virginia plates with a '93 sticker. "Haven't driven it in four years," he says. He leaves the garage and walks toward the fence, where a black Ford pickup is parked. The seat is too close to the steering wheel for him, and he has a difficult time squeezing in. It takes him a few minutes, but now he is there, behind the wheel, and he has a key that fits and the engine starts and he motions to climb in.

As the truck reaches the front entrance, Ali stops, waiting for the electronic gate to open. His eyes close. He starts snoring. He can fall asleep any time of day, his doctors say, but he often only pretends to, and people around him can never be sure if he is dozing or duping.

Only a trick this time. The gate opens. The black pickup goes flying up the road, free and swaying. He always loved to speed. In the old days he might take the wheel of the press bus at training camp and scare the daylights out of the boxing scribes. He is doing it again. What is going on here? No reason to fear. Muhammad Ali is heading out to see the world. He is hungry, and he knows what he wants: some love and affirmation and a quarter-pounder with mustard and onions at the local McDonald's.

The love is there the moment he pulls in the parking lot. Everyone wants an autograph, and he joyfully obliges. They call him champ and hero and pat his back and shake his hand and kiss him and smile at him and show him pictures and stare at him. They talk about how much he means to them. They say they will miss him if he moves, as he and Lonnie plan to do before the year is out, down to Louisville, his hometown, where he is setting up a Muhammad Ali center. He smiles back with his eyes.

No need to feel sorry for the champ, he wants you to know. "My life is a party," he says softly, chewing his quarter-pounder.

"Every day. Imagine. Every day. Things are quiet here. Imagine how it must be when I go to New York. Harlem. Detroit. Philly. Walk into a gym. The streets. Look at me. Imagine what it's like."

After lunch, Ali returns to the farm and resumes a tour of the grounds. He comes to a barn and slides open the door and looks inside. There, in the dim darkness, is an extraordinary thing. Look up in the rafters. Trophies lining the hayloft beam, one bigger than the next. Gathering dust. And attached to the wall: a huge blackandwhite blowup of the young Ali, gloved hands aloft in triumph, after one of his title matches with Frazier. He stares at his own image, the greatest of all time.

People often wonder about the past; how beautiful it would be if they realized the present. Ali turns and steps out of the barn. He slides the wooden door to the right. Is it closed? He notices an opening on the left. He slides it to the left. Now there is an opening on the right. He decides to leave it that way, a ray of light filtering in, and walks down the path to his home.

[June, 1997]

Please note that this piece has been edited for this volume and does not appear in its entirety.

COPYRIGHT ACKNOWLEDGMENTS

The 1980s

The 1990s

ABOUT THE EDITOR

GERALD EARLY is the author of *The Culture of Bruising: Essays on Prizefighting, Literature, and Modern American Culture,* winner of the 1994 National Book Critics Circle Award, and *Tuxedo Junction: Essays on American Culture,* both published by Ecco. A recipient of the Whiting Writer's Prize and the General Electric–CCLM Foundation Award, Early is Merle Kling Professor of Modern Letters at Washington University in St. Louis, where he also heads the African and Afro-American Studies Program.